Arguing With Historians

Also by Richard Nelson Current

Old Thad Stevens: A Story of Ambition

Pine Logs and Politics: A Life of
  Philetus Sawyer, 1816–1900

The Typewriter and the Men Who Made It

Secretary Stimson: A Study in Statecraft

Daniel Webster and the Rise of National Conservatism

Lincoln the President: Last Full Measure.
  With J. G. Randall.

The Lincoln Nobody Knows

American History: A Survey.
  With T. Harry Williams and Frank Freidel.
  7th Ed., also with Alan Brinkley.

Great American Thinkers: John C. Calhoun

Lincoln and the First Shot

Three Carpetbag Governors

United States History. With Alexander DeConde
  and Harris Dante.

The History of Wisconsin: The Civil War
  Era, 1848–1873

Wisconsin: A Bicentennial History

Unity, Ethnicity and Abraham Lincoln

Speaking of Abraham Lincoln: The Man and
  His Meaning for Our Times

Northernizing the South

Richard Nelson Current

Arguing With Historians
Essays on the Historical and the Unhistorical

 Wesleyan University Press
Middletown, Connecticut

Chapter 1 appeared originally in *The North Carolina Historical Review* 54, no. 2 (April 1977). Chapter 2 appeared originally in Richard N. Current, *Lincoln and the First Shot*, Lippincott, 1963. Reprinted by permission of Harper & Row, Publishers, Inc. Chapter 3 appeared originally in *Papers of the Abraham Lincoln Association* 6 (1984). Chapter 4 is a paper originally presented at the "Lincoln 175" Conference at Gettysburg College, September 1984. Chapter 5 appeared originally in David L. Wilson and John Y. Simon, eds., *Ulysses S. Grant: Essays and Documents*, Southern Illinois University Press, 1981. Chapter 6 appeared originally in *Pennsylvania History* 14, no. 4 (October 1947). Chapter 7 appeared originally as the introduction to James W. Garner, *Reconstruction in Mississippi*, Louisiana State University Press, 1968. Chapter 8 appeared originally in David Pinkney and Theodore Ropp, eds., *A Festschrift for Frederick B. Artz*, Duke University Press, 1964. Chapter 9 appeared originally in Richard N. Current, *John C. Calhoun*, Washington Square Press, 1963. Chapter 10 appeared originally in *The Journal of Southern History* 52, no. 1 (February 1986). Chapter 11 appeared originally in *The History Teacher* 15, no. 1 (November 1981).

LIBRARY OF CONGRESS CATALOGING-IN-PUBLICATION DATA
Current, Richard Nelson.
  Arguing with historians.
  Bibliography: p.
  Includes index.
  Summary: An imaginary Declaration of Independence, 1775–1975—Who started the war, Abraham Lincoln or Jefferson Davis?—The myth of the jealous son—[etc.]
  1. United States—Historiography. 2. United States—History—Civil War, 1861–1865—Historiography. 3. Reconstruction—Historiography.
4. Sectionalism (United States)—Historiography. 5. United States—Race relations—Historiography. 6. United States—Ethnic relations—Historiography. I. Title.
E175.C87 1987   973'.072   87-13682
ISBN 0-8195-5187-2 (alk. paper)

All inquiries and permissions requests should be addressed to the Publisher, Wesleyan University Press, 110 Mt. Vernon Street, Middletown, Connecticut 06457.

Distributed by Harper & Row Publishers, Keystone Industrial Park, Scranton, Pennsylvania 18512.

Manufactured in the United States of America

First Edition

To the memory of
three great teachers of American History
Robert S. Fletcher
Frederick Merk
William B. Hesseltine

Contents

Introduction   3

1. An Imaginary Declaration of Independence,
   1775–1975   9
2. Who Started the War, Abraham Lincoln or
   Jefferson Davis?   31
3. The Myth of the Jealous Son   52
4. Lincoln Biographies: Old and New Myths   61
5. President Grant and the
   Continuing Civil War   71
6. Love, Hate, and Thaddeus Stevens   83
7. Reconstruction in Mississippi   97
8. Carpetbaggers Reconsidered   115
9. Neo-Calhounism and Minority Rights   132
10. Fiction as History: Vidal, Haley, Styron   147
11. The "New Ethnicity" and American History   162

Notes   175
Index   199

Arguing With Historians

Introduction

These essays deal with a variety of subjects, ranging from Abraham Lincoln to Alex Haley and from the Mecklenburg Declaration to the melting pot. Yet the collection possesses a certain unity by virtue of shared themes and a common approach. Each of the essays touches upon one or both of two themes familiar in American history—nationalism and sectionalism—especially as these relate to a third theme, the changing relationship between blacks and whites. And all the essays take a historiographical approach, setting out to distinguish between the historical and the unhistorical in what writers on the various subjects have previously said.

The essays respond, positively or negatively, to some of the main historiographical trends of the last half-century. During that time, "revisionism" as applied to the Civil War reached flood tide and then receded. It was essentially a pro-Confederate line of thought (though many of its proponents were Northerners), one that characterized the war as unfortunate and unnecessary and blamed it on the North—on abolitionist fanatics and often on Lincoln himself. "Counterrevisionism" undertook to restore the essentials of the older interpretation, the one that had been revised. This view held that, in preserving the Union and destroying slavery, the war had accomplished important and desirable results.

The term *revisionism* as applied to Reconstruction meant the opposite of what it did as applied to the Civil War. It meant revising a pro-Southern interpretation. In regard to Reconstruction the view prevailing in the North as well as the South had been pro-Southern and antiblack. It had received elaboration and documentation most notably at the hands of Professor William A. Dunning, a Northerner, and his students, many of them Southerners, at Columbia University. Reconstruction "revisionists," among whom the black historian William E. B. Du Bois was a pioneer, tried to show that the congressional program for remaking the postwar South was by no means so vicious as the Dunningites maintained.

White historians had neglected or minimized the role of blacks in slavery and antislavery, in war and Reconstruction, and in American history generally. Black history, under the impetus of both black and white historians, began to flourish along with the agitation for civil rights. Black studies inspired other ethnic studies, as Native, Hispanic, Oriental, and various European Americans followed the example of African Americans in cultivating group pride. And psychobiography gained practitioners, especially after the acclaim that Erik Erikson won for his psychoanalytic study *Young Man Luther* (1958).

These essays were written at different times during a fairly long period, the latest of them four decades after the earliest. In the present collection, the first essay, "An Imaginary Declaration of Independence, 1775–1975" (first published in 1977), traces an endless controversy over the claim that a citizens' committee of Charlotte, North Carolina, adopted a declaration of independence more than a year before the Continental Congress in Philadelphia got around to doing so. In this story the theme of sectionalism appears only incidentally, but the theme of nationalism figures prominently. To be sure, it figures in a rather strange way, as local people with the pride of patriotism insist that Mecklenburg County was the real birthplace of American nationhood.

Civil War revisionists were divided on the question of whether Lincoln was to blame for starting the war. Some of them reasserted and attempted to document the Confederates' charge that, in sending his 1861 expedition to Fort Sumter, Lincoln schemed to provoke the Confederates into firing the first shot. Other historians, including some revisionists, maintained that his object was to hold the fort without jeopardizing peace. "Who Started the War, Abraham Lincoln or Jefferson Davis?" (1963) reviews the argument and concludes that neither peace nor war was precisely what Lincoln was aiming at.

Psychobiographers also blamed the war on Lincoln, though by a different process of reasoning (if *reasoning* is the word). Some of them said he suffered from an Oedipus complex, which made him ambitious to slay the Founding Fathers and take their place. This he could do only by effacing their work and refounding the Republic—only by bringing about secession and then reunion. In "The Myth of the Jealous Son" (1984) Lincoln's words and deeds are compared with what fanciful psychobiographers have made of them.

Other writers, too, have stretched Lincoln's words to fit their own predilections. White supremacists used to quote him in support of the segregation and disfranchisement of blacks. More recently, advocates of civil rights have brought Lincoln to their side or, rather, to their front. They have hailed him as a president who, by the time of his death, had become as radical as the most radical of congressmen and senators. If he had lived, his latest interpreters say, he would have insisted upon full black rights, including black suffrage, in the reconstructed South. Are his new, prointegration admirers tending to err almost as much in one direction as his old, prosegregation admirers did in the opposite direction? This question is discussed in "Lincoln Biographies: Old and New Myths" (1984).

While historians generally have rated Lincoln as the greatest of presidents, they have ranked Ulysses S. Grant among the very worst. Lincoln and others of the highly regarded occupants of the White House were war presidents or warrior presidents (Washington, the two Roosevelts, Wilson, Jackson,

Polk). "President Grant and the Continuing Civil War" (1981) argues that Reconstruction was essentially a continuation of the war and that Grant therefore was a war president as well as a warrior president. It argues, further, that he made a commendable effort to enforce the Radical program with its provision for black voting—hence the low opinion of him among historians who were influenced by the Dunning school. The conclusion is that Grant deserves a better political reputation than he has had.

The Dunningites contended that the Radical Republicans, in granting civil and political rights to blacks during Reconstruction, were "Vindictives" who sought to heap humiliation upon defeat for Southern whites. Friends of Thaddeus Stevens, the Radical leader of the House of Representatives, insisted that he, at least, was motivated by idealism, by a desire to see justice done to blacks and to the downtrodden of all races and colors. "Love, Hate, and Thaddeus Stevens" (1947) suggests that neither love for Southern blacks nor hatred of Southern whites accounted for Stevens's Reconstruction policies.

Of all the Dunning students, perhaps the most objective was James W. Garner, a Mississippian who wrote his dissertation at Columbia on Reconstruction in Mississippi. From the viewpoint of a Northern sympathizer with the Radicals, Garner might seem like a rather extreme Southern racist. But from the viewpoint of some of his conservative fellow Mississippians he appeared a traitor to the traditions of the South. "Reconstruction in Mississippi" (1968) appraises his treatment of the subject.

Practically no historians, either integrationists or segregationists, had a good word for the "carpetbaggers," those Northerners who cooperated with blacks and "scalawags" in forming and running the Republican party in the reconstructed South. Carpetbaggers are remembered as political adventurers who took advantage of the Negro vote to gain power in the Southern states and despoil the already impoverished Southern people. "Carpetbaggers Reconsidered" (1964) raises doubts about the familiar stereotype.

John C. Calhoun was the very personification of the proslavery argument and the secessionist doctrine. It seems incredible that by the 1950s, a hundred years after his death, both Northerners and Southerners, liberals and conservatives, should have looked to Calhoun for the political technique to be applied in protecting minorities, even blacks. Yet prominent historians, political scientists, politicians, and journalists did so. They misread both Calhoun's philosophy and contemporary politics, according to "Neo-Calhounism and Minority Rights" (1963).

To describe Calhoun as a champion of racial minorities, or Lincoln as an enemy of the Republic, would seem to require the kind of imagination that we usually ascribe to novelists. Through fictional history, some novelists have exerted a greater influence than most historians on popular conceptions of the American past. This influence has increased with the growth of television and the "docudrama." Many people have looked to Gore Vidal for their picture of Lincoln as president, to Alex Haley for the ancestral heritage of blacks, and to William Styron for the personality of the slave-rebellion leader Nat Turner. "Fiction as History" (1986) shows to what extent these authors have written history and to what extent fiction.

The ideals of nationalism that Lincoln embodied and expressed have come under attack from champions of the "new ethnicity," a kind of ethnic chauvinism inspired at least in part by black assertions of group pride. Ethnic chauvinists have presented an interpretation of history in which Americans of older stock are the villains and more recent immigrants the heroes. Writers of this persuasion assert, among other things, that "WASPs" were responsible for antiblack prejudice and that the foreign-born, especially the Irish and the Germans, were responsible for the Union victory in the Civil War. The truth of these assertions is questioned in "The 'New Ethnicity' and American History" (1981).

None of the essays here pretends to say the last word, though a few of them may come close to doing so. It seems unlikely that future historians will give a great deal of attention to the Mecklenburg Declaration, or to the notion that Calhoun has a special message for latter-day Americans, or to the question of Lincoln's role in regard to Fort Sumter. Still, it would perhaps be premature to declare any of those issues historiographically dead. All the rest of the topics will no doubt continue to engage the attention of historians or biographers, and there is no predicting in what directions the discussion may go. History, after all, is not an agreed-upon list of names, events, places, and dates. It is an ongoing argument about the meaning of the past.

Chapter 1. An Imaginary Declaration of Independence, 1775–1975

Happy is the land that has no history. So it has been said, but historyless North Carolina was not an entirely happy land during the early decades of her statehood. The "first forty-five years of the Republic of North Carolina," one native son recalled, "did not produce even a pamphlet on any subject of her history, except the abortive effort of Williamson," that is, Hugh Williamson's *History of North Carolina* (1812), which filled two volumes and yet was incomplete. The "utter want of a history was felt as a public misfortune by the intelligent men of the State," and by none more than Archibald D. Murphey, the great advocate of transportation improvements and popular education as means of building up the state's prosperity. Around 1819 Murphey conceived the project of writing a comprehensive account of the North Carolina past (a task he was never to find the time or energy to carry out). "Such a work, well executed, would add very much to our standing in the Union, and make us respectable in our own eyes," he believed. "Knowing nothing of ourselves, we have nothing in our history to which we can turn with conscious pride."[1]

Certainly, in those days, the reputation and the self-image of North Carolina were sadly in need of bolstering. Newspapers in the rest of the country began to refer to her as the "Rip Van Winkle State" after the appearance, in 1819, of Washington Irving's story of the man who slept for years without waking while progress transformed the world around him.

Sleepy, shiftless, backward—such were Carolinians in the eyes of other Americans and especially in the eyes of the neighboring Virginians. Many Virginians still took the supercilious attitude that William Byrd had assumed a century earlier when, in his "History of the Dividing Line," he made much of the "Slothfulness of the People" to the south of the line and referred to their colony as "Lubberland."[2]

Virginians bragged, among other things, that Virginia had led the way to the American Revolution. When, in 1819, the question came up in Congress, men from Massachusetts disputed the Virginia claim. And then a North Carolinian stepped forth to assert that neither Massachusetts nor Virginia had started the movement for independence. No, indeed; the honor rightfully belonged to North Carolina. This assertion met with sneering disbelief.

So the long-serving senator from North Carolina, Nathaniel Macon, and the freshman representative from the Mecklenburg district, William Davidson, wrote home for documentary proof. Joseph McKnitt Alexander, of Mecklenburg County, responded by providing a manuscript that his late father, John McKnitt Alexander, had left. Joseph's brother William Alexander apologized for the lack of original documents. "Nearly all of my father's papers," he explained, "were burned in the spring of 1800, [in a fire which destroyed his house and] which destroyed the papers now wanted."

Senator Macon nevertheless forwarded the Alexander manuscript to the *Raleigh Register*. "It is probably not known to many of our readers that the citizens of Mecklenburg County, in this State, made a Declaration of Independence more than a year before Congress made theirs," the *Register* announced in its issue of April 30, 1819. "The following Document on the subject has lately come to the hands of the Editor from unquestionable authority, and it is published that it may go down to posterity." There followed Alexander's account of a meeting in Charlotte on May 19–20, 1775, and his list of the meeting's resolutions, the most striking of which ran: "That we do hereby declare ourselves a free and independent people."[3]

This amazing news, first given to the world forty-four years after the event, apparently aroused no public expression of doubt except on the part of a single Massachusetts editor. To quench that one little spark of skepticism, William Polk, son of a reputed leader in the Charlotte meeting of 1775, gathered testimony from several men who said they had been present on that occasion, though some were not sure of the exact date. The *Raleigh Register* published this testimony in 1819, and Polk had it reprinted as a pamphlet three years later.

The Polk pamphlet suggested to Polk's family and friends in Charlotte "the propriety of signalizing the event by an annual celebration on the 19th of May." Polk's son Thomas led in organizing the semicentennial in 1825. An "immense concourse" was on hand to hear the Reverend Humphrey Hunter of the Presbyterian church read the Mecklenburg Declaration and recount the circumstances of its first public reading— which, he said, he himself had heard a half century before. Two other survivors and avowed witnesses presided over the day's festival, and sixty or seventy aging veterans of the Revolutionary War marched at the head of the parade.[4]

For a whole decade, from 1819 to 1829, nobody openly questioned the historicity of the event that the Mecklenburgers celebrated. Consequently, Mecklenburgers in particular and North Carolinians in general felt thoroughly justified in accepting and treasuring it as a historic fact. Suddenly they received a shock. The *Works* of Thomas Jefferson, which came out in 1829 after Jefferson's death, contained a letter dismissing the Mecklenburg Declaration as a hoax. In the letter Jefferson had conceded that he could not prove it to be one. "But I shall believe it such until positive and solemn proof of its authenticity shall be produced."[5]

The state legislature, at its 1830–1831 session, responded to Jefferson's challenge by setting up a committee and placing

Thomas G. Polk, the organizer of the recent semicentennial, at the committee's head. "The impression in the Legislature," one of the lawmakers later recalled, "was that Gen. Polk, the chairman, was allowed to have his own way on a subject that he was so much interested in."[6] Polk and his fellow committeemen determined, as they said, "to usher to the world the Mecklenburg Declaration, accompanied with such testimonials of its genuineness, as shall silence incredulity." The world must not be allowed to forget that "a few gallant North Carolinians . . . earned for themselves, and for their fellow-citizens of North Carolina, the honor of giving birth to the first Declaration of Independence." So the committee gathered some new statements from presumed witnesses still living and added these statements to the materials that the *Raleigh Register* had published in 1819. The legislature then gave the state's imprimatur to the Mecklenburg Declaration by issuing the committee's report, along with the supporting evidence, in an official pamphlet.[7]

A far more pointed reply to Jefferson came from the pen of Joseph Seawell Jones, one of the state's Federalist-Whigs who, as such, were anti-Jeffersonian to begin with. Jones produced a book with the title *A Defence of the Revolutionary History of the State of North Carolina from the Aspersions of Mr. Jefferson* (1834). Jefferson, according to Jones, had set North Carolina back not only by depriving her of her glorious past but also by placing her under the domination of his party and hence under the domination of Virginia. "I do look upon it as the most fatal stroke ever aimed at the dignity and honor of my own country," Jones expostulated, "and I would willingly lay the first stone of a Chinese wall to divide for ever the physical and intellectual resources of the two states."[8]

The North Carolina Whigs could secure no monopoly, however, on the Mecklenburg Declaration. The Democrats also claimed it as their own, and when James K. Polk ran for the presidency they asserted—and the Whigs denied—that his grandfather had been one of the declaration's signers.[9] Faith in the sacred document transcended politics.

It also transcended religion. The reputed signers were practically all Scotch-Irish Presbyterians, and so were the original promoters of the cause. But by 1835 it had captivated even Judge William Gaston, the state's most prominent Roman Catholic. Gaston reflected the popular belief when he wrote the words for his song "The Old North State": "Carolina! Carolina! . . . Tho' the scorner may sneer at and witlings defame her, Still our hearts swell with gladness when ever we name her. . . . Tho' she envies not others their merited glory, Say whose name stands the foremost in liberty's story."[10]

The continuing annual celebrations were great occasions for Charlotte and its vicinity, and they were assuming a more than local significance. Thus, on May 20, 1835, Gov. David L. Swain lent his presence and with it the authority of the state to the sixtieth anniversary observance, which was much the biggest yet. Some Revolutionary veterans were still spry enough to march, and one of them, Gen. Joseph Graham, retold the wonderful story of Mecklenburg's priority in independence.[11] Seemingly North Carolinians had succeeded in exorcising the baneful spirit of Thomas Jefferson and in restoring their declaration to its former position, high above all doubt and disbelief.

Faith, except on the part of the most faithful, was again shaken when, in 1838, the pioneer archivist Peter Force discovered a copy of the *Massachusetts Spy* for July 12, 1775. Reproduced in this paper was part of a series of resolutions reportedly drawn up in Charlotte and dated May 30, 1775. Force published the resolutions in the Washington *Daily National Intelligencer*, thus giving them wide publicity. Several years later, in 1847, the whole series, bearing the correct date of May 31, 1775, was found in the June 13, 1775, issue of the *South Carolina Gazette*.

These resolutions were not the same as those the *Raleigh*

Register had brought to light back in 1819. Not only were the dates different—May 20 and May 31—but so were the contents. In the May 20 resolutions the people of Mecklenburg County declared themselves unequivocally "free and independent." In the May 31 resolutions the county committee (of public safety) stated that royal commissions in all the colonies were suspended and that the powers of government were vested in the various provincial congresses "under the direction of the great Continental Congress." The committee directed that the citizens of Mecklenburg County should proceed to elect military officers who would exercise power "independent of the Crown of Great-Britain." But the committee also provided, in the eighteenth of the twenty resolves, that all twenty would cease to have effect if and when Great Britain should "resign its unjust and arbitrary pretensions with respect to America."

Had Mecklenburg County produced two sets of resolutions only eleven days apart in May 1775? At the time the May 31 set came to light, none of the participants or witnesses was still alive to answer that question. When they had testified, in 1819 or 1831, all of them had referred to only a single set, for which most of them had been willing to accept the date of May 20. Not one of them had mentioned two separate meetings or two separate documents. Peter Force concluded that when those old men thought they were remembering a declaration of May 20 they really had in mind the resolves of May 31.[12] The Mecklenburg Declaration of Independence promptly lost credibility except among North Carolinians.

One native Tar Heel living in New York City, the Episcopal minister Francis L. Hawks, replied to Force in an 1852 lecture before the New York Historical Society, a lecture that was to be published as part of a book the following year. The Reverend Dr. Hawks set out to prove that the resolves of May 30 (i.e., May 31) were not the ones the participants had recalled. "But," he noted, "it is, in truth, of little moment, inasmuch as in either case, whether they declared themselves independent ten days sooner or ten days later in May, 1775, they are at any rate anterior to the National Declaration of July 4, 1776, by more than a year." Then, contradicting himself, Hawks went on to say there was indeed a big difference between the two documents of May 1775. The one of May 20, he said, is a forthright assertion of independence. The other, "in which the word *independence* does not even occur," is only a "delicate insinuation" of independence and "is avowedly to be of force *but for a time*"; it provides for no more than "a *temporary* independence" at most.

Hawks ended his lecture with an expression of the pride that North Carolinians were beginning to feel in the economic and social progress they thought their state was making during the 1850s. One citizen had said in a letter to the *Raleigh Register*, ". . . Old Rip may wipe the dew out of his eyes and wake up to a sense of his real dignity." Another wrote to the *Fayetteville Observer* that a Tar Heel need no longer expect "to have his feelings wounded at the sneering remarks of scoffers and witlings as they defamed the Old North State." And Hawks told his New York audience: "Rip thinks he was wide awake on the 20th of May, 1775. . . . Really, he does not seem to have been such a drowsy character, after all "[13]

The case for Mecklenburg, however, was about to receive another blow, one that was to have a long-lasting, reverberating effect. This blow was especially effective and especially bitter because it came from a North Carolina source—the *North Carolina University Magazine*. The magazine's issue for May 1853 contained an essay with the title "May 1775." The author was the first to make use of a copy of the Alexander manuscript (including the putative resolutions of May 20) that Alexander had given to William R. Davie, the Revolutionary leader and educational statesman. According to the magazine writer, the Davie copy bore the following notation under the date of September 3, 1800: ". . . the foregoing statement, tho' fundamentally correct; yet may not literally correspond with the original records . . . as all those records and papers were burnt" (in the fire that destroyed the Alexander house in the spring of 1800). So, the author concluded, the May 20 resolutions, as first published in 1819, had not been reproduced from any document; they had been reconstructed from memory; and in the process the real document, the one of May 31, had been misdated and distorted.[14]

This iconoclastic article, like other contributions to the *North Carolina University Magazine,* was unsigned. The anonymous author was Charles Phillips, a professor of mathematics at Chapel Hill (and a brother of Cornelia Phillips Spencer, who was to gain fame as the university's savior after the Civil War). Though the Phillips family had a distinguished North Carolina future, it had no North Carolina past to speak of. No native Tar Heel, Charles Phillips had been born in New York City, and his father in England. Charles became a Presbyterian minister, but he was no Scotch-Irish Presbyterian, nor was he a descendant of any of the Revolutionary patriots of Mecklenburg County.

A few months after the publication of Phillips's unsigned article, another essay on the same subject appeared in the *Nassau Literary Magazine,* a Princeton student periodical. The author, Peter Force's son Samuel, wrote in regard to the Mecklenburg Declaration, "The genuineness is a point on which the people of North Carolina are extremely sensitive (needlessly, we think, extremely sensitive)." Needlessly, young Samuel Force thought, because they could take just as much pride in the May 31 resolutions, and these without any question were bona fide.

So sensitive were North Carolinians that Professor Phillips dared not avow his views. A correspondent of his, forwarding to the historian George Bancroft a letter from him, admonished, ". . . you will of course take good care that he is not brought into danger by his frankness. The publication of his remarks would probably cost him his professorship."[15]

Bancroft was enough influenced by Phillips to eschew the date May 20 when recounting North Carolina events in the fourth volume of his *History of the United States* (1858). Yet Bancroft accepted other elements of the Mecklenburg story, and these he blended in with the Phillips version. His readers throughout the country learned that, on May 31, more than a year ahead of the rest of the colonists, the liberty-loving Scotch-Irish Presbyterians of Mecklenburg County had adopted what "formed in effect a declaration of independence, as well as a system of government."[16]

Among North Carolinians of the 1850s the Phillips article gained little credence. Hinton Rowan Helper, in his *Impending Crisis* (1857), disputed the state's claims to recent progress, but even Helper had no doubts about the Mecklenburg achievement. Indeed, he made quite a point of it in his book. North Carolina, he argued, ought to be the first of the slave states to abolish slavery because, though she was now the last of all the states in literacy and wealth, she once had been the first in freedom. On that historic May 20 she had "set her sister colonies a most valorous and praiseworthy example," and they had followed it. "To her infamous slaveholding sisters of the South, it is now meet that she should set another noble example of decency, virtue, and independence."[17]

Instead of leading the way toward that kind of independence, North Carolina of course followed other slaveholding states in seeking independence of a quite different sort. Her 1861 convention borrowed glory for secession by passing the ordinance on the Mecklenburg anniversary. Then the convention emphasized the parallel between 1775 and 1861 by means of the state flag it adopted, a flag bearing the two dates May 20, 1775, and May 20, 1861.[18] The two reinforced each other, and for a time there was a double significance in the twentieth of May.

Yet, with the distractions of war and reconstruction, the day ceased to be one of grand celebration, even in Charlotte. Finally, as the centennial of 1875 approached, the Mecklenburgers began to prepare for a joyous renewal of the occasion. In the midst of their preparations they were thrown on the defensive by the most scholarly attack yet launched against the authenticity of what they were about to celebrate.

The salvo came from a prestigious magazine, the *North American Review*, and from a prominent writer and educator, James C. Welling. A New Jerseyite by birth, a Princeton graduate, and a former editor of the *National Intelligencer*, Welling was the president of Columbian University (later to be known as George Washington University) in the District of Columbia. How he had got interested in the Mecklenburg question is not clear, but he was certainly well informed about it, and he was especially well acquainted with Phillips's position on it.

According to Welling, in the April 1874 issue of the *North American Review*, the Mecklenburg myth was an understandable expression of state character and state pride. "The emulous North-Carolinian, noted among his countrymen as much for his modesty as his merit, not unnaturally dreamed again the dream of Joseph, and, as in a vision, saw his sheaf standing upright, and the sheaves of his brethren standing around and doing obeisance to his sheaf." Still, Welling thought, the myth would never have taken hold of the state if, when Alexander's supposed declaration was first published, it had been accompanied by his admission that it was not a true copy. "The apocryphal recollections of an old man, who is careful to premise that they may not literally correspond with the original record, would have been received by all for what they were worth, without flinging at his head charges of forgery on the one hand, and without making them the gospel of North Carolina patriotism on the other."[19]

The promoters of the Mecklenburg centennial determined to neutralize the Welling artillery in advance of the celebration. Accordingly, they lined up their most powerful gun to return the fire from Charlotte on February 4, 1875. William Alexander Graham, then seventy years old, was one of the most distinguished of living North Carolina statesmen. He was a prominent attorney and a former governor, Navy secretary, United States senator, and Confederate senator. He was a son of Gen. Joseph Graham, who had recalled witnessing the Mecklenburg events of May 19–20, 1775, and a grandson of Maj. John Davidson, who was remembered as one of the signers of the Mecklenburg Declaration. The centennial commit tee saw to the publication of a book containing both Graham's long, eloquent address in reply to Welling and the materials of the 1831 pamphlet that the legislature had issued in reply to Jefferson.

Graham began his address by saying that, if his kinship with the Mecklenburg heroes might "induce a suspicion of bias," he hoped it would also be recognized as giving him the benefit of information "not accessible to strangers." He went on to urge the indispensability of the "oral evidence of living witnesses" when dealing with a time and place where "no printing press existed" and where "printed documentary proof" was therefore not to be found. He stressed the credibility of the witnesses—would all those patriotic and sagacious men of the Revolution have deceived either themselves or others? Lawyer that he was, he relied on a lawyer's rather than a historian's rules of evidence, maintaining that "a witness who makes positive affirmation of an event is to be credited in preference to one who does not remember it."

With a touch of sarcasm, Graham said he was "thankful to the last learned critic in the *North American Review*" for granting that "'the people of Mecklenburg were the first to cut the "gordian knot" of the political situation by their incisive declaration made on the 31st of May, 1775.'" But this to Graham (as earlier to Hawks) was not enough, and he insisted on May 20 and on outright resolutions of *independence*. "The word implies so grand and stupendous an idea to the subjects of a monarchy, that there is little liability to mistake it for anything else, on the part of witnesses of ordinary intelligence." It was time, Graham concluded, "on the approach of the hundredth birthday of the event, when all of the old thirteen States seem to be brushing off the dust from their armor, and brightening their escutcheons for display on the great Centennial of the Union, that we should review history and see the foundations on which our faith in it may rest."[20]

On May 19 and 20, 1875, Charlotte enjoyed the biggest celebration it had ever seen. According to one enthusiastic estimate, more than forty thousand visitors crowded into the town of five or six thousand. There was the obligatory reading of the Mecklenburg Declaration, and there were speeches, parades, brass bands, fireworks, a hundred-gun salute, horse races, and a fancy dress ball. There was even a program of cockfights between North and South Carolina birds.[21]

For the next twenty-five or thirty years a comparative calm descended upon the Mecklenburg controversy. The newer, "scientific" historians of national repute, such as Justin Winsor and Edward Channing, dismissed the May 20 declaration as spurious, and it continued to have little credence outside of North Carolina.[22] Inside the state it became a stronger article of faith than ever. The legislature of 1881 made May 20 a legal holiday. The legislature of 1885 removed from the state flag the date of May 20, 1861, and replaced it with April 12, 1776 (the time of the Halifax Resolves), but retained on the flag the beloved date of May 20, 1775.[23]

Meanwhile, in North Carolina, the popular belief expanded to embrace the idea that on that famous date, the Mecklenburg patriots had proclaimed independence not merely for the county but for the entire colony. The widely traveled reporter Edward King reflected this belief in his comments (1875) regarding the stretch between Charlotte and Greenville, South Carolina. "The better class of people all through this section, and especially in North Carolina, possess and manifest that boldness of spirit which made the colony the first of the original thirteen to claim independence . . . ," King wrote with approval. But he hastened to add, "There is a good deal of ignorance and prejudice among the low class of whites; they are hardly the stuff of which the old heroes were made."[24]

The State Board of Agriculture, in its efforts to promote the economic development of North Carolina, enlarged the scope of the Mecklenburg Declaration even further. The board filled its annual handbooks with data to show the greatness of the state's past as well as the promise of her future. The volume for 1896 credited North Carolina with several Revolutionary firsts. One of these represented a fairly recent claim: "The first pitched battle against governmental tyranny was at Alamance, May 12, 1771." Another greatly stretched the old claim: On May 20, 1775, "the patriots of Mecklenburg met in convention and declared the independence of the colonies"— the independence of all thirteen of them![25]

The continuing anniversary celebrations in Charlotte presented no problems of conscience for native speakers but imposed a dilemma upon an outsider such as Sen. David Bennett Hill of New York, the main orator for 1892. Senator Hill had prepared himself by a careful reading of both Welling's negating essay and Graham's affirmatory address. He did his best to weave the two together. Enigmatically he remarked, "It is the credulity of opposing partisans, sectarians, bigots, which the muse of history now mocks with her wise smile." The dispute, he went on to say, really concerned nothing more than two dates, and these "less than a fortnight" apart "Which one of the thirteen States, finding such a record as that among its archives, never questioned, undisputable, authentic and contemporaneous, would not regard the Mecklenburg Resolves of the 31st of May as a perfect title to all that was ever claimed for North Carolina's sons as the forerunners of American Independence?"[26]

Though polite enough to Senator Hill, the Mecklenburgers were unconvinced by him. At the 1898 celebration they dedicated the monument that had finally been erected after a campaign of more than half a century. The man who made the dedicatory speech was the vice-president of the United States, Adlai E. Stevenson, himself a blood relative of one of the famous declaration's "signers."[27] And the monument unequivocally confirmed the date—May 20, 1775.

After a generation of quiescence the controversy erupted with greater volume if not greater violence than ever before or since. More words on the subject were printed during the years 1905–1909 than during any other five-year period from the beginning of the debate to the present. Reopening the argument was Dr. George W. Graham of Charlotte, a descendant of the pioneer Mecklenburg family. Dr. Graham explained to the Scotch-Irish Society of America, at its 1895 meeting in Lexington, Virginia, *Why North Carolinians Believe in the Mecklenburg Declaration of Independence*. The theme, he said, was "of deep interest to the Scotch-Irish fraternity, as the first men in America to cast off the British yoke were members of that brotherhood." This address promptly appeared in print and later, in 1905, was published in a book along with brief biographies of the reputed signers.

Dr. Graham thought he had discovered new evidence that would "remove all doubt." This consisted of various supposed early references, occurring between 1777 and 1809, to the Mecklenburg Declaration. There was, for example, a boy who was born on May 20 (1787) and whom his father therefore called "My Independence Boy."

Dr. Graham was positive there existed—or had once existed—still other evidence that would absolutely clinch the case. The June 3, 1775, issue of the *Cape-Fear Mercury* of Wilmington, he contended, would be found to contain the resolutions of May 20. Unfortunately, no copy of that particular issue could be located anywhere. The last colonial governor of North Carolina had sent a copy to his superiors in London, and that copy had since disappeared. An American minister to England, a friend of Jefferson's, had borrowed it and kept it. Obviously, the "Jefferson partizans" were trying to hide the embarrassing fact that Jefferson had "plagiarized several of the Mecklenburg phrases when drawing the National Declaration"![28]

Providence seemed to be on Dr. Graham's side when, in 1905, *Collier's Magazine* suddenly came out with an apparent facsimile of the long-missing copy of the *Cape-Fear Mercury*.

Sure enough, on the front page of the paper, as reproduced in *Collier's,* were the familiar Mecklenburg resolutions of May 20. Here at last was the contemporary documentation that skeptics and scoffers had been demanding for so long. Or was it? In the accompanying *Collier's* article Dr. S. Millington Miller said he had found the paper among the effects of the diplomat who had been accused of stealing it. But the secretary of the South Carolina Historical Commission soon charged that Dr. Miller had fabricated the interesting document himself. Dr. Miller was willing to sell it for $5,000. To talk with him and look at it, Dr. Graham led a committee of three from Charlotte to Baltimore. The three agreed to buy the paper on one condition—that the document expert Worthington C. Ford certify its genuineness. After investigating, Ford pronounced the thing a barefaced forgery.[29]

To the Mecklenburgers, that revelation was disappointing enough, but worse was to come—the most thorough and scholarly of all attacks on the authenticity of the May 20 declaration. A youthful graduate of Fordham College, William Henry Hoyt, was writing his master's thesis on the subject at the University of Vermont. G. P. Putnam's Sons, of New York and London, published the thesis as a book in 1907. In the preface Hoyt acknowledged he was taking some risk: ". . . it is inevitable today that a publication which discredits the proudest page in the history of North Carolina should engender in some quarters an unkindly feeling for its author." But he protested that he had written "simply as a student of history, inspired with a special love for the history of the 'Old North State,' and with profound veneration for the Mecklenburg patriots of 1775." In the monograph, elaborating on the Force-Phillips-Welling line of argument, Hoyt undertook to show "that all the evidence, new and old, which is cited in support of the genuineness and authenticity of the Mecklenburg Declaration, should be understood as relating to a series of resolves of similar import, which were adopted in Mecklenburg County May 31, 1775, and that the several versions of the supposititious paper of May 20, 1775, trace their origin to rough notes written from memory in 1800 by John McKnitt Alexander, who believed these resolves to be a declaration of independence and attempted to set forth their substance."[30]

Reviewers in national periodicals judged, overoptimistically, that Hoyt had said the "final word," or almost the final word, on the subject.[31] A defender of the Mecklenburg Declaration quickly turned out a book in reply,[32] but not a single academic historian, even in North Carolina, spoke out to disagree with Hoyt. North Carolina now had her share of specialists who were trained in the new, critical, "scientific" historical discipline.

Foremost among these scholars was Stephen B. Weeks. Born in Pasquotank County, a member of a Methodist family of English and Huguenot lineage, Weeks graduated from the university at Chapel Hill, earned a Ph.D. in English there, and went on to get a history doctorate from Johns Hopkins, the leading center of the new historiography. While Trinity College was still in Randolph County, Weeks served on its faculty as the first full-time professor of history in any southern institution of higher learning. He helped Hoyt with the latter's research. Reviewing Hoyt's book most favorably, he revealed that Hoyt was a great-grandson of no less a man than Archibald D. Murphey. "It can hardly be imagined then," Weeks wrote, "that a descendant of this protagonist of intellectual life in North Carolina could come to a study of any phase of history of that State in any spirit except one seeking for the truth."[33]

Weeks also assisted Samuel A. Ashe in the preparation of Ashe's two-volume *History of North Carolina*, the first volume of which was published in Greensboro in 1908. When Ashe, in the course of his narrative, came to the problem of May 1775, he made a concession to the advocates of the twentieth by first telling their version of the story. Then, after presenting the evidence on the other side, he decided in favor of the thirty-first.[34] His was the first history of the state in almost a century—the first since Williamson's incomplete work of 1812—to treat the Mecklenburg Declaration as anything other than a historical fact.

The advocates of the twentieth were not appeased by Ashe's presentation of their case. In the next session of the North Carolina assembly, his history became the object of a legislative contest, one that pitted Mecklenburg against Guilford. A senator from Greensboro—the place of publication of the first volume—introduced a bill merely authorizing and advising (but not appropriating any money for) the purchase of a copy for each of the rural school libraries in the state. A senator from Charlotte moved to strike out the reference to advising, and the senate passed the bill as thus amended and weakened. When it went to the other chamber, the speaker of the house, A. W. Graham, a descendant of one of the May 20 "signers," left his chair to oppose the measure both in committee and on the floor. The house finally rejected it.

"The opponents of the bill did not think argument necessary," Weeks disgustedly reported to the *Nation* magazine. "Their speeches were directed to showing what would follow in the wake of the bill: The date, May 20, is on the State flag and the State seal; a monument has been erected in Charlotte to commemorate this event; the children have been taught this date, and, as one member put it, its authenticity 'has been established by the Legislature already as thoroughly as the Legislature can establish anything.' Then why not leave good enough alone without questioning its correctness?"[35]

While the legislature insisted on May 20 as official dogma, a semiofficial repudiation of it came from R. D. W. Connor, the pioneer secretary of the state-supported North Carolina Historical Commission. In a 1909 article Connor said the controversy over the Mecklenburg Declaration had attracted more attention than it deserved and had "tended to throw into obscurity the more significant action of the Congress at Halifax in April of the next year," when ahead of all the other provincial congresses, North Carolina's authorized its delegates in the Continental Congress to join in a general declaration of independence. Connor reasoned that the state's claim to priority must rest on the resolutions of April 12, 1776, not on those of May 20, 1775. But he cautioned, "This claim must not be considered as an assertion that the idea of independence originated in North Carolina."[36]

Thus, by 1909, though the Mecklenburg Declaration still had the support of many politicians throughout the state, it had the endorsement of practically no scholars outside of Mecklenburg County. But it was about to get its greatest champion, one of the most energetic and versatile scholars that North Carolina has ever produced, Archibald Henderson. Long ago, a Chapel Hill professor of mathematics, Phillips, had labored to tear down the declaration's credibility. Now another Chapel Hill professor of mathematics, Henderson, was to devote himself to building it back up.

Henderson launched his campaign of rehabilitation when he delivered the anniversary address in Charlotte on May 19, 1916. His great-great-grandfather Moses Alexander, he began, had been a Mecklenburg pioneer but had died in 1772, three years before the remarkable declaration was made. "The fact that I have no relationship, even in a remote degree, to any of the actors in the scene commemorated here tonight, clarifies my vision of all prejudice, I trust." Henderson proceeded to demonstrate, to the satisfaction of his audience, that the news of the Battle of Lexington, April 19, 1775, had arrived in Charlotte exactly one month later. From this he drew the conclusion that the Mecklenburg citizens must have met on May 19 and must have adopted the independence resolutions (which allude to the battle) on the next day.[37]

On the next day in 1916 the Charlotte orator of the occasion was the president of the United States, Woodrow Wilson. A Scotch-Irishman by descent, a Presbyterian of the Presbyterians, and a one-time Davidson College student—but also a historian and the holder of a Johns Hopkins doctorate—Wilson chose not to speak on the favorite theme of the Scotch-Irish Presbyterians of the locality. He talked, instead, of current national affairs. Only once did he mention the event he was commemorating by his presence, and then he mentioned it parenthetically and with a light touch. Quoting the Declaration of Independence, he said, "(I am now referring to the minor declaration at Philadelphia, not to the Mecklenburg declaration)."[38]

Undaunted, Professor Henderson continued year after year to look for new evidence that would vindicate the Mecklenburgers for all time. In 1939 he announced his greatest discovery. The Davie copy of the Alexander manuscript, a copy presumed to be no longer extant, had turned up in the Southern Historical Collection at Chapel Hill. Till then, nobody had examined that piece of paper since 1853, when Phillips had made use of it with such telling effect. Other critical writers, notably Welling and Hoyt, had taken Phillips's word that the Davie copy bore a notation in Alexander's own hand indicating it had been reconstructed from memory (and hence the other copies also had been). Now Henderson discovered that the manuscript also contained another and quite different note in Alexander's penmanship. This note, underscored and inserted after Alexander's account of the May 20 proceedings of the Mecklenburg committee, read, "Thus far from the Journals and records of sd. Committee." The previously revealed notation—"that the foregoing statement . . . may not litterally correspond with the original records"—was presumably intended to apply only the next part of the manuscript, a part that had nothing to do with the resolutions themselves. So, Henderson inferred, the Mecklenburg Declaration was not a figment originating in the fallible memory of man. Not at all! It had come directly from a contemporary document. And all these years the doubting historians had been misled.[39]

As author and editor of the first two volumes of the five-volume *North Carolina: The Old North State and the New* (1941), Henderson made a point of insisting "that a meeting was held [in Charlotte] on May 19 and 20, 1775; and that the convention, on the latter date, made an outright declaration of

independence and appointed a committee of safety which met
for the first time eleven days later," to adopt a temporary plan
of government in the resolves of May 31. The doubting historians still had their doubts, and James W. Patton, then teaching
at Converse College, expressed some of them in his review of
Henderson's volumes. In a long and indignant reply, Henderson
reemphasized his discoveries and said that "one finds incredible, from a teacher of history, the casual dismissal of these
documents and their revolutionary character." Patton stood
his ground, retorting that Henderson's conclusions were "in-
triguing" but whether they were "persuasive or merely plausible" depended on one's point of view.[40]

The claim to priority in independence had met an understandable need on the part of North Carolinians when, in the
early nineteenth century, the state first began to assert the
claim. By the early twentieth century the psychological need
was no longer so apparent. Gone was the obloquy pertaining
to a backward, Rip Van Winkle state. North Carolina now had
a reputation as the most progressive state in the South and
one of the most progressive in the entire country. According to
numerous reports she was going ahead faster than any of her
southern sisters in the development of schools, highways, and
industries. No more need Tar Heels feel any sense of inferiority when they glanced at Virginia or South Carolina. They
were, as one commentator put it in 1924, "so full of hope,
courage, and honest pride," that they had "reversed the old
definition of North Carolina as 'a valley of humility between
two mountains of conceit'" and had "made it a model for the
envy and the emulation of their neighbors."[41]

Yet, despite this transformation of the North Carolina spirit,
a great majority of the state's people still clung to the glorious
and reassuring story of Mecklenburg. It continued to be taught
in the schools. Writing in 1941, Jonathan Daniels recalled an
occasion when, in Raleigh, he had "stood with other little
boys and girls in the dim rotunda of the Capitol and pulled
back a drape from a plaque" reaffirming that the state had

been earliest in independence. "(That was one of the things about North Carolina the whole country seemed conspiring to forget.)" Students who went on to college might learn to favor May 31 over May 20. "Controversy concerning these two dates," a Tar Heel wrote in the *American Mercury*, "has divided families and estranged friends and kinsmen." But North Carolina as a whole retained her old reputation for self-delusion, along with her new reputation for progressiveness.[42]

As always, the least skepticism was to be found in Mecklenburg County. Anniversary celebrations kept on reminding the world that Charlotte had been more than a year ahead of Philadelphia. In 1925, for the sesquicentennial, there was a big pageant, and in 1948 an even bigger one—the symphonic drama *Shout Freedom!*, the work of LeGette Blythe, a descendant of one of the "signers."

In 1954 the main speaker was President Dwight D. Eisenhower, and present with him were the secretary of the army and about thirty-five generals. Warplanes roaring overhead saluted the guests and the occasion. The speech proved to be a fine example of Eisenhower's elocution. "And we have met, in addition, for the purpose, the additional purpose of honoring those men of long ago who, patriots in their time, signed the Mecklenburg Declaration," the president said. "It matters not that part of the document had to be reconstructed from memories of those who were present. The fact is that it was an important step in our development because today people venerate the occurrence."[43] Thus Eisenhower managed to hold on to both horns of his dilemma.

The dilemma for an outsider had become even sharper by 1975 when Charlotte was readying for a grand bicentennial, to be climaxed by another speech by a president of the United States. Again there was to be a play by LeGette Blythe. This time there were also to be commemorative coins, a mock battle against British troops, and a reenactment of the ride of Capt. James Jack, who was supposed to have carried a copy of the May 20 resolutions to the Continental Congress in 1775.

The state's two senators and eleven congressmen, as well as the governor, were to be on hand.

But the affair was to be lacking in the sanction of scholarship. With the exception of Chalmers Davidson of Davidson College, no academic historian in the state was willing to say a good word for the Mecklenburg Declaration. Leading authorities, such as Hugh Lefler and William Powell of the University of North Carolina at Chapel Hill and Blackwell Robinson of the University of North Carolina at Greensboro, questioned its authenticity. Even a historian at the University of North Carolina at Charlotte, a Massachusetts native, Edward S. Perzel, made bold to speak out against it. Local citizens, Perzel soon realized, did not take kindly either to him or to his views. "This is very, very serious to a lot of people here," he said. "When they figure out who I am, they're just not nice."[44]

What would President Gerald R. Ford have to say on the subject? He could have taken a cue from Gov. James Holshouser, who escaped the dilemma in a way that some others had done before him. At a press conference on the eve of the celebration the governor said the only question was whether the date was May 20. "Far more important than the date is the fact that we were first." But the president preferred to keep clear of controversy—to avoid acknowledgment of its very existence. His prepared speech lauded North Carolina as a "showcase" state, one that revered the past while leading the way toward a progressive future. The speech, as distributed in advance copies, barely mentioned the Mecklenburg Declaration, cautiously characterizing it as a "symbol of pride."[45] At the last minute the president decided to omit even this noncommittal reference, and in delivering his address on May 20 he made no mention of his reason for being in Charlotte. Nor did either of the national news magazines specify the occasion in reporting his presence there.[46] Though still a live issue in North Carolina, the question of her priority in independence no longer aroused any interest in the rest of the country.

Chapter 2. Who Started the War, Abraham Lincoln or Jefferson Davis?

To most Northerners of the Civil War generation, it seemed obvious that the Southerners had started the war. The Southerners had fired the first shot and, what was worse, had done so without real provocation. They had begun the bloodshed on being informed that the Federal government would attempt to carry food to a few dozen hungry and beleaguered men.

To certain Northerners, however, and to practically all Southerners, it seemed just as obvious that Lincoln was to blame. While the war was still going on, one New York Democrat confided to another his suspicion that Lincoln had brought off an "adroit manoeuver" to "precipitate the attack" for its "expected effect upon the public feeling of the North." A one-time Kentucky governor, speaking in Liverpool, England, stated that the Republicans had schemed to "provoke a collision in order that they might say that the Confederates had made the first attack." The Richmond journalist E. A. Pollard wrote in his wartime history of the war that Lincoln had "procured" the assault and thus, by an "ingenious artifice," had himself commenced the fighting. "He chose to draw the sword," the *Petersburg Express* asserted, "but by a dirty trick succeeded in throwing upon the South the *seeming* blame of firing the first gun."

When, soon after the war's end, Alexander H. Stephens wrote his memoirs, he had no doubt as to who the real aggressor had been in 1861. In the book, he conducted an imaginary colloquium. "Do you mean to say, Mr. Stephens, that the war was inaugurated by Mr. Lincoln?" he had one of his listeners ask. "Most assuredly I do," Stephens replied. "Why, how in the world . . . ?" the incredulous one persisted. "It is a fact that the *first gun* was fired by the Confederates," Stephens conceded. Then he patiently explained that the aggressor in a war is not the first to use force but the first to make force necessary.

Jefferson Davis, in his account of *The Rise and Fall of the Confederate Government* (1881), agreed with Stephens on this point, though he had agreed with him on little else while the two were president and vice president of the Confederacy. "He who makes the assault is not necessarily he who strikes the first blow or fires the first gun," Davis wrote. Referring to the Republicans and the Sumter expedition, he elaborated: "To have awaited further strengthening of their position by land and naval forces, with hostile purpose now declared, would have been as unwise as it would be to hesitate to strike down the arm of the assailant, who levels a deadly weapon at one's breast, until he has actually fired."[1]

Some Northerners, defenders of Lincoln, took a view rather similar to that of his Southern critics but presented it in a very different light. They praised Lincoln for essentially the same reasons that Davis, Stephens, and others blamed him.

In a book (1882) purporting to give the "true stories" of Sumter and Pickens, and dedicated to the "old friends" of Robert Anderson, a lieutenant colonel of the United States Army maintained that the advice of General Winfield Scott and Secretary of State William H. Seward to withdraw from Sumter was quite sound from a merely military standpoint. "But Mr. Lincoln and Mr. [Postmaster General Montgomery] Blair judged more wisely that it would be better to sacrifice the garrison of Sumter for political effect." They sent the expedition "with the knowledge that it would compel the rebels to strike the first blow. If the last man in the garrison of Sumter had perished, it would have been a cheap price to pay for the magnificent outburst of patriotism that followed."

In their ten-volume history (1890) Lincoln's former private secretaries, John G. Nicolay and John Hay, wrote that Lincoln cared little whether the Sumter expedition would succeed in its provisioning attempt. "He was not playing a game of military strategy with [P. G. T.] Beauregard [the Confederate commander in Charleston]." He was playing a game for much higher stakes than Sumter itself. "When he finally gave the order that the fleet should sail he was master of the situation . . . master if the rebels hesitated or repented, because they would thereby forfeit their prestige with the South; master if they persisted, for he would then command a united North." He was "looking through and beyond the Sumter expedition to the now inevitable rebel attack and the response of an awakened and united North." The government, of course, was in the right. "But to make the issue sure, he determined in addition that the rebellion should be put in the wrong." His success entitled him to the high honors of "universal statesmanship."

In later generations a number of writers repeated the view that Lincoln himself had compelled the Confederates to fire first. Most of these writers inclined to the opinion that, in doing so, he exhibited less of universal statesmanship than of low cunning. Not till 1935, however, did a professional historian present a forthright statement of the thesis with all the accoutrements of scholarship. In that year Professor Charles W. Ramsdell, of the University of Texas, reading a paper at the annual meeting of the American Historical Association, thus summed up the case:

"Lincoln, having decided that there was no other way than war for the salvation of his administration, his party, and the

Union, maneuvered the Confederates into firing the first shot in order that they, rather than he, should take the blame of beginning bloodshed."

According to the Ramsdell argument, Davis and the rest of the Confederate leaders desired peace. They were eager to negotiate a settlement and avoid a resort to arms. But Lincoln, not so peaceably inclined, refused to deal with them.

During the weeks that followed his inauguration Lincoln was beset on two sides. Coercionists demanded that he take forceful action to rescue Fort Sumter. Moderate men advised him to yield the fort. If he should use force, he might impel the states of the Upper South to secede, and perhaps the border states as well. If he should abandon the fort, the majority of his party would probably abandon him. While he hesitated, his fellow Republicans bickered among themselves, his administration declined in prestige, and the country drifted toward ruin. He had to make up his mind soon, before the Sumter garrison was starved out.

At last he hit upon a way out of his dilemma. The thought occurred to him—*must have* occurred to him—that he could induce the Confederates to attack the fort. Then, the flag having been fired upon, he would gain all the benefits of an aroused patriotism. Republicans and Democrats would forget their quarrels of party and faction, the border states would respond with an upsurge of loyalty, and wavering millions throughout the North would rally to the Union cause. The party, the administration, and the Union would be saved.

The stratagem was a shrewd one, worthy of the shrewd man that Lincoln was. He decided to send the expedition and—most cleverly—to give advance notice. A genius with words, he could make them mean different things to different people. This is what he did with the words he addressed to the governor of South Carolina. To Northerners these words would seem quite innocent. The government was taking groceries to starving men and would not use force unless it had to. That was all. To Southerners the same words carried a threat, indeed a double threat. First, Sumter was going to be provisioned so that it could hold out. Second, if resistance should be offered, arms and men as well as food were going to be run in!

The notice was timed as carefully as it was phrased. It was delivered while the ships of the expedition were departing from New York. They could not reach their destination for three days at least, so the Confederates would have plenty of time to take counteraction before the ships arrived. Already the Confederates had news that a sizable expedition was being prepared, and they were left to suppose that the entire force (including the part of it actually being dispatched to Pensacola) was heading for Charleston. With such a large force presumed to be on the way, they had all the more reason to move quickly.

The ruse worked perfectly. True, the expedition neither provisioned nor reinforced Sumter; it gave the garrison no help at all. But that was not the object. The object was to provoke a shot that would rouse the Northern people to fight.

This Ramsdell thesis was elaborated, with variations, in a book written by a Southern lawyer, John S. Tilley, and published during that fateful year 1941 (when another President was to be accused of a first-shot "maneuver"). Writing in a spirit more appropriate to a criminal court than a scholarly forum, Tilley contended that, at the time of Lincoln's inauguration, there existed no real need for provisioning Sumter. Indeed, Tilley left the impression that Lincoln had invented the story of short supplies at the fort so as to have an excuse for forcing the issue with the Confederacy. One of Tilley's chapter titles announced, "Lincoln Got What He Wanted." The implication was that Lincoln wanted war and went out of his way to get it.[2]

While the Ramsdell thesis has attracted other and more responsible adherents, it has also been challenged by formidable critics. Professor James G. Randall, of the University of Illinois, maintained in the *Abraham Lincoln Quarterly* (1940) and in two books on Lincoln (1945, 1947) that Lincoln intended and expected a peaceful provisioning of the fort. After an independent study of *Lincoln and His Party in the Secession Crisis* (1942), Professor David M. Potter, then of Yale University (now of Stanford University), presented essentially similar conclusions. Lincoln counted upon a resurgence of unionism in the South to overcome secession eventually, without war. To facilitate reunion, he planned to refrain from forcible assertion of Federal authority so long as he could do so without an obvious and outright surrender of it. He would have evacuated Fort Sumter if he had been able promptly enough to reinforce and secure Fort Pickens, so that it could serve as a substitute symbol of Federal authority. Events, however, compelled him to act. Finally, he accepted the necessity of the Sumter expedition, but he took care to make it as unprovocative as possible. By means of it he hoped merely to preserve the existing status in Charleston Harbor. His policy was a failure, since it culminated in war. Such is the contention of Professors Randall and Potter.

In between the Randall-Potter thesis of the peace policy and the Ramsdell-Tilley thesis of the war maneuver, there is yet a third interpretation that sees Lincoln's policy as aiming at neither war nor peace, as such, but as risking the chance of war. Professor Kenneth M. Stampp, of the University of California, stated this thesis of the calculated risk in the *Journal of Southern History* (1945) and restated it in his book *And the War Came* (1950). According to Stampp, Lincoln's primary purpose was to preserve the Union and to do so by a "strategy of defense" which would avoid even the appearance of initiating hostilities.[3]

2

One version of the Sumter story—Tilley's insinuation that Lincoln faked the hunger crisis at the fort—may be immediately ruled out. This insinuation was based mainly upon the absence of evidence. Tilley could not find the letter, or even a copy of the letter, that Lincoln was supposed to have seen on the day after his inauguration, the letter in which Major Anderson, in command at Sumter, revealed shortages of certain essential supplies and the necessity of either replenishing these or abandoning the fort. Now, it may be good legal practice to argue from the absence of evidence. It is not sound historical scholarship. Even at the time Tilley wrote, there were documents available referring to the Anderson letter and indicating clearly enough that it actually had been written and sent. Later, after the opening of the Robert Todd Lincoln Collection of Lincoln papers in the Library of Congress, in 1947, lo! there was the missing letter that Tilley had been at such pains to prove nonexistent.[4]

The Ramsdell thesis itself does not necessarily fall with the collapse of Tilley's case, though much of Ramsdell's evidence is either inconclusive or irrelevant. He devoted a considerable part of his essay merely to showing that various pressures or supposed pressures had induced Lincoln to decide in favor of sending the Sumter expedition, but this line of argument has little bearing upon the main issue to which Ramsdell had addressed himself. As his critic Randall aptly commented, "The inducing-to-attack argument does not proceed very far before it involves a subtle change of approach, so that the very decision to send the expedition is treated as the aggressive or provocative thing, whereas the point at issue . . . is whether the sending of supplies to feed the garrison was not in Lincoln's mind compatible with continued peace efforts."[5]

This is indeed a crucial question. It may be restated thus: Did Lincoln think, or did he have good reason to think, that he could send his expedition to Sumter and his advance notice to the South Carolina governor without encountering resistance on the part of the Confederate forces at Charleston? Unfortunately, there is no direct, contemporary evidence to show

what Lincoln *actually thought* about the probable Confederate reaction. There is, however, plenty of evidence to indicate
what he *had good reason to think.*

Lincoln was familiar with the news of recent events at
Charleston—events illustrating the readiness of the Confederate batteries to open up. He knew that in January his prede-
cessor, President James Buchanan, had sent an unescorted and
unarmed merchant steamer with provisions and (below deck)
troops for Sumter, and that the Charleston batteries had fired
upon this vessel and compelled her to turn back. Now, Lincoln
was sending not one ship but several, including warships. He
had reason to expect that his expedition would meet with at
least the same degree of hostility as Buchanan's had met with,
if not more. Before Lincoln's expedition had actually sailed,
he received confirmation of this probability in the report that,
on April 3, the Confederate batteries fired upon the Boston
schooner *R. H. Shannon,* which innocently had put in at
Charleston Harbor to get out of the ocean fog.

When Lincoln called upon his cabinet for written advice,
on March 15 and again on March 29, he got little assurance
the first time and still less the second time that a peaceful provisioning would be likely. The first time only two of the seven
members favored making the attempt, and only one of the
two, Secretary of the Treasury Salmon P. Chase, was confident
that it could be made without armed conflict. The second
time only one definitely opposed the attempt, but even Chase,
who still favored it, had lost his confidence that it could be
carried out peaceably. Secretary of the Navy Gideon Welles,
who had changed from opposition to approval, now expressed
an opinion similar to Chase's. "There is little possibility that
this will be permitted," Welles stated, "if the opposing forces
can prevent it."

The objection may be raised that, nevertheless, Lincoln had
reason to think *his* Sumter expedition, unlike Buchanan's,
might be tolerated by the authorities in Charleston because
he intended to give, and did give, advance notice of its coming,

whereas Buchanan had not done so. Though Ramsdell has characterized this notice as a threat, and a double-barreled one at that, his critics have replied that it was no such thing. They say it was given "to show that hostile surprise was not intended" and to make clear Lincoln's "non aggressive pur pose." Whether the notification, with its reference to "men, arms, or ammunition," constituted a threat, we need not stop to debate. We need only to recall what Lincoln had learned recently from Stephen S. Hurlbut, his secret emissary to Charleston. Hurlbut reported his conclusion "that a ship known to contain *only provisions* for Sumpter would be stopped & refused admittance." In the light of this information, Lincoln would have had little ground for expecting that his notice would mollify the Confederates even if he had confined it to a simple announcement that he would attempt to supply "provisions only."

If Lincoln had intended and expected nothing but a peaceful provisioning, he no doubt would have been surprised and disappointed at the actual outcome. In fact, however, he repeatedly expressed a feeling of at least qualified satisfaction and success. When he replied to the Virginia delegates at the White House, on April 13, he said in an almost triumphant tone that the "unprovoked assault" would set him "at liberty" to go beyond the self-imposed limitations of his inaugural and to "repossess" as well as "hold, occupy, and possess" Federal positions in the seceded states. When he consoled Gustavus Vasa Fox, the frustrated commander of the expedition, on May 1, he wrote, "You and I both anticipated that the cause of the country would be advanced by making the attempt to provision Fort-Sumpter, even if it should fail; and it is no small consolation now to feel that our anticipation is justified by the result." When he drafted his first message to Congress, for the July 4 session, he emphasized the point that, by the "affair at Fort Sumpter," he had succeeded in making good his earlier declaration that, if war should come, the seceders would have to be the aggressors. And when he read the message to his Illinois friend, Senator Orville H. Browning, on July 3, he went on to remark, as Browning paraphrased him, "The plan succeeded. They attacked Sumter—it fell, and thus, did more service than it otherwise could."

In short, it appears that Lincoln, when he decided to send the Sumter expedition, considered hostilities to be *probable*. It also appears, however, that he believed an unopposed and peaceable provisioning to be at least barely *possible*. It is reasonable to suppose that he shared the expectation of his attorney general, who wrote in his diary at the time Fox was leaving New York for Charleston, "One of two things will happen—either the fort will be well provisioned, the Southrons forebearing to assail the boats, or a fierce contest will ensue." If the first rather than the second of the two possibilities had materialized, then Lincoln doubtless could have said afterwards, just as he said when the second of the two occurred, that his plan had succeeded. Doubtless he would have been equally well satisfied, perhaps even better satisfied. Either way, whether the Confederates resisted or not, he would have been (in the words of Nicolay and Hay) "master of the situation."

It follows, then, that neither the Randall-Potter nor the Ramsdell view of Lincoln's intentions and expectations seems quite accurate. On the one hand, Lincoln did not count confidently upon peace, though he thought there was a bare chance of its being preserved for the time being. On the other hand, he did not deliberately provoke war. He thought hostilities would be the likely result, and he was determined that, if they should be, they must clearly be initiated by the Confederates. "To say that Lincoln meant that the first shot would be fired by the other side *if a first shot was fired*," as Randall has most admirably put the matter, "is not to say that he maneuvered to have the first shot fired."[6]

3

The Ramsdell thesis, with its war-maneuver charge, is essentially an effort to document the rationalizations of Davis,
Stephens, and other Confederates or Confederate sympathizers. Similarly, the Randall-Potter thesis, in one of its important
aspects, is essentially an effort to substantiate the explanation
that Lincoln gave after the events, in his July 4 message to
Congress.

Interestingly, Potter observes that to understand Lincoln's
plans at the time of his inauguration, "it is necessary to ex-
clude the misleading perspective of hindsight, and to view the
problem as he viewed it at the time, rather than as he later
viewed it." Yet, in dealing with Lincoln's policy after the inauguration, Potter neglects this very principle. Like Randall, he
bases his argument largely on the misleading perspective of
hindsight, on the way Lincoln viewed the problem in July
rather than the way he viewed it in March and April.

According to Potter, who paraphrases Lincoln's July 4 message, the Sumter expedition was only tentative, the Pickens
expedition definite. The Sumter expedition "was withheld
until the fort was almost starved out, and it was withheld because Lincoln still hoped that he could transfer the issue of
Union to Fort Pickens before the Sumter question reached a
crisis." To both Potter and Randall the critical date is April 6.
This was the date when, as Lincoln said in the message, he
received a report that his order to land the troops already on
shipboard in Pensacola Harbor, to reinforce Fort Pickens, had
not been carried out. And this was the date when Lincoln sent
to Major Anderson, by special messenger, the letter informing
him that the expedition was going ahead (though the letter
was dated April 4). "Up to April 6, then," Randall says, "the
expedition, though prepared, could have been held back." And
the plain implication of Randall and Potter, as well as of Lincoln himself, is that if the troops had been landed at Fort Pick-

ens, and if Lincoln had known of it by April 6, he would have called off the Sumter expedition.[7]

There is undoubtedly an element of truth in this story of a Sumter-for-Pickens sacrifice. During March and early April the idea was discussed in the newspapers, was recommended by a number of Lincoln's Republican correspondents, and was urged again and again by Seward. At one time or another, Lincoln must have given some consideration to it. He could hardly have avoided doing so. Possibly, if he had been assured before March 29 that the troops had been landed and Fort Pickens was safe, he might not have decided at that time to prepare the Sumter expedition. But it appears (in the light of contemporary evidence) that having ordered the Sumter preparations on March 29, he did not thereafter make his policy for Charleston contingent upon events at Pensacola.

Actually, the key dates regarding the Sumter decision are March 29 and April 4, not April 6. After the order for preparations had been given on March 29, there followed a period of vacillation and delay that was exasperating to Fox. The causes were twofold: the fears that visible preparations would hurt the prospects on the New York money market for the government loan to be subscribed on April 2, and the hopes (on the part of Seward) that a last-minute Sumter-for-Virginia deal could be arranged. After the successful sale of the bonds, and after the fiasco of Lincoln's conversation with the Virginia representative, Lincoln decided definitely to go ahead with the Sumter plans. On April 4 he arranged the details with Fox and wrote the letter informing Anderson that supplies would be on the way. That same day a copy of the letter was mailed to Anderson, and Anderson received it three days later. Not sure that the mail had got through, Lincoln sent the second copy by special messenger on April 6. His sending it on that day is no indication whatever that he waited until then to make his final decision regarding Sumter.[8]

True, on April 6, Lincoln learned that his nearly month-old order to land the troops at Pensacola had not been executed.

But, to him, this was hardly unexpected news: it was merely a confirmation of what he already had guessed. As early as March 29 he had suspected that the order somehow had gone astray. On April 1 he was informed, by a communication from Pensacola, that the forces there had (as of March 21) been out of touch with the government. When the report of April 6 arrived, it had only one visible effect upon the administration: it caused the prompt dispatch of a messenger overland to Pensacola with new orders from Secretary Welles to land the troops already there.

Meanwhile, Seward had never given up his obsession with the idea of yielding Sumter and holding Pickens as a kind of substitute. The idea was Seward's, not Lincoln's. Seward stressed it in his brash April 1 memorandum, "Some Thoughts for the President's Consideration," and Lincoln in his written reply on the same day said his own domestic policy was the same as Seward's "with the single exception, that it does not propose to abandon Fort Sumter."

Why, then, did Lincoln tell Congress, in the July 4 message, that he *had* proposed to abandon Fort Sumter if Fort Pickens could be made secure in time? One conceivable reason is that, after the months of preoccupation with the widening war, he had forgotten some of the chronological details of his earlier policy formation. He may well have remembered that on some occasion or other, possibly in mid-March, he had actually given at least fleeting consideration to the proposal. He may not have remembered exactly when, or how seriously. Another conceivable reason is that he was still concerned, in July, about the opinions of those peace-minded Northerners, including many Republicans, who in March and early April had been willing or even eager for Sumter to be evacuated on the condition that Pickens be firmly held. Lincoln may have felt it advisable now to reassure those timid and hesitant ones that he had, indeed, exhausted all the possibilities for peace and, in particular, had carefully considered the Sumter-for-Pickens alternative.

In stressing this alternative as an essential element of Lincoln's April policy, Randall and Potter confuse Lincoln's March and April thinking with Seward's. They make the same error in characterizing Lincoln's overall approach to the secession problem. Potter, for instance, asserts that "Republican policy was consistent" and that party leaders "insisted that delay and avoidance of friction would create a condition under which the Unionists in the South could regain the ascendancy"[9]— certain party leaders, yes, and above all Seward, but Lincoln never fully shared Seward's faith in the do-nothing panacea.

In truth, Republican policy was far from being consistent. The policy of Seward was, at many points, inconsistent with that of Lincoln. The assumption that time would heal all wounds, the hints and promises of an early withdrawal from Sumter, the notion of bargaining Sumter for Virginia, the proposal to abandon Sumter and concentrate on Pickens—all these were hobbies of Seward's. Lincoln had great respect for Seward's abilities and for his political value to the administration. He listened to Seward's suggestions and urgings. To some extent he was influenced by them, but he was by no means converted. Nor did he authorize all of Seward's undertakings. Some of them he knew nothing about until after they had been well advanced.

4

The worst fault in the Ramsdell thesis is a lack of balance and perspective. Ramsdell makes Lincoln appear too much the warmonger, Davis too much the peace lover; Lincoln too much the controlling force, Davis too much the passive agent. Ramsdell argues that the Confederate government "could not, without yielding the principle of independence, abate its claims to the fort." He fails to see that, likewise, the Federal government could not abate its claims without yielding the principle of Union.

Davis made the decision that led directly to war. True, early on the morning of April 12, Beauregard sent Roger A. Pryor, James Chestnut, and two others from Charleston to the fort to present Davis's final terms, and these men on their own rejected Anderson's reply—which was that he would hold his fire and evacuate in three days, unless he should meanwhile receive "controlling instructions" or "additional supplies." Instead of taking responsibility upon themselves, Pryor and the other hot-headed underlings might have referred Anderson's reply to Beauregard, and he in turn to Leroy P. Walker, the Confederate Secretary of War, and Davis. Since Pryor and his colleagues went ahead without thus referring to higher authority, the story arose that they and not Davis had made the real decision. The story seemed to be confirmed by the testimony that Pryor gave to an historian many years later, in 1909. Accepting Pryor's account, the historian wrote, "Pryor and his associates did not report to the General, but, thinking that Davis was trying to reconstruct the Union and negotiate with Seward to that end and that the chance of war was about to slip away forever, they conferred together and decided to give the signal to the gunners to fire—and war began, and such a war!"[10] War began, all right, but the main point of Pryor's testimony has no foundation in fact. When Pryor and his associates rejected Anderson's reply, they were faithfully following the line of Davis's policy, and Davis afterwards fully approved what they had done. The real decision was his, not theirs.

Davis justified his decision on the ground that "the reduction of Fort Sumter was a measure of defense rendered absolutely and immediately necessary." In fact, however, Sumter in April 1861 offered no immediate threat to the physical safety of Charleston or of South Carolina or of the other six Confederate states. Nor did the approach of Fox's small fleet suddenly create such a threat. The landing of supplies—or even of men, arms, and ammunition—would have made little difference in the existing power balance.

Writers of the Ramsdell school insist that there was no

military reason for Lincoln's effort to provision the fort. They cannot have it both ways. If there was no military reason for Lincoln's attempt, there could have been none for Davis's effort to forestall it.

Indeed, the Ramsdell thesis, turned inside out, could be applied to Davis with as much justice as it has been applied to Lincoln. One could argue that political and not military necessity led Davis to order the firing of the first shot. The very life of the Confederacy, the growth upon which that life depended, was at stake. So were the pride, the prestige, and the position of Davis. Ramsdell himself, a distinguished authority on Confederate history, might appropriately have devoted his talents to an essay on "Davis and Fort Sumter" instead of "Lincoln and Fort Sumter."

Biographers of Davis and historians of the Confederacy have evaded or obscured their hero's role in the Sumter affair. They have digressed to levy accusations or innuendoes at Lincoln. If they have any concern for historical objectivity, however, they should face frankly the question of Davis's responsibility for the coming of the war. Upon them, upon *his* partisans, should rest the burden of proof. It should not have to be borne forever, as it has for far too many years, by Lincoln's champions. After all, Lincoln did not order the guns to fire. Davis did.[11]

5

Authorities agree pretty well as to what actually happened in March and April 1861. They disagree about the meaning of the events and, in particular, about the aims of Lincoln. To judge historical significance involves a certain amount of guessing, and to ascertain a man's intentions (especially when the man is so closemouthed as Lincoln or, for that matter, Davis) requires a bit of mind reading. For these reasons, the true inwardness of the Sumter story will, in some of its aspects, always be more or less moot. The probable truth may be summarized as follows:

At the time of his inauguration Lincoln was determined to retake the Federal positions already lost to the seceding states as well as to hold the positions not yet lost. When he revised his inaugural, so as to announce only the "hold, occupy, and possess" objective, he did not really change or limit his original purpose. He meant to achieve this purpose, however, without appearing to initiate the use of force. He did not yet know precisely how he was going to manage so delicate a task, but he assumed that he would have plenty of time in which to deal with the problem.

Then, for about three weeks, he hesitated with regard to Fort Sumter, though not with regard to Fort Pickens, which he promptly ordered to be reinforced by means of the troops already available there. In the case of Sumter, the bad news from Anderson and the deterring counsel from Scott and the cabinet gave him pause. During the period of hesitation he considered alternative lines of action as at least temporary expedients—the collection of customs on ships off Southern ports, the evacuation of Sumter if and when Pickens had been made absolutely secure, the provisioning (with advance notice) but not the reinforcing of Sumter.

On March 29 he gave orders for the preparation of an expedition to provision Sumter—and also, conditionally, to reinforce it. He had decided to act because, from various sources of advice and information, he had concluded that a retreat at any point (except in the face of superior force) would lead eventually to a retreat at all points. If he were to yield to the demand for Sumter, he would still face the demand for Pickens and the other Florida forts, to say nothing of the demand for recognition of the Confederacy. True, if he took a stand, he would run the risk of antagonizing and losing Virginia and other still-loyal slave states. But if he declined to take a stand, he would still risk losing those states, through conferring new prestige and attractiveness upon the Confederacy. And, besides, he would surely alienate many of his adherents in the North.

Soon afterward, at Seward's urging, Lincoln ordered also the preparation of another expedition, this one to be secret, unannounced, and intended for the immediate reinforcement of Fort Pickens. Even its sponsor, Seward, did not expect the enterprise to be peaceably received: he merely thought Pensacola a better place than Charleston for war to begin. The Pickens expedition got off first, the Sumter preparations running into various snags, including Seward's efforts at sabotage.

On April 4, in consultation with Fox, Lincoln made the final arrangements for the Sumter effort. According to these carefully laid plans, Fox's men would try to run in supplies by boats or tugs. If challenged, the pilot would hand over a note explaining that the aim was only to take food to the garrison, and that if the Confederates fired upon the boats, they would be firing upon unarmed and defenseless men. Already the South Carolina governor would have received his notice. Thus the arrival of the boats would put the Confederates in a dilemma. If they fired, they would convict themselves of an atrocity. If not, they could hardly prevent the fort from being supplied. Either way, they would lose.

And if they fired, the guns of the warships offshore and of the fort itself would fire back and, hopefully, clear the way for the supplies to be taken in, along with reinforcements. This would, no doubt, entail a certain amount of bloodshed, but surely the Federal government would appear to be justified, in the eyes of most Northerners and of many Southerners as well. Even the majority of Virginians, under these circumstances, would possibly think twice before countenancing the secession of their state.

In certain respects the outcome was not to be quite what Lincoln anticipated.

The policy of the Montgomery government was less passive, less cautious, than he supposed. That policy aimed to get control of Sumter and the other forts as soon as it could be done, by negotiations if feasible, by siege or assault if not. The mission to Washington had a twofold function: on the one hand, to seek recognition of the Confederacy and a peaceful transfer of the forts and, on the other, to gain time for military preparations to be used in case diplomacy should fail. Once the preparations had proceeded far enough, the termination of diplomacy was to be the signal for the beginning of military measures. By early April, in Charleston, Beauregard was ready. Soon he would have begun actual operations for taking Sumter—even if Lincoln had never planned or sent an expedition of any kind (unless Anderson should promptly have given up, which was a possibility, or Lincoln should have invited the commissioners to talk with him, which was not).

When Davis heard of Lincoln's notice to the South Carolina governor, on April 8, his immediate response was to order Beauregard to prevent the landing of the supplies. It is interesting to speculate about what might have happened if Davis had stuck to this decision. Most likely, Beauregard then would have waited for the actual approach of the provisioning boats. But Fox, considering the storm-caused delays and the non-appearance of the flagship, *Powhatan*, probably would have decided not to send the boats in. In that event, the Sumter expedition would have proved an utter fiasco. Lincoln would have lost prestige and Davis gained it. Or, after hesitation, Fox might have made a token effort. Then things would have happened pretty much as Lincoln had calculated, except that the expedition would not have had the power to open the way for the supplies.

But Davis and his advisers did not remain content with their decision of April 8. Two days later they made a new one, and orders went to Beauregard to demand a surrender and, failing to get that, to reduce the fort.

This reaction, though more than Lincoln had counted on, was somewhat better, from his point of view, than the previous one. If the Confederates were going to fire at all, it was well that they should do so without even waiting until the food-laden boats were in sight. The eagerness of the Confederates would the more surely convict them of aggression, and this was all to the good, even though it would mean that Sumter would have less chance of being actually reinforced and held.

The first shot having been fired, the response of the North more than reconciled Lincoln to the loss of the fort, if not also to the loss of Virginia, Arkansas, Tennessee, and North Carolina. The response of the North certainly went far toward making possible the ultimate redemption of the Union.

In those early April days both Lincoln and Davis took chances which, in retrospect, seem awesome. The chances they took eventuated in the most terrible of all wars for the American people. Lincoln and Davis, as each made his irrevocable decision, could see clearly enough the cost of holding back. Neither could see so clearly the cost of going ahead. Both expected, or at least hoped, that the hostilities would be limited in space and time. Lincoln thought of blockade and boycott and a few seaborne operations against coastal forts. Davis thought of accessions and allies—in the slave states, in foreign countries, and in the North itself—that would make the Confederacy too strong for its independence to be long contested.

The Sumter incident itself did not lead at once to general war. Neither side was yet prepared for that. By a kind of escalation, however, war rapidly developed, and the lines were soon drawn. Through his proclamation of April 15, calling for 75,000 volunteers, Lincoln unintentionally contributed to the growth of the martial spirit on both sides. Perhaps if in that proclamation he had stressed his defensive purposes, especially the need for troops to protect the capital, he might at least have strengthened the unionists in Virginia and the other nonseceded slave states.

The charge of "aggression," which has been bandied for so long, should not concern historians except as it figured in the propaganda of 1861 and after. From the Confederate point of view the United States had made itself the aggressor long before Lincoln acted to strengthen any fort. It was aggression when, on December 26, 1860, Major Anderson moved his small force from their exposed position at Fort Moultrie to the somewhat more secure one at Fort Sumter. Indeed, it was a continuing act of aggression every day that United States forces remained in Sumter or any other place within the boundaries of the Confederacy. And from the Union point of view the Confederacy had committed and was committing aggression by its very claim to existence, to say nothing of its seizures of Federal property and its preparations to seize Sumter and Pickens. Viewed impartially, both sides were guilty of aggression, and neither was.

When Lincoln expressed his desire for peace he was sincere, and so was Davis when he did the same. But Lincoln thought of peace for one, undivided country; Davis, of peace for two separate countries. "Both parties deprecated war," as Lincoln later put it, "but one of them would *make* war rather than let the nation survive; and the other would *accept* war rather than let it perish. And the war came."[12]

Chapter 3. The Myth of the Jealous Son

Believe it or not, the Civil War came because Abraham Lincoln suffered from an Oedipus complex. He had no use for his father, refused to visit him in his last illness, subconsciously wished him dead. He found a surrogate in George Washington, the Father of His Country. Still, Lincoln was a jealous as well as a worshipful son, for he was inordinately ambitious, and he had to compete with Washington's incomparable fame. No longer could any American gain immortality as a founder of the Republic, but there remained the possibility of making oneself the savior of it. Lincoln indulged in fantasies of saving it from a would-be destroyer and dictator—fantasies, that is, of saving it from himself. Consciously or unconsciously he aspired to destroy and refound the Republic, to slay the Founding Fathers and take their place. "The way that Lincoln cast himself into the center of the political conflict between the sections over slavery transformed that conflict into a civil war that created a modern nation while it destroyed forever the old Republic of the fathers."[1] In the process he won the immortality he sought, and he won it "by becoming the very tyrant against whom Washington had warned in his Farewell Address."[2]

Lincoln the tyrant! Lincoln the father killer! If he was Oedipus Rex, one wonders who, in this latter-day scenario, was Jocasta, the Mother whom he married. More seriously, one wonders whether all this amounts to anything more than the latest in a long series of base and baseless characterizations of Lincoln. Certainly he has taken Washington's place as first in the hearts of his countrymen. Since 1948, historians have rated the presidents in at least a half-dozen polls, and in every one of them Lincoln has emerged as the greatest.[3] Yet, 175 years after his birth, he continues to be, as he was during his lifetime, the subject of denigrating myth.

A pioneer among the myth makers and psychologizers was, of course, Lincoln's one-time law partner William H. Herndon. "If there is anything that a poor ignorant Sucker like myself can arrogate to myself," Herndon once wrote, "it is this, namely, an intuitive seeing of human character." He thought he, if anyone, could look right into Lincoln's very "gizzard." From Herndon's remarkable insight came a number of familiar stories, among them the story that Lincoln never loved any woman except Ann Rutledge and that Mary Todd married him not out of love but out of revenge.

Though not adopting those particular themes from Herndon, the recent psychologizers look to him for much of their information and insight, especially in regard to Lincoln's ambition—that "little engine that knew no rest," as Herndon called it.[4] But mainly they draw their inspiration from Sigmund Freud and other psychoanalysts, most notably Erik H. Erikson, author of *Young Man Luther: A Study in Psychoanalysis and History* (1958). The new interpreters of Lincoln also acknowledge a debt to the literary critic Edmund Wilson, who included a Lincoln essay in his study of Civil War literature *Patriotic Gore* (1962). For Wilson and his psychologizing followers, the key document in Lincoln's self-revelation is his address before the Young Men's Lyceum of Springfield on January 27, 1838.

On that occasion, about two weeks before his twenty-ninth birthday, Lincoln took as his topic "The Perpetuation of Our Political Institutions." We the "legal inheritors" of "fundamental blessings" from our Revolutionary forefathers, he proceeded to orate, now face a possible threat to our republican inheritance, not from some enemy abroad but from developments at home. Recent lynchings in various parts of the country indicate a trend toward "mob law." If this should reach a point where government can no longer protect lives and property, citizens generally may become alienated from government. Then, promising law and order, some extraordinarily ambitious man may take over as dictator. "Many great and good men sufficiently qualified for any task they should undertake, may ever be found, whose ambition would aspire to nothing beyond a seat in Congress, a gubernatorial or a presidential chair; *but such belong not to the family of the lion, or the tribe of the eagle.* What! think you these places would satisfy an Alexander, a Caesar, or a Napoleon? Never!" The way to avert this danger, Lincoln concluded, is to cultivate a "political religion" that emphasizes "reverence for the laws" and puts reliance on "reason, cold, calculating, unimpassioned reason."[5]

Reading between the lines, Edmund Wilson says "it is evident that Lincoln has projected himself into the role against which he is warning" here. According to Wilson, the young Lincoln already was "extremely ambitious" and "saw himself in the heroic role." So he issued an "equivocal warning against the ambitious leader, describing this figure with a fire that seemed to derive as much from admiration as from apprehension." Not only was he revealing his own self-perception but he was also being "startlingly prophetic" when he spoke of a "towering genius" who would "burn for distinction" and if possible would "have it, whether at the expense of emancipating slaves or enslaving freemen."[6]

One of the recent psychobiographers, George B. Forgie, in his *Patricide in the House Divided* (1979), concedes that "Wilson was partially correct, for Lincoln's image of danger is on the one hand so precise and on the other so far removed from any plausible threat that it must have appeared first on some inner mirror." But Forgie insists that, to "clarify or amend" Wilson's proposition that Lincoln was identifying with the would-be dictator, it is important to add that "Lincoln was doing so *unconsciously*. So close is the description to certain traits of the describer that only a man completely unconscious of what he was doing would have presented it." Forgie maintains that, at a "conscious level," Lincoln was "among the most devoted of all sons of the revolutionary fathers. There is no evidence that at this level he ever questioned that it was his duty to preserve"—not to destroy the republican edifice the fathers had erected.[7]

Another of the new interpreters, Charles B. Strozier, in *Lincoln's Quest for Union* (1982), accepts the Wilson thesis but agrees with Forgie that Lincoln was expressing only his "unacknowledged (or unconscious) wishes." "His desire to be the greatest and most powerful leader of all time, to be the towering genius, appears in the speech as motivating someone else," Strozier explains. "The other figure he feared because it spoke for his forbidden self; the wish, as Freud has observed, is father to the fear." Strozier underscores the "oedipal implications" of the speech. After quoting Lincoln's metaphor comparing the fathers of the republic to "giant oaks . . . shorn of . . . foliage . . . with mutilated limbs," he comments, "The imagery here suggests emasculation and castration at the hands of the aspiring son."

Strozier freely indicates the influence of Erik H. Erikson. His chapter title "Young Man Lincoln" obviously derives from Erikson's book title *Young Man Luther*. To his own analysis of Lincoln he applies principles that Erikson uses in analyzing his subject—for example, the principle that avoidance of personal commitment and intimacy "may lead to a deep sense of isolation and consequent self-absorption," which, Strozier says, "fits well with what we know about Lincoln." Strozier finds a significant similarity between Luther's and Lincoln's paths to greatness. "After 1854 Lincoln turned outward and attempted, as Erik Erikson might say, to solve for all what he could not solve for himself." That is to say, after failing to overcome the divisive forces within his own personality, he succeeded in his "quest for union" by overcoming the divisive forces in the nation at large.[8]

A third analyst, Dwight G. Anderson, in *Abraham Lincoln: The Quest for Immortality* (1982), states frankly that his "definition of the subject matter is dependent upon Freud's theory of the origins of monotheism and Erik Erikson's study of Martin Luther." Monotheism is presumably relevant because, according to Anderson, Lincoln wanted to be God. "His project of becoming 'God' worked itself out in both a private and public context, against both his natural father and his political father, with the result that a personal death anxiety became transformed into a symbolic immortality both for himself and for the nation." Anderson adds, "Some assistance in understanding Lincoln's preoccupation with death is offered by Erik Erikson's comments on the 'young great man' in the years before he becomes the 'great young man.' Erikson had Martin Luther in mind, but his words describe Lincoln just as well."

Anderson agrees with Forgie and Strozier in accepting the Edmund Wilson thesis but disagrees with them by insisting that Lincoln *consciously* identified himself with the "towering genius," the potential tyrant. To clinch the point, Anderson directs attention to one particular clause in the Lyceum speech. Lincoln is saying that many have sought and achieved fame in pursuit of independence and the new government. "But," he continues, "the game is caught; *and I believe it is true*, that with the catching, end the pleasures of the chase." Anderson provides the following gloss: "Here was Lincoln . . . projecting himself ('and I believe it is true') into the very role against which he warned his audience—a Caesarean role in which the player would have his distinction no matter what the cost—whether by freeing slaves or enslaving free men."

Anderson is not content with disagreeing with Forgie but goes on to denounce him and his views with considerable virulence. Anderson declares:

Forgie's work is an illustration of why psychohistory is so widely held in disrepute. He argues that Lincoln created the tyrant out of "undesirable wishes he could not recognize in himself," which "he expelled and then reified . . . into the image of the bad son." In a footnote he explains, "Psychoanalysts call this operation 'projection.'" Actually, however, it is Forgie's projection rather than Lincoln's that is the relevant factor in this interpretation. For not only does Forgie ignore Lincoln's explicit statement of identification with those who might become tyrant ("and I believe it is true . . ."), it is hardly bold to assume that he may also have been unconsciously hostile to Lincoln's actual words, because his central thesis is that Stephen A. Douglas is the "bad son" of the Lyceum Address whom Lincoln symbolically killed in the 1850s. This preposterous conclusion . . . would seem to be a monumental case of intellectual regression in service of the professional ego (to alter slightly a characterization Forgie applies to Lincoln).[9]

Now that is surely an instance of the pot calling the kettle black. If Forgie, as charged, reads Lincoln in the light of private preconceptions, Anderson certainly does the same—and with results that are even more farfetched. Nowhere does Lincoln make, as Anderson claims, an "explicit statement of identification with those who might become tyrant." Lincoln's words "and I believe it is true" lead up to no such statement. Lincoln is *not* saying, "I believe it is true that I am one of those aspiring dictators." He is merely saying, "I believe it is true that the pleasures of the chase end when the game has been caught." His meaning is perfectly plain to any reader who is neither riding a hobby nor being ridden by one.

Anderson's book lacks the redeeming qualities that both Forgie's and Strozier's possess. Dealing not only with the words of Lincoln but also with those of many of his contemporaries, Forgie has sought out the metaphor of the house and the family in a wide range of antebellum American writing, and he has shown imagination and skill in arranging the quotations to fit a Freudian pattern. Strozier, generally a careful historian as well as a competent psychiatrist, has written what is on the whole a warm, sympathetic, and moving as well as illuminating account, one that adds to our understanding of Lincoln's private motives and their relation to his public stance.

It seems too bad that these two historians should have taken at face value the *ipse dixit* of Edmund Wilson, illustrious though he may have been as a fiction writer and a literary critic. The credulity of Anderson is perhaps more understandable, since he is a political scientist, not a historian. All three authors, in adopting Erik Erikson's model, abandon the historian's standards. According to Erikson, "the making of legend is as much part of the scholarly rewriting of history as it is part of the original facts used in the work of scholars. We are thus obliged to accept half-legend as half-history, provided only that a reported episode does not contradict other well-established facts; persists in having a ring of truth; and yields a meaning consistent with psychological theory."[10]

Well, the assertion that Lincoln aspired to dictatorship, even to godhood, contradicts no known facts—except perhaps for the fact that as president he showed great restraint in the exercise of his powers and great respect for the constitutional limits on them. The assertion has the "ring of truth" for those who think it has, and it yields meanings that appear to be consistent with one psychological theory or another. Thus it may meet the requirements of "half-history," but it does not meet those of whole history. Historians are taught to accept only the testimony that two or more independent and competent witnesses confirm. The hypothesis of Lincoln the would-be patricide and tyrant gets no support whatever from historical evidence. Rather, the record of his career suggests that he himself was one of those "great and good men" he referred to in the Lyceum speech—one of those who would have been satisfied with a presidential chair or even a senatorial seat.

We may reasonably conclude that in this speech Lincoln means exactly what he says. If we are to draw inferences from his remarks, we ought to keep in mind the context of the time. When he speaks of a rising "mobocratic spirit" he gives examples of it, and we could easily add other examples. When he warns against a leader who may seek power and fame "whether at the expense of emancipating slaves, or enslaving freemen," we do not have to jump to the conclusion that he is prophesying his own future, as Edmund Wilson does. We may safely assume that he in thinking of the abolitionist and pro-slavery feelings of the very moment—feelings that accounted for the recent mob murder of Elijah Lovejoy in nearby Alton, Illinois.[11]

And when Lincoln talks of overweening ambition—of a homegrown Alexander, Caesar, or Napoleon—we do not have to probe his psyche to find out what he really means. He was a Whig, and the Whigs were used to referring to Andrew Jackson as "King Andrew the First," a veritable tyrant or at least an incipient one, as they saw him. Whigs and other Americans—those of them with even a bit of schooling—were familiar with the name of Julius Caesar and with the fate of the Roman republic. They were even better acquainted with the career of Napoleon Bonaparte, who after all was nearly a contemporary, having been dead less than seventeen years when Lincoln addressed the Lyceum.

How curious it is that any present-day American historian should think, as Forgie does, that Lincoln's "image of danger" was "so far removed from any plausible threat that it must have appeared first on some inner mirror"! Whether plausible or not to Forgie, the potential threat was real enough in the view of early-nineteenth-century Americans who knew something of the history of republics, ancient, medieval, and modern. Politicians from the generation of George Washington and John Adams to that of Daniel Webster and John C. Calhoun made their constituents aware of the possible danger. To discover it, Lincoln did not have to peer into his inner consciousness or subconsciousness.

Not for any cryptic meanings but for its manifest message the Lyceum speech is a remarkable production to have come from a twenty-eight-year-old man of Lincoln's background. One of its insights, neglected by commentators, qualifies the author as something of a psychologist, a social psychologist, himself. In explaining why it was easier to maintain republican institutions during the Revolutionary period than in his own time, he says that during the Revolution "the deep rooted principles of *hate,* and the powerful motive of *revenge,* instead of being turned [by Americans] against each other, were directed exclusively against the British nation." Since then, however, in the absence of a menacing external foe, the "*passions* of the people" could be expected to divide and weaken the republic rather than to unite and strengthen it. Here Lincoln is adumbrating the sociological law that the degree of solidarity of the in-group is more or less proportional to the intensity of conflict with an out-group. As a practical proposition, this had been familiar to politicians from time immemorial. Lincoln as president was to decline to apply the principle when Secretary of State William H. Seward, in his memorandum of April 1, 1861, recommended foreign war as a means of preventing civil war.[12]

Psychologizers of Lincoln today ought to exercise at least as much caution as the first of them, William H. Herndon, advised. "He was the most secretive—reticent—shut-mouthed man that ever existed," Herndon said of Lincoln. "You had to *guess* at the man after years of acquaintance, and then you must look long and keenly before you *guessed* or you would make an ass of yourself."[13] And all of us who are eager for the truth ought to heed Lincoln's own request of 1858: "I only ask my friends and all who are eager for the truth, that when they hear me represented as saying or meaning anything strange, they will turn to my own words and examine for themselves."[14]

Chapter 4. Lincoln Biographies: Old and New Myths

Recent single-volume biographies of Abraham Lincoln include one of the best and one of the worst. Admirable despite serious flaws is Stephen B. Oates's *With Malice Toward None* (1977), some themes of which the author makes more explicit in his collection of essays subtitled *The Man Behind the Myths* (1984).[1] Undeserving of even faint praise is Oscar and Lilian Handlin's contribution (1980) to the Library of American Biography, a series of brief, interpretative volumes of which Oscar Handlin is founder and editor.[2]

According to Handlin's specifications, each book in the series is to illuminate the intersection between the subject's life and the nation's history. In such terms the Handlins justify their small contribution to the vast Lincoln literature. They declare that "there is something more to say," and they are confident that they have said it. "Our research has uncovered no facts, but it has encompassed all the facts known," they assert. "And it has provided us with the means of understanding Abraham Lincoln, his times, and the meaning of both."[3]

Certainly there is room for a new short life of Lincoln, an interpretative one that would do what the Handlins claim to have done. Such a volume, to justify itself, would need to distill the best of recent Lincoln scholarship and present the distillation with at least a bit of dramatic flair and literary grace. This the Handlin book fails to do. Three-fourths of its pages are given over to a rather plodding, unimaginative account of the prepresidential years. The treatment of the presidency is not only skimpy but poorly organized. In a chaos of chronology, Lincoln's assassination comes before Lee's surrender, which precedes the 1864 election, which in turn arrives ahead of the 1863 announcement of the 10-percent plan. The ill-told story lacks any clear and consistent theme or combination of themes, and it contains all too many dubious or erroneous statements, including opinions once widely believed but now discredited. A couple of examples: Lincoln as an Illinois legislator in 1835 was "swapping railroads, canals, turnpikes, and bridges for votes" to move the state capital to Springfield; he decided not to run for Congress a second time because of the Illinois reaction to his stand on the Mexican War. In sum, the Handlin volume does not fulfill the promises of its preface, nor does it meet the aim that Handlin himself set for the series.

Oates's Lincoln deserves much more attention than the Handlins'. Indeed, Oates's must be considered as, on the whole, the finest of the one-volume biographies. Among the other notable ones of this century, Lord Charnwood's (1917)[4] and Nathaniel W. Stephenson's (1922)[5] now seem completely outdated and almost quaint. Even Benjamin P. Thomas's (1952)[6] and Reinhard H. Luthin's (1960)[7] appear somewhat old-fashioned by comparison. For instance, neither Thomas nor Luthin included an index entry for Frederick Douglass, Negroes, race, or racism. Oates does list these topics in his index, and he gives them considerable attention in his text, in accordance with his announced intention to reveal Lincoln's "racial views in the context of his time and place."

On matters other than race, the Thomas or the Luthin biography may sometimes be more useful, or at least handier, as a work of reference. But Oates is probably somewhat more readable than Thomas and certainly much more readable than Luthin. Not that Oates's style is flawless. He likes slangy expressions (on one occasion Lincoln "wasn't too interested"; on another he "griped"). He uses overfamiliar terms (surely the hatchet-faced, hard-bitten Montgomery Blair would resent the author's chumminess in always referring to him as "Monty"). He mixes his metaphors (someone once "waded into Lincoln's speech . . . with both fists, flaying it"). He falls into misusages ("by-elections" for "midterm elections") and even into mala propisms ("expostulated" for "expounded"). But gaffes of this kind will probably offend no one except perhaps some old-maidish composition teacher. Nearly all readers will, no doubt, agree with the jacket blurb, which describes the book as "lyrical, engrossing and thoroughly moving." They are likely to get from it a warm sense of sympathy with Lincoln— and with Mrs. Lincoln—in their many trials.

Unlike the Handlins, Oates has kept abreast of the writing on Lincoln and his times. He avows that, in preparing the biography, he has "utilized scores of published source materials and unpublished manuscript collections" in addition to numerous scholarly studies. In his "reference notes," however, he actually cites very few manuscript sources. Essentially the book is a synthesis of recent scholarship and a remarkably comprehensive one. At some points, where scholarship remains divided or uncertain, the Oates account has an assurance and a precision that the sources hardly warrant. But more about that later.

In *With Malice Toward None* the author announces his intention to present the "real Lincoln" in place of the "Lincoln of mythology." He undertakes to carry the exposure further in *Abraham Lincoln: The Man Behind the Myths*, which we may view as a supplement to the biography. "In shaping it," he says of the newer volume, "I benefited enormously from a growing library of modern Lincoln studies. In fact, the last couple of decades have witnessed a veritable renaissance of Lincoln scholarship." Much of this "hasn't reached a broad literary audience. I am addressing that audience, because I want lay readers to rediscover Lincoln as the scholars have."[8]

Oates, then, does not pretend to be offering a strictly original interpretation. Perhaps the most innovative idea in the two books is his characterization of the Radical Republicans as "liberals." According to him, Senators Charles Sumner, Benjamin F. Wade, and Zachariah Chandler "belonged to a loose faction incorrectly categorized as 'radicals,' a misnomer that has persisted through the years." Republicans of this faction "were really progressive, nineteenth-century liberals who felt a powerful kinship with English liberals like John Bright and Richard Cobden."[9] Well, Sumner did feel a certain kinship with Cobden and Bright. He was a free-trader, as they and the rest of the English liberals were, but most members of Sumner's faction were protectionists. Some of them, most notably Sumner himself, were to join the so-called Liberal Republican movement of 1872, but they did not refer to themselves as Liberal Republicans in Lincoln's time. For us now to call them liberals is inappropriate and anachronistic.

Oates apparently prefers to call the Radicals liberals so as to minimize the difference between them and Lincoln, whom he looks upon as another progressive, nineteenth-century liberal. He agrees with those scholars who see Lincoln as lagging only a little behind, and quickly catching up with, the members of his party who took the most advanced position in regard to emancipation, Negro suffrage, and the reconstruction of the seceded states. He is an advocate of what might be called the Donald-Hyman-Trefousse-McPherson-Belz-McCrary-Cox thesis, its foremost proponents being David Donald, Harold Hyman, Hans Trefousse, James McPherson, Herman Belz, Peyton McCrary, and LaWanda Cox.[10] Each of those historians has taken issue with the once generally held belief that Lincoln and the Radicals differed significantly on questions of black rights. To Oates, that belief is the worst of the Lincoln myths, the one that he is at the greatest pains to dispel.

"My interpretation," Oates says, "is similar to that in Peyton McCrary, *Abraham Lincoln and Reconstruction: The Louisiana Experiment*." He adds, "Several older historians, especially those in or from the South, have faulted McCrary's inescapable conclusions that Lincoln stood with his advanced Republican colleagues on critical reconstruction questions; apparently these historians prefer the mythical version."[11] I dislike getting personal, but I cannot help recognizing myself as one of those "older historians," one who lived for nearly thirty years in the South and, while living there, wrote a review that "faulted McCrary's inescapable conclusions." I now submit that the question whether those conclusions are "inescapable" is, to say the least, open to debate, as is the identity of the historians who "prefer the mythical version" of the events.

Consider what Oates has to say, in *The Man Behind the Myths*, about the Emancipation Proclamation. It was, he contends, "a sweeping blow against slavery as an institution in the rebel states, a blow that would free *all* slaves there—those of secessionists and loyalists alike."[12] The fact is that the proclamation did not apply to the rebel states as a whole—not to the areas under Union occupation, but only to those still under Confederate control. Even at its most efficacious, the proclamation therefore would fall far short of freeing all the slaves in the rebel states.

Oates quotes the famous passage in Lincoln's December 1862 message to Congress beginning: "Fellow-citizens, we cannot escape history." Then he says, "That message provoked a fusillade of abuse from congressional Democrats, who blasted Lincoln's projected Proclamation as unconstitutional."[13] Thus he gives the impression that Lincoln uttered those eloquent words in support of his forthcoming proclamation. In fact, Lincoln was urging the adoption of a constitutional amendment that would authorize his favorite emancipation plan. According to this plan, the states themselves would have to free the slaves. They could take their time about it, delaying final freedom until as late as 1900. They would have to compensate the slave owners but could get financial aid from the federal government. And they would induce the freed blacks to resettle in Africa, Haiti, or some other place outside the United States. This was hardly a plan that the Radical Republicans could approve, and they did not approve it.

"As Union armies pushed into rebel territory, they would tear slavery out root and branch, automatically freeing all slaves in the areas and states they conquered," Oates continues. "By war's end, all three and a half million slaves in the defeated Confederacy could claim freedom under Lincoln's Proclamation and the victorious Union flag."[14]

Maybe so. Maybe not. Lincoln himself had doubts about the lasting effect of the proclamation even in the still rebellious areas to which he confined it. On September 22, 1861, exactly one year before he issued his preliminary proclamation, he had defended his revocation of General John C. Frémont's Missouri emancipation proclamation by asking, "Can it be pretended that it is any longer the government of the U.S.—any government of Constitution and laws—wherein a General, or a President, may make permanent rules of property by proclamation?"[15] By September 22, 1862, he had persuaded himself to make permanent rules of property and to base his action on his constitutional authority as commander in chief of the army and the navy.

It is very doubtful that the framers of the Constitution, when they made the president the commander in chief, had anything more in mind than to assure the supremacy of the civilian over the military. By the time of the Civil War, some students of the Constitution had begun to argue for a presidential "war power." Today we take that power pretty much for granted, but when Lincoln became the first president to exercise it, its constitutionality was very much in doubt. Would the federal courts approve? Even if they accepted the proclamation as a war measure, what would they think of its efficacy once the war was over? Lincoln did not know the answers to these questions, and neither do we. What we do know is that, after Appomattox, the future of slavery remained unclear until the final ratification of the Thirteenth Amendment near the end of 1865.

Consider, next, what Oates has to say about the proclamation of December 1863 in which Lincoln announced his 10-percent plan for reconstructing the Southern states. This, Oates declares, "made emancipation the very basis of reconstruction, thus placing him on the side of Sumner and the advanced and moderate members of his party."[16] In fact, it did no such thing. It required that at least 10 percent of a state's voters swear to abide by all congressional acts and presidential proclamations with regard to slavery. As yet, no act of Congress called for complete abolition. The Emancipation Proclamation, as we have seen, exempted those parts of the Confederacy that the Union armies had already recovered—the only parts where reconstruction could possibly begin. By no means did Lincoln's announcement place him on the side of the "advanced" Republicans, the Radicals. They showed their disagreement by passing a quite different reconstruction plan, the Wade-Davis bill, which Lincoln pocket-vetoed. Then they denounced him in the Wade-Davis manifesto and plotted to get rid of him as the party's presidential candidate.

Consider, finally, what Oates has to say about Lincoln and Negro suffrage. "Over the winter of 1864–65," he writes, ". . . Lincoln approved some form of Negro suffrage for other rebel states if Congress would accept his Louisiana regime"—without Negro suffrage. "But the compromise fell apart because most congressional Republicans opposed even limited Negro suffrage as too radical."[17] Now, even McCrary, whom Oates closely follows, concedes that "there had been some misunderstanding on the precise nature of the compromise."[18] The evidence for such a compromise is unconvincing. One thing seems clear enough: Lincoln insisted on the removal of the Negro suffrage provision from the proposed reconstruction bill.

Oates sums up his case as follows: "Not only did the historical Lincoln side with Sumner and Stevens on most crucial reconstruction issues; by 1865 he was prepared to reform and reshape the South's shattered society with the help of military force."[19] But the historical Lincoln spoke "with malice toward none, with charity for all," of "binding up the nation's wounds." Thaddeus Stevens talked of compelling Southerners to "eat the fruit of foul rebellion"; of confiscating plantations, driving off the owners, and dividing the land among the freedmen; of revolutionizing the South. Neither Sumner nor Stevens thought the Constitution a hindrance. Sumner held that the Southern states, by seceding, had committed suicide and had reverted to territories. Stevens argued that, having been defeated in war, those states were nothing but "conquered provinces." But Lincoln said the question whether they were still states or not, whether they were in or out of the Union, was a "merely pernicious abstraction." The important thing, he thought, was to restore them to their "proper practical relation" with the Union as soon as possible.

Why should we even expect Lincoln to have taken positions as extreme as those of some Radicals in Congress? In the White House he could hardly afford to be so far advanced or so single-minded. He had to hold the North together and direct the war effort so as to achieve a victory that would reunite the nation. He had to act as the president of the Conservatives as well as the Radicals, the Democrats as well as the Republicans, the Southerners as well as the Northerners, the whites as well as the blacks. None of the Radicals represented any such broad constituency. Stevens, for one, had a very narrow power base; he was responsible only to the Republican majority within a small portion of a single state—the Lancaster district of Pennsylvania.

All this is, emphatically, not to suggest that Lincoln leaned toward the other extreme from that of the Radicals. The black historian Lerone Bennett, Jr., was quite unhistorical in denigrating him as a man notable for racism.[20] The antiblack historian J. G. deRoulhac Hamilton, a North Carolinian of the

Dunning school, was equally wrong in praising him as one who shared conservative white Southerners' "belief in the natural inferiority of the negro" and who, if he had lived, would have managed to "check the radicals in Congress" so as to save the reconstructed states from the horrors of "Negro rule."[21] James G. Randall was perhaps the greatest of all Lincoln scholars, but he was mistaken in saying that the Radicals were "the precise opposites of Lincoln" and that he planned an "easy reconstruction" but was "confronted with the hateful opposition of anti-Southern radicals."[22] Not Lincoln, but his party foes, the Democrats, were the confirmed racists of the North. Not he but they were the true friends of the white supremacists in the South.

Oates and other recent writers who emphasize Lincoln's growing radicalism are much closer to the truth than were the earlier historians who portrayed him as the reluctant destroyer of slavery but the willing preserver of a caste system. There can be no doubt as to the direction in which he was moving during the presidential years. Under the pressure of events he tended to advocate the more and more immediate realization of the promise of equality. But doubts persist as to exactly where he stood at particular times. At various points, as I have just undertaken to show, Oates and like-minded writers make him appear to have been farther advanced than the evidence warrants.

When Lincoln said, in his last public address, that he might soon "make some new announcement," what did he have in mind? Even McCrary recognizes that Lincoln's assassination a few days later "makes it impossible to know precisely what direction his proposed shift in policy might have taken."[23] More than that, it makes it impossible to know whether he was actually contemplating any shift in policy.

This uncertainty has left ample room for speculation among historians, novelists, and politicians ever since Lincoln's death. Consciously or not, they have manipulated his memory to suit their own necessities. Opponents as well as proponents of

Radical Reconstruction tried to get him on their side. Later, Southerners appealed to his name to legitimize state laws and constitutional amendments disfranchising and subordinating blacks. Then, as the renewed movement for civil rights gained momentum, sympathetic (white) historians attempted to enlist him in this cause.

Years ago, when William H. Herndon and the preachers were quarreling about Lincoln's religious beliefs, one of the preachers pointed out that "the faith and future of the Christian religion in no wise depends upon the sentiments of Abraham Lincoln."[24] Today we might add that the justice and prospects of the civil rights movement in no wise depend upon his sentiments. In any case, those who rewrite the past to serve a present cause, no matter how worthy the cause may be, are engaged in the very essence of myth making. In destroying the old myth of Lincoln the pro-Southern-white conservative, they are in the process of creating a new myth of Lincoln the most radical of Radicals.

Chapter 5. President Grant and the Continuing Civil War

"Let us have peace." That was the plea of Ulysses S. Grant, a plea he made at the beginning of his presidency and repeated from time to time thereafter. "Let us have peace." But President Grant stuck to his "Southern policy," and as a consequence there was no peace so long as he remained in office. He ended his second term with a sense of frustration and defeat. In his eighth and last annual message to Congress he did something that few if any other outgoing presidents have ever done: he confessed that he had made "mistakes."

This touch of candor—so utterly lacking in our chief magistrates of more recent times—ought perhaps to have disarmed historians and given them a little charity in judging President Grant. It has, of course, done nothing of the sort. Instead, it has been taken as a self-confirmation of wrongheadedness and incompetence. When the late Arthur M. Schlesinger polled his fellow historians, in 1948 and again in 1962, they rated Grant on both occasions as one of two "failures" among all the presidents, placing him next to the very bottom of the list, only a notch above Warren G. Harding.

Those whom the historians ranked the highest were the *war* presidents, with Abraham Lincoln at the top. On this ground alone, if on no other, Grant deserves reconsideration, for he too may be viewed as a war president. He was commander in chief during the Reconstruction phase of the continuing Civil War.

A possible renewal of hostilities had been far from General Grant's thoughts when, at Appomattox, he gave his generous terms to the surrendering army of Robert E. Lee. "I am satisfied that the mass of thinking men of the South accept the present situation of affairs in good faith," Grant wrote a little later, after his southern tour in the summer of 1865. "The questions which have heretofore divided the sentiments of the people of the two sections—slavery and States' rights, or the right of a State to secede from the Union—they regard as having been settled forever by the highest tribunal—arms— that man can resort to." But Grant's friend William T. Sherman took a quite different view, predicting a kind of guerrilla war. "Now," Sherman said, after his even more liberal terms to Joseph E. Johnston had been overruled, ". . . we will have to deal with numberless bands of desperadoes, headed by such men as Mosby, Forrest . . . and others, who know not and care not for danger and its consequences." Time was to prove Sherman's prediction accurate.

General Grant began to change his mind as President Andrew Johnson defied Congress and persisted in trying to restore the Southern states according to his own plan. This involved the return of ex-Confederates to office, the passage of the black codes to provide a substitute for slavery, vetoes of congressional bills for assuring civil rights and protection to the freedmen, riots in which blacks and loyal whites were the victims, and the rise of the Ku Klux Klan. In the fall of 1866, as the congressional elections approached, it seemed to Grant that Johnson had aroused the lately subdued rebels to a point where a military clash with the adherents of Congress was a real possibility. "Commanders in Southern States," he advised Major General Philip H. Sheridan, "will have to take great care to see, if a crisis does come, that no armed headway can be made against the Union."

By the time the first Reconstruction Act was passed, in March of 1867, Grant was ready to give his full endorsement to its provisions, Negro suffrage and all. His conversion to the suffrage cause had resulted neither from a love for Southern blacks nor from a hatred of Southern whites. He now had no more vindictiveness toward his late enemies than he had had at Appomattox. His conversion to black enfranchisement was like his earlier conversion to black emancipation. In 1862 he had faced the question of what to do with the thousands of slave refugees flocking into his Tennessee camp. Though no abolitionist in principle, he then decided that he must not return the slaves to their owners but must set them free so as to weaken the enemy and win the war. Similarly, in 1867, he concluded that giving the suffrage to the freedmen was (to quote Adam Badeau) "the only practical means of securing what had been won in the field." Otherwise, the late rebels of the South in combination with the "Copperheads" of the North would regain control of the federal government, and "the results of the war would be lost."

After his inauguration, President Grant reversed the obstructionist tactics of President Johnson and set out to execute wholeheartedly the congressional reconstruction plan. He was enthusiastic when the plan was capped by the Fifteenth Amendment, so enthusiastic that he departed from custom to announce the ratification in a special message, on March 30, 1870. In a sentence breathtaking both for its length and for its exaggeration, he declared,

A measure which makes at once 4,000,000 people voters who were heretofore declared by the highest tribunal in the land not citizens of the United States, nor eligible to become so (with the assertion that "at the time of the Declaration of Independence the opinion was fixed and universal in the civilized portion of the white race, regarded as an axiom in morals as well as in politics, that black men had no rights which the white man was bound to respect" [a quotation, of course, from Chief Justice Roger B. Taney's opinion in the Dred Scott case, of 1857]), is indeed a measure of grander importance than any other one act of the kind from the foundation of our free Government to the present day.

Very few Southern whites shared Grant's enthusiasm for the Fifteenth Amendment. This amendment, together with the reconstruction acts, only intensified the spirit of rebellion in the South. The campaign of violence and terror increased, with the aim of depriving the freedmen of the vote, overthrowing the reconstructed state governments, and thus frustrating federal law. The masked night riders of the Klan and other Klan-like groups had their day and then were succeeded by less ritualistic but even more effective organizations of armed and mounted men, such as the White Leagues of Louisiana, the rifle clubs of Mississippi, and the Red Shirts of South Carolina.

By 1870–71, Grant confronted a situation resembling the one that Lincoln had faced a decade earlier, and Grant responded to it in much the same way. Like Lincoln, he invoked an old statute of 1795 that authorized the president, "in case of an insurrection in any state," to "call out the militia of any state to suppress such insurrection." He soon felt, however, that he needed powers more specifically designed for dealing with the existing disorders in the South. Accordingly, Congress passed a series of three "force acts," which empowered him to use military and other means to enforce the Fourteenth and Fifteenth Amendments wherever "unlawful combinations and conspiracies" were to be found, and which declared such combinations and conspiracies to be "rebellion against the Government of the United States." In successive proclamations invoking these acts from 1870 to 1876, Grant used language reminiscent of Lincoln's in 1861. Again, a president was calling upon troops to put down "combinations" that could not be "controlled or suppressed by the ordinary course of justice."

Until the end of Grant's second term the federal troops remaining at Southern posts were kept fairly busy in assisting civilian officials, especially at election times. More than two hundred detachments were made in a single year. In nine counties of South Carolina the president, under the authority of the force acts, briefly suspended the writ of habeas corpus and imposed martial law. He used the army to the greatest extent in Louisiana, where, as he said, the "lawlessness, turbulence, and bloodshed" were the worst. When the Louisiana Democrats threatened to make good their claim to victory in the 1872 election, he dispatched soldiers to New Orleans to protect William Pitt Kellogg's Republican regime. He sent them again after the Democrats and their White League allies had killed dozens of black and white Republicans in the Colfax and Coushatta massacres, had risen in armed revolt, and had driven Kellogg and his followers out of the statehouse.

Southern conservative newspapers kept denouncing Grant and complaining of federal "tyranny and despotism." Northern Democratic papers called him "Kaiser Ulysses" and said he was "puffed up with a sense of his despotic authority." Anti-Grant Republicans talked about his assumption of "enormous and irresponsible powers" and warned against the dangers of "Caesarism"—or "Grantism," which to his critics meant much the same thing. The Democratic and Liberal Republican propaganda gave the impression that the president, out of sheer cussedness, was making war on the people of the South. No doubt this propaganda helped to account for Northern disillusionment with the whole idea of Reconstruction. It helped to account also for the Democrats' gains in the elections of 1874, gains which gave them control of the national House of Representatives in 1875.

Nothing could have been farther off the mark than the charges of militaristic excess against Grant. The truth is that, in the execution of his Southern policy, he showed remarkable self-restraint. Only in a small area and only for a short period did he resort to martial law. On several occasions, despite urgent appeals, he held back military aid and tried to settle electoral disputes by mediation. On other occasions he sent troops not to assist Republicans against Democrats but merely to keep the two from going into armed combat with one another. He was quick, perhaps at times too quick, to withdraw the soldiers once the immediate threat to law and order had appeared to subside.

Thus, in the case of Louisiana, he might have prevented the worst of the violence if, from the beginning of the trouble in that state, he had maintained a large force there and had ordered it to break up the pretended government and the paramilitary organizations of the Democrats. From New Orleans, Sheridan begged for permission to treat the White Leaguers as "banditti"—to shoot them as outlaws. There was (at least as seen in retrospect) a good deal of merit in Sheridan's proposal, but the president declined even to consider it, though appreciating the general's point of view.

Grant kept his use of military force to a minimum for several reasons. For one thing, he had constitutional and legal scruples—which were reinforced when the strict constructionist Edwards Pierrepont became his attorney general in 1875—and he was willing to take action only when assured that it was within the letter of the law. Then, too, he had doubts about the rights and wrongs in some of the electoral disputes, where fraud appeared to be rife on both sides, and these doubts gave him pause. Moreover, he had to take into account the swell of adverse opinion in the North. Thus, in 1875, when the desperate Republicans of Mississippi were pleading in vain for federal support, Attorney General Pierrepont sent them a telegram that quoted Grant as saying, "The whole public are tired out with these annual autumnal outbreaks in the South, and the great majority are ready now to condemn any interference on the part of the Government." Besides, after the congressional elections of 1874, Grant was handicapped by the predominance of Democrats in the House. They tried to embarrass him with calls for information about his use of soldiers, and they turned down his request for new legislation—for yet another force act—which would have clarified and amplified his power to employ the army.

Finally, even if Grant had been inclined to intervene more actively than he was, he would have been limited by the unavailability of troops. The total of those stationed in the South had shrunk from nearly 200,000 in mid-1865 to about

11,000 in late 1869 and only 6,000 at the end of 1876. These 6,000 were widely scattered in small garrisons. After the disputed 1876 election, Grant declared that "if there had been more military force available" he would have been justified in using it in several of the Southern states.

Restrained though he was in resorting to military might, Grant held deep convictions about what he considered the basic issues of the conflict in the South. One was the issue of actual freedom for the former slaves. The question whether the Fourteenth and Fifteenth Amendments were to be "practically enforced," a convention of Alabama blacks declared in 1874, was a question whether emancipation was to be a "reality or a mockery" and whether the blacks themselves were to be "freemen in fact or only in name." At almost exactly the same time, Grant was saying, in response to complaints about "interference by Federal authority," that if the Fifteenth Amendment and the force acts did not provide for such interference, then they were "without meaning" and the "whole scheme of colored enfranchisement" was "worse than mockery and little better than a crime."

At stake was not only freedom but also union, as Grant saw the matter. It was a question "whether the control of the Government should be thrown immediately into the hands of those who had so recently and persistently tried to destroy it," he said in his last annual message to Congress. "Reconstruction, as finally agreed upon, means this and only this, except that the late slave was enfranchised, giving an increase, as was supposed, to the Union-loving and Union-supporting votes. If *free* in the full sense of the word [and Grant underlined the word *free*], they would not disappoint this expectation."

By 1877, the Republicans of Mississippi had already fallen before the terrorism of the Democrats. In the three Southern states where Republicans still managed to hold on, they did so only with the support of federal troops. Grant kept these soldiers in place to the very end of his presidency. Then he saw, with dismay and disgust, his Southern policy reversed by his successor, Rutherford B. Hayes. Under Hayes, the troops were removed, the force acts ignored, and the Fourteenth and Fifteenth Amendments nullified. For the rest of the century the Republicans talked off and on of enforcement but did nothing about it. By the early 1900s, all but seven of the forty-two sections of the three force acts had been repealed or superseded or declared unconstitutional, and the seven remaining sections were dead letters.

Writing in the early 1900s, historian William A. Dunning said, "Grant in 1868 had cried peace, but in his time, with the radicals and carpet-baggers in the saddle, there was no peace; with Hayes peace came." Dunning and his followers (along with nearly all their white contemporaries, Northern as well as Southern, Republican as well as Democratic) were convinced that the attempt to impose Negro suffrage on the South had been a horrible mistake. According to those historians, the attempt had provoked such disorder and violence as actually existed in the South. But the lawlessness, they said, was exaggerated for "political effect," to suit the propaganda needs of the Radical Republicans. Insofar as the Ku Klux Klan and similar organizations had a "political motive" of their own, Dunning insisted, this "was concerned with purely local incidents of radical misrule, and was ridiculously remote from any purpose that could be fairly called 'rebellion' against the United States."

Though "peace" (in the Dunning view) did not come until 1877, the war itself had long since ended. The Civil War was one thing and the Reconstruction quite another—an unfortunate aftermath, a sequel and yet a kind of non sequitur. For all its undeniable aspects of meanness, the Civil War was a credit to both sides, and the participants were ennobled by courage, sacrifice, and high ideals. But Reconstruction disgraced the victors. Not content with winning the war, preserving the Union, and emancipating the slaves, a ruling faction of Northern vindictives proceeded to "reconstruct" and, in the process, to humiliate and despoil the already ruined and chastened

South. These Republican Radicals, thousands of them, now invaded the defeated land. They went as penniless adventurers, as "carpetbaggers," to mislead the newly enfranchised Negro, misgovern the reconstructed states, and misappropriate whatever wealth remained. Thus, in the role of conqueror, the greedy politician replaced the brave soldier: the jackal came in the track of the lion. More than the war itself, this time of terrible peace embittered the Southern people and left lasting scars upon their memory.

Such, in outline, is the story as Dunning, James Ford Rhodes, and most other writers once told it. That version still has its believers, and no doubt it contains some elements of historical truth, but we may question whether it represents the whole truth, or even the essential truth. There is another way of looking at the events of the 1860s and the 1870s. This way, we may discover at least a few significant themes that extend from the wartime through the "postwar" period and give a common character to both. Thus we may see Reconstruction as essentially a continuation of the Civil War.

One continuing theme is violence. The war was not to be ended by a treaty, of course, or even by a general cease-fire agreement (though that was the kind of agreement that Sherman hoped to make with Johnston). Repeatedly President Lincoln had said the war would cease, on the part of his government, when it had ceased on the part of those who were resisting the government's authority. The rebels had only to lay down their arms. Though the Confederate armies surrendered in 1865, the South remained an "occupied country," and before long it showed signs of being a hostile one as well. President Johnson proposed to withdraw the occupying troops, and on August 20, 1866, he proclaimed that peace had been restored in all the states formerly in rebellion. This proclamation the Supreme Court later took as marking the legal end of hostilities.

Yet, throughout the South, resistance to federal authority continued on the part of well-armed and well-organized bodies of men. With uniformed, gun-wielding horsemen on the prowl, it was sometimes hard to tell the difference between a political and a military campaign. So, if formal fighting ended in 1865 and legal hostilities in 1866, irregular warfare went on for years afterward. And if, during these years, there was no such wholesale bloodshed as at Antietam or Gettysburg, there were nevertheless a great many casualties in countless engagements of one kind and another.

A second continuing theme is personnel. Confederate veterans made up the core of the persisting opposition to federal authority in the South. Nathan Bedford Forrest, the one-time slave trader who had gained fame as a commander of Confederate cavalry, founded and led the Ku Klux Klan. The berobed Klansmen pretended to be ghosts of the Confederate dead but were, in considerable numbers, flesh-and-blood survivors of the Confederate army. Former rebel soldiers also officered and manned the rifle companies such as the Red Shirts, whose hero and guiding spirit, Wade Hampton, had been like Forrest a leader of Southern cavalry.

On the other side, the army of occupation consisted largely of men who had served in earlier campaigns against the Confederates. Small and scattered as this force was, its members often were remote from the scenes of actual combat. More active than the regular soldiers, on the new firing lines, were the carpetbaggers and their scalawag and Negro allies, sometimes organized as state militia. The carpetbaggers were, almost to a man, veterans of the Union army. Whatever else they may have been, they were men who formerly had worn the blue, and they now had to pit themselves against men who, whether at present wearing white robes or red shirts, once had worn the gray.

A third continuing theme is purpose. By 1865, the North had not yet quite achieved its war aims of Union and freedom. Not that the rebel Southerners intended to try secession again, but they did intend to go on running their own affairs, with as little interference as possible from the outside. The war from 1861 to 1865, though bringing about the collapse of the Confederacy, had not destroyed but had strengthened the belief in state's rights and the sense of sectional distinctiveness, the sense of devotion to the South. Though no longer fighting for their national independence, the Southerners, in resisting Reconstruction, were fighting for their separate identity and for a large measure of local and regional autonomy.

Nor did the Southerners propose to reestablish the institution of chattel slavery, though they had gone to war in 1861 to preserve it. At that time the vice-president of the Confederacy, Alexander H. Stephens, was only stating the obvious when he declared that the idea of Negro inferiority, with its institutional expression, Negro slavery, formed the "corner-stone" of the new government. This cornerstone remained after the rest of the edifice had collapsed: the dogma of racial inequality survived the defeat of the Confederacy. The black codes, together with other outrages against the Negro, convinced the Radical Republicans that the freedman would have to be given civil and political rights if he was to be truly free. The conservative Southerners were determined to cancel those rights and, as they put it, to restore "white supremacy." With them, it was a matter of maintaining customs and institutions that would correspond to the belief in black inferiority.

Taking into account the continuity of violence, of personnel, and of aims, we may look upon Lee's surrender as more a transitional than a terminal point. At that time (in April 1865) the Lost Cause was not yet wholly lost, the Union victory not yet fully won. Afterwards there might have been much less bitterness and bloodshed if President Johnson had got away with his program for a quick and easy peace. But in that case the South would have been, to a considerable extent, victorious in defeat. In the end the South was to be partly victorious despite the passage of the Radical Reconstruction plan. The Compromise of 1877 left the former slaves to their former masters, and the South pretty much to itself.

That was not the fault of Ulysses S. Grant. That was not the outcome that he wanted to see. But the conquering hero of the Civil War failed in his efforts to confirm the victory through Reconstruction.

Grant's low repute among historians has been largely a product of the Dunning school. His fame continues to suffer even though the Dunning interpretation as a whole has long been discredited. It is time that revisionist scholars, having already revised practically every other phase of Reconstruction, should reconsider the role of President Grant.

There can be no doubt that, in the future, he will rank much higher than he has in the past. If he was not one of the more successful war presidents, he was, in a certain respect, one of the greatest, if not the greatest of all presidents. In this respect, only Lyndon B. Johnson can even be compared with him. None of the others carried on such a determined struggle, against such hopeless odds, to give reality to the Fourteenth and Fifteenth Amendments and to protect all citizens of this country in the exercise of their constitutional rights.

Chapter 6. Love, Hate, and
Thaddeus Stevens

One day in February 1866, when Thaddeus Stevens was just
starting the Radical Reconstruction program in Congress, he
got a letter from a man in Virginia who impertinently asked,
"Now, Thad . . . Which feeling is strongest & uppermost in
your Abraham's bosom, *love* of the *negro,* or *hatred* of the
white man of the South?"[1] Old Thad's reply to the inquiring
Virginian, if he gave any, is not on record. But since Stevens's
death the question in one form or another has interested biographers and historians, and they have tried to find answers
to it.

Nearly all of them have stated or implied that love or hate or
both moved Stevens in his political career. They have disagreed, however, about which feeling was strongest and uppermost in his bosom. Most Stevens biographers have believed
the strongest feeling was love for the Negroes and indeed for
all the oppressed of the world, white as well as black. One of
the earliest biographers labeled him a great "commoner." The
late Professor J. A. Woodburn averred that he was a born democrat, that he had antislavery convictions arising from the "innate bent" of his character. A more recent biographer dubbed
him a "great leveler," and a Marxist author called him a "mili-
tant democrat and fighter for Negro rights." In a new and
partly fictional life, the Pennsylvania novelist Elsie Singmaster depicted imaginary as well as actual scenes to show that

he was a sincere friend of the Negro and of all mankind—altogether a loving and a lovable person.[2]

Historians of the Civil War and Reconstruction have not been so nearly unanimous as the biographers of Stevens. James Ford Rhodes thought Stevens had a "profound sympathy" for the Negro "coming straight from the heart," but was also "bitter and vindictive" and showed "virulence toward the South." William A. Dunning taught his followers that Stevens was merely "truculent, vindictive, and cynical." In the same spirit the popular historian Claude G. Bowers said of Stevens, "Because of his obsession on Negro rights . . . and his inveterate hatred of Southern whites, his relation for many years to Lydia Smith, a mulatto, and until his death his housekeeper, cannot be ignored." Lloyd P. Stryker, one of the revisionist biographers of Andrew Johnson, carried this idea still farther. Taking as a fact what Rhodes had treated as an opinion, Stryker wrote, "Thaddeus Stevens . . . could not forget . . . that during the Confederate invasion of Pennsylvania in 1863 his iron works near Chambersburg were burned. It was therefore with peculiar zest and flaming personal malevolence toward Southerners that he demanded the confiscation of their estates. . . . His hatred and jealousy of the slave owners were only matched by his professed affection for the negro race,—some said a very personal affection for some members of it." In more moderate terms Professor J. G. Randall, a careful scholar and leading authority, referred to the "partisan character of the Vindictive program" under Stevens and also to "the domineering force of this hater of the South."[3]

While not necessarily denying that Stevens was capable of hatred and vengeance, other students of Reconstruction have put more emphasis on what they consider Old Thad's idealism, his social and economic radicalism. The Negro historian W. E. Burghardt DuBois characterized Stevens as "a leader of the common people" who, though a politician, was "never a mere politician" but "a stern believer in democracy, both in politics and in industry." The Marxist historian James S. Allen considered Stevens the "revolutionist" who best represented both "the industrial bourgeoisie and the Abolitionist democracy." Though not at first impressed by Stevens as the leader of a popular revolution, Howard K. Beale was later inclined to concur with DuBois and Allen. Beale wrote, "Thad Stevens and Charles Sumner agreed with the businessmen who backed the party in wanting a high tariff, which the South's return might endanger. But Stevens and Sumner were idealists in their concern for the Negro and human rights. Stevens at least was genuinely a radical. He wanted to confiscate planter property and divide it among Negroes." Even more than Beale, Louis M. Hacker has emphasized the role of Stevens and the Radical Republicans in using their party to effect the triumph of American capitalism. But Hacker also said, "Stevens envisaged a new South based upon egalitarian property rights. He was a vengeful man and fearful of the recapture of political power by the old ruling class of the South. But he was, as well, the honest friend of the Negro." Hacker added that the "New Radicals" sympathized with the Negro "for expediency only," but the "Old Radicals" (and Stevens was one of these) did so for "emotional reasons." These Radicals, Hacker insisted on another occasion, "labored in the great democratic tradition of the West that goes back to the Levelers of Puritan England."[4]

As has been seen, none of the more sophisticated writers has sought the meaning and motivation of Stevens's career solely in terms of love and hate. All the newer historians have recognized that he had important partisan and economic interests. It should be noted, however, that they have not presented a political and economic interpretation to refute or provide a substitute for the love-hate thesis but merely to supplement and enlarge upon it.

One Stevens biography took a basically different point of view toward his motivation. This book, bearing the subtitle *A Story of Ambition*, admitted that Stevens "did his part in bringing about the age of Big Business" but maintained that, of all the historians and biographers treating him, "None has taken adequately into account the simple fact that he was, above everything else, a man of politics seeking always to get and exercise the powers of public office."[5] Apparently, however, this book did not state its case very clearly or argue it very cogently. One of the book's ablest reviewers, Robert H. Woody, commented, ". . . the reinterpretation is one of degree rather than kind. It reminds one of Claude G. Bowers' graphic portrait, though it is much more fully developed."[6] But the book had intended, in part, to refute or at least to question the Bowers view that Stevens was motivated by vindictiveness toward the South, as well as the opposite view that he was motivated by regard for the Negroes in particular and the oppressed of all races in general.

The present paper attempts in a brief space to make this refutation somewhat more explicit and perhaps more convincing. It is a dangerous and difficult thing, of course, for historians to pry into the motives of any historical figure. To find out what really made their subjects go, the historians would need the combined aid of two experts from outside the profession—a psychoanalyst and a spiritualist. Until historians can get the cooperation of reliable mediums and analysts, they are going to find much to baffle them in their efforts to understand the personalities of people no longer living. This does not mean that they have to give up in despair. They can learn something about a historical figure's dominating interests, even if they cannot learn everything, from a study of what the person actually said and did when alive.

About Stevens it should be remembered, again, that his greatest activity and interest lay in the field of politics. That is to say, he was a politician. The business of politicians is to get votes. One way they get votes is to hold up to the voter ideals against idols—ideals to be cherished, idols to be smashed.[7] They point with pride and they view with alarm. To take an example, Hamilton Fish held up a species of "Americanism" as the ideal and "Communism" as the dangerous idol.[8] Today all our politicians seem to have become "Ham Fishes." In the day of Thaddeus Stevens the behavior of politicians was the same but their materials were different. With Stevens the true god for electioneering purposes came to be the idea of "democracy" and "freedom." The false god came to be the idea of "aristocracy" and "slavery."

It can be demonstrated that Stevens fairly consistently used the symbols of "democracy" and "aristocracy" to gain political power. (It cannot be demonstrated that he consistently used his political power to gain the ends of democracy as against those of aristocracy.) The way to make this demonstration is to compare the *public* Stevens and the *private* Stevens, the explicit and the implicit meanings of his words and actions. It will be revealing to compare the public and the private aspects of his career at several points, giving attention first to the years 1835–1838, when he was as yet prominent only in Pennsylvania, and then to the years 1865–1868, when he had become conspicuous throughout the whole country.

By 1837 Stevens had gained a reputation as a defender of free public schools and as a scourge of the secret, exclusive, "undemocratic" society of Masons. He was just becoming famous as a friend of the slave and a foe of the slaveholder. After having been elected three times to the Pennsylvania legislature, he had recently been defeated for reelection. As a kind of consolation prize, however, he had won election as a delegate to the state constitutional convention of 1837–38. If his immediate personal concerns during the 1830s are examined in the light of his reputation, some interesting contrasts appear.

When, for instance, Stevens delivered his famous speech (in 1835) that saved the new educational system of Pennsylvania, he was interested not only in schools but also in politics. He was determined that his party of Whigs and Antimasons should elect their candidate for governor in the approaching elections. The Democratic party was splitting on the school question. The Democratic governor, George Wolf, himself a candidate for reelection, was an advocate of public enlightenment at state expense. Another Democratic candidate, Muhlenberg, who had strong Lutheran support, opposed the levying of taxes for public education. By forcing the school issue Stevens could hope to widen the rift in the Democratic party and so enable the Whigs and Antimasons, who combined were still a minority, to elect their man as governor. This they succeeded in doing.[9]

While Stevens was noisily condemning the Masons, for all to hear, he was more quietly interesting himself in quite other things than the destruction of the Freemasonic lodge. His closest friend in Gettysburg, the banker John B. McPherson, was a leader of the local Masons, and Stevens's tirades against Masonry did not ruffle this friendship in the least. In the legislature, while Stevens cried out in vain for laws to suppress the damnable society, he was busily getting laws passed to benefit McPherson and other bankers, among them the biggest of all, Nicholas Biddle. The grateful and realistic Biddle wrote to Stevens, "You are a magician greater than Van Buren, & with all your professions against Masonry, you are an absolute right worshipful Grand Master."[10] But Antimasonry had lost its magic for Stevens when he was defeated for office in 1836. Then and only then did he begin to turn seriously to antislavery.[11] One may reasonably doubt whether he was motivated by love for the Negro or hatred for the slave owner when he turned to antislavery, any more than he was motivated by love for the common man or hatred for the aristocratic Mason when he earlier took up Antimasonry.

One can be certain at least that Stevens was no "leveler" in those days. It is true that on the hustings and in the legislative hall he sometimes sounded like a rabid democrat, especially when he denounced that pretended friend of the common people, Andrew Jackson. But in the relative privacy of the constitutional convention of 1837–38, he sounded quite different. There he was afraid the Loco Focos might put through an amendment limiting the freedom of bankers or extending the power of voters. Demanding protection for "vested rights," he inveighed against "the wild visions of idle dreamers," "the wild, revolutionary, and agrarian folly of modern reformers." He deplored the "inflammatory harangues from raw Irishmen and imported democrats" who might induce "mobs to lay violent hands on the institutions of the country." He condemned the revolutionists of the past and present, who with their "levelling doctrine" had always begun their attack on "order" and "virtue" by "arraying the poor against the rich and the laborer against the capitalist." Certain pages of the thirteen-volume report of this convention ought to be required reading for all those Marxists who make a pet of Thaddeus Stevens.[12]

Even though they concede a point about Stevens of 1837, however, the Marxists and other proponents of the love-hate thesis may object that the Stevens of 1867 was a different man. But there is little, in actual fact, to indicate that Stevens had changed his dominant interests in the interim. During the years before the Civil War, he continued to busy himself with a politician's chores—bribing editors, combining party ballots in deceptive ways, herding voters to the polls, and doing whatever else was needful to win elections.[13] And in 1867, elections were still the things he was most concerned about. Early in that year he suffered the biggest disappointment of his life when Simon Cameron bought from the Pennsylvania legislature the United States senatorship that he himself desperately wanted. Later in the year he was chagrined to see the Democrats coming back strong to win state and local elections in Pennsylvania, Ohio, and elsewhere. These affairs of politics, as will be seen, had a very real bearing upon the things Stevens was meanwhile saying and doing about Negro suffrage, the impeachment of President Johnson, and Reconstruction, "confiscation," and the punishment of the South.

Congress by its legislation of 1867 gave the vote to Negroes in the Southern states, which were in what Stevens called a "territorial condition." But Congress could not do the same for Negroes in the sovereign states of the North, a number of which, including Stevens's own Pennsylvania, still kept black men away from polling places. (Much has been said of Stevens's refusal to sign the revised state constitution of 1838, which introduced the word *white* as a voting qualification. The truth is that, though Stevens did not sign, he also did not protest, as did the president of the convention, John Sergeant. The Pennsylvania Anti-Slavery Society published a thinly disguised rebuke to Stevens for his "neutral course.")[14] In 1866, Stevens had broken with Charles Sumner when the latter demanded immediate and universal Negro suffrage.[15] To Old Thad that was bad politics. Few Pennsylvania Republicans, to say nothing of Democrats, would be willing to let Pennsylvania Negroes vote.

In 1867, however, Stevens began to feel that a Fifteenth Amendment giving the vote to Negroes everywhere, North as well as South, had become a political necessity. Foreseeing in August the Democratic victories in the fall, he wrote to his confidant Edward McPherson, "We must establish the doctrine of National jurisdiction over all the States in State matters of the Franchise, or we shall be finally ruined. We must thus bridle Penna. Ohio Ind et cetera, or the South, *being in*, we shall drift into democracy." Before the end of 1867 he was preparing public statements in which, forgetting his recent quarrel with Sumner, he said "universal suffrage" was an "inalienable right." He added, ". . . without it I believe the government will pass into the hands of the loco focos"—or, as he cunningly corrected the words before publication, "into the hands of the rebels and their friends."[16] In this rather sudden conversion of Stevens to the cause of general Negro suffrage, there is plenty of evidence that he was thinking about his own political fortunes and those of the Republican party, but there is little or no evidence that he was thinking about the welfare of the nation's Negroes or about the injury of Southern whites.

Granting all that, the unconvinced may still ask: But did not Stevens have good reason for hating Southerners? What about his affection for Lydia Smith, his mulatto housekeeper?

What about the burning of his ironworks by Confederate troops? Do not his public actions reveal a strong hostility toward the white South, even if they do not show any real humanitarian regard for the Negro? What about his attacks on President Johnson, whom he condemned as the agent of unreconstructed rebels? What about his repeated demands that Southerners must suffer "just retribution for their hellish rebellion," including the loss of their political rights and the confiscation of their estates?

As for Lydia Smith, it would obviously be hard to find documents that would show precisely her relationship to Stevens or her effect upon his attitudes. (There does exist one document that proves he got from her no deep and abiding affection for all members of her race or even of her family. That is a note he left in 1867 for one of Lydia's sons, ordering him to get out of the house and stay out.)[17] As for the destruction of Stevens's ironworks, it had no noticeable effect upon his policies, for his speeches were as "vindictive" before as after. And if his public remarks were vengeful, his private letters at the time were quite otherwise. In his personal correspondence he observed that "the chivalry" were disappointed in not getting him too when they burned his establishment and took his horses and mules; he expressed concern for the immediate welfare of his workmen; and, viewing his loss calmly and philosophically, he said it was the sort of thing one must expect in war. All talk of vengeance he saved for the place where it would get some votes—the public platform.[18]

There is a similar revealing contrast between Stevens's public actions and his private actions in regard to President Johnson. In confidential notes to Sumner in 1865, Stevens worried about the fate of the nation under its new president, but he also worried about Johnson's political power and its possible meaning for his own political future. "John[son] has the reigns," he complained. "With illegal courts, and usurping 'reconstruction,' I know not where you and I shall be." "The danger is that so much success will reconcile the people to almost any thing." One of the first things Stevens openly attacked Johnson for was the president's liberal policy in granting pardons to former Confederate leaders. But previously Stevens himself had signed a petition to President Lincoln for the pardon of a leading secessionist, and he used to inquire in a friendly way about the health of Roger A. Pryor, a captured Confederate officer who had been released to the custody of John W. Forney.[19] These facts imply that Old Thad's "vindictiveness" was not so much personal as political.

This point is better established in the frank avowal Old Thad made in June 1867 to a *New York Herald* reporter. For some time the judiciary committee of the House of Representatives had been investigating Johnson's private life in an effort to find grounds for impeachment. "What chance would an impeachment resolution have?" the *Herald* man asked. Stevens replied that it could not possibly be carried, for if Johnson were removed his successor would be the president of the Senate, Ben Wade, and Wade's election to that position had aroused the jealousy of all the friends of his chief competitor, W. P. Fessenden. Yet, despite its futility, Stevens favored keeping up an agitation for impeachment, and he explained why. "I fear that we shall lose Pennsylvania this next election," he said. The people were "disheartened" and the party was disunited and demoralized because of Cameron's recent notorious corruption of the state legislature. "This corruption will certainly beat us here next election, unless we draw out the Republican strength by getting up a furor and excitement on impeachment."[20] Thus to Old Thad, in 1867 at least, violent condemnation of Johnson as a representative of the unrepentant South was primarily a means of strengthening the Republican party and winning the next election in Pennsylvania!

The following year, as Republicans were preparing for the campaign of 1868, Stevens displayed a similar spirit toward another supposed pro-Southerner, James Buchanan. After Buchanan's death, the House of Representatives was composing a resolution honoring the former president. Cynically Old

Thad moved to delete from the statement, already cautious and perfunctory enough, the words "ability and patriotic motives." But all that was for public consumption. In private, Stevens was much more charitable. He had recently told a Democratic acquaintance that those who had "fawned on Mr. Buchanan in the day of his power" and had since deserted him were base and contemptible men. During the war Stevens once sent Buchanan a letter of apology for implying that Buchanan as president had been extravagant in furnishing the White House. Earlier, at a time when the two men used to exchange scurrilities on the stump but refused to exchange civilities on the streets of Lancaster, their mutual home, Buchanan once requested a favor of Stevens and the latter politely responded by recommending Buchanan's nephew to the Whig President Taylor for an appointment to West Point.[21] Between these politicians there secretly existed a professional camaraderie which suggests that much of their denunciation of each other was only for political effect.

It seems likely that Stevens again had political effect in mind when he harped upon his favorite Reconstruction theme— "confiscation." At the end of the war he was only one of several Radicals, prominent among whom were also Sumner, Wade, Henry Winter Davis, and Ben Butler. To make himself stand out as the Radical of Radicals, Stevens had to go to unusual extremes. But did he really intend to impoverish the Southern planters and give 40 acres to every freedman? Some features of his confiscation plan cause one to doubt whether he himself took the whole of it seriously. He told his fellow Lancastrians that after the land had been taken from its former owners and 40 million acres given to the freed slaves, 354 million acres would be left and could be sold to raise three and a half billion dollars toward paying the national debt. He was estimating that the government could get on the average ten dollars an acre for this land. But could the government sell worn-out lands at that price in the ruined South at a time when it was giving away under the homestead law good lands

in the virgin West? Horace Greeley thought the plan was im-
practicable, the whole idea absurd. Though the proposal might
appeal to Pennsylvania voters who had suffered property damage in the war, could Stevens have believed in it as a program
to be put into actual practice? Anyhow, while he always kept
the confiscation idea hanging in the air, he never pressed it
very hard as a concrete piece of legislation. In 1867, an edi-
torial writer in the *New York Herald* scoffed at the notion
that Stevens was motivated by his "apparent vindictiveness"
toward the South or by an "avaricious longing" to make good
the loss he had incurred in the destruction of his ironworks.
"His ambition," the writer pointed out, "induces him to run
to extremes in his confiscation programme; but we believe it
to be prompted more by his desire to retain the position of the
leader of the extremists than by any settled determination to
push it to the bitter end."[22]

From Stevens's point of view the whole reconstruction program seems to have been a matter of political expediency
rather than one of settled principle. It was not a case of pun-
ishing whites and rewarding blacks; instead, it was a case of
keeping Democrats down and Republicans up. Ever since Andrew Jackson's first election Stevens had been fighting Democrats. To him the words *Democrat, Loco Foco, slaveowner,*
rebel, and *Copperhead* were all synonymous. The prewar crisis and the war itself gave him and others like him their first
real chance to crush the opposition. After the war, and especially after the adoption of the Thirteenth Amendment, he
feared that the Southern and Northern Democrats, reunited,
would soon get back into power. Unless something was done,
he said, "They will at the very first election take possession of
the White House and the halls of Congress." He schemed to
prevent this by the provisions of the Fourteenth Amendment
that reduced the basis of Southern representation in Congress
and disfranchised and disqualified the leading Southerners. In
1867, he deliberately planned to make the process of reconstruction so complicated and confusing as to postpone the res-

toration of the seceded states indefinitely. When he changed his mind soon afterward and decided to hurry the "recon-structed" states back into the Union, he did so because of considerations of politics—first, the hope for more Republican senators to vote Johnson guilty in the impeachment trial, later, the need for additional Republican electors in the election of 1868.[23]

So at different points in his long career there is a contrast between the public Stevens and the private Stevens. The one— the public man—preached hatred and retribution for Freema-sons, slave owners, doughfaces, and rebels successively while he preached love and vindication for common men both white and black. The other—the private individual—was thinking in terms of party advantage and personal advancement.

The conclusion to be drawn from the evidence and argu-ment here presented is not, in the first place, that Stevens disliked Negroes and liked Southern white people. On the contrary, a politician like Stevens may come, if only through autosuggestion, to believe his own speeches. The only pur-pose here is to question whether these feelings of love or hate, if any, are relevant as motivations of Stevens's political career. In the second place, the conclusion is not that his aid to Northern industrialists was inconsiderable or unimportant. But it can be shown that his economic measures were often as much a means as an end of politics. In Congress, he demanded a high tariff in 1861, for instance, as a means of saving the Re-publican party in Pennsylvania. During the war years, he did not insist on higher duties for ironmakers in disregard of the needs of railroad builders; he acted as an honest broker har-monizing the conflicting interests and holding the loyalty of both. And he supported a Northern Pacific railroad land grant with the understanding that the company was going to bring laborers from northern Europe and colonize them along the right of way—"men who [would] always be on the side of free-dom"; men who would constitute a population in the North-west that "with the people of the great North, [might] be a counterpoise to the rebellious South"; men who, in other words, would vote as faithful Republicans.[24] In the third place, the conclusion is not that Stevens was unique among politicians of his time in attacking the idols of another section and defending the ideals of his own. Far from it. Indeed, it may be argued that the activities of politicians both North and South in turning domestic discontent away from home—and deflecting it to the opposite side of Mason and Dixon's line— were important causes of the sectional controversy, the Civil War, and the Reconstruction bitterness.

Regardless of the merit of this speculation, there is one conclusion that the student can scarcely avoid after a careful study of the life of Thaddeus Stevens. One could give in a single word an honest answer to the Virginian who asked Old Thad, "Which feeling is strongest & uppermost in your Abraham's bosom, *love* of the *negro*, or *hatred* of the *white man* of the South?" That one word would be *neither!*

Chapter 7. Reconstruction in Mississippi

James W. Garner's *Reconstruction in Mississippi*, originally published in 1901, was the first and is generally considered the best of the books that members of the "Dunning school" wrote on Reconstruction in various Southern states. The head of this school, William A. Dunning, who had been born in New Jersey, taught history at Columbia University from the 1880s to the 1920s. Though Dunning produced only a few books of his own, these were quite influential, and so were his lectures and his conversations at Columbia. A remarkably effective teacher, he inspired his graduate students, many of them Southerners, to apply his approach to the Civil War and Reconstruction in a number of specialized studies. His students, in turn, influenced him through their research, and he acknowledged the writings of some of them in his general account *Reconstruction, Political and Economic, 1865–1877*, published in 1907.

Garner, born in Pike County, Mississippi, on November 22, 1871, had earned a B.S. degree from Mississippi Agricultural and Mechanical College and a Ph.M. from the University of Chicago before he entered Dunning's seminar at Columbia in 1900. He readily appreciated the qualities of Dunning, whom he was to remember as an excellent teacher, one who "not only knew his subject, but had the rare gift of presenting it in an attractive and forceful manner." Garner had already gained some teaching experience at Bradley Polytechnic Institute in Peoria, Illinois, and after receiving his Ph.D. he taught briefly at Columbia and at the University of Pennsylvania. Then, in 1904, he took a position as professor of political science at the University of Illinois, a position he was to hold until his death in 1938.

While at Illinois, Garner made for himself a distinguished career as a political scientist. He built up the university's political science department, of which he was at first both the head and the sole member, to one of the largest and most active in the country. He traveled abroad on a succession of honorific lectureships in England, France, Switzerland, The Netherlands, India, and other parts of the world. He received honorary degrees from the University of Calcutta, the University of Lyons, Oberlin College, and Columbia University, and he was made a Chevalier of the French Legion of Honor. Meanwhile, his fellow political scientists recognized him as a leader of the profession when, in 1924 (two years after having recognized his mentor Dunning in the same way), they named him president of the American Political Science Association.

During these years Garner was a prolific writer, though in a field rather remote from that of his dissertation at Columbia. He contributed nearly three hundred articles to encyclopedias and professional journals, and he produced a dozen scholarly books. Almost all of these articles and books dealt with international relations or with general political science. In *Who's Who* he listed those of his works that he considered noteworthy. Among them were the following: *American Government* (1911), *Idées et Institutions Politiques Américaines* (1921), *Prize Law During the World War* (1927), *American Foreign Policies* (1927), and *Law of Treaties* (1935); but he included in this bibliography only one historical work, a four-volume history of the United States that he had written in collaboration with Henry Cabot Lodge (1906). Curiously, he made no mention of the book that will probably endure the longest—his first book, *Reconstruction in Mississippi.*[1]

From the outset, this work has received the sober, if qualified, approval of a wide variety of critics, and it continues to do so. A contemporary reviewer in the *Nation* thought that the "dismal story" had been "told impartially by Mr. Garner." Dunning himself commented on the "rigidly judicial spirit" his former student had shown. Years later, the outstanding Negro historian W. E. Burghardt DuBois characterized several of the Dunning-school studies as "thoroughly bad" but conceded that some, and especially Garner's, "though influenced by the same general attitude" of hostility to Radical Reconstruction, had a certain "scientific poise" and other redeeming qualities. Garner's *Reconstruction in Mississippi*, DuBois added, "conceives the Negro as an integral part of the scene and treats him as a human being." Howard K. Beale opined that a few of the Dunning students, "to a certain extent, and Garner, notably, escaped from the restricting frames of reference of the others." David Donald described the Garner book as "accurate, thorough, and generally impartial." Vernon L. Wharton wrote,

Little that has been learned in the succeeding sixty years would serve greatly to alter or even to add to Garner's story. However, Garner did assume that Radical Reconstruction was wrong in principle and practice and that the restoration of native white rule was essential to the peace and progress of Mississippi. These assumptions resulted in some lack of consideration of the experiences, needs, and aspirations of the Negro majority, and in tendencies to discredit the character and testimony of those who took part in the Radical movement and to magnify the virtues of those who fought against it.[2]

In fact, Garner's book seems to have got a reasonably favorable reception in all quarters except one. Some of his fellow Mississippians were horrified to find him saying anything in exculpation of the Republican regime they had hated and had fought to overthrow. One of his severest critics was John S. McNeily, who prided himself on his ancestors' having settled in Mississippi in the time of Spanish rule. After serving in the Confederate army, McNeily became a professional journalist and an amateur historian. He edited a Democratic newspaper in Greenville and later in Vicksburg, and wrote a long and vigorous essay on "The Climax and Collapse of Reconstruction in Mississippi." In it he undertook to correct what he considered "grossly misleading deductions and errors" in Garner's work. McNeily was particularly offended by Garner's taking at face value a certain statement of a carpetbag official. The carpetbagger, McNeily said, "could never have dreamed that his flimsy fiction would be accepted in a history of reconstruction, whose author is a native of Mississippi."[3]

In comparison with other natives of Mississippi who, before Garner, had written on Reconstruction in that state, he appears to be well balanced in his opinions and carefully restrained in his expression of them. One of the most important of the earlier writers was Ethelbert Barksdale, who had helped to lead the Democrats in overthrowing Republican rule and who afterward had served as a Democratic congressman from Mississippi. Barksdale contributed the Mississippi chapter to a collection of essays on the results of Reconstruction in the various states, a book that was put together and published as propaganda against a movement to secure congressional legislation for enforcing the Fifteenth Amendment in the South. This volume, *Why the Solid South?* (1890), probably did more than anything else to crystallize the Southern white, Democratic version of Reconstruction history. "In a word," Barksdale wrote of Mississippi (though he must have meant "in three words"), "mongrelism, ignorance and depravity were installed." Republicans "ruled and robbed," while "ignorance and knavery" prevailed over "intelligence and honesty." The Negro-and-carpetbagger government pretended to set up an educational system, but this was only "the convenient cover for all kinds of plundering schemes." Republican finances as a whole provided "a model of profligacy and extravagance." To all this, there could have been but one outcome. "The attempt of sectional agitators and philonegrists to reverse the abnormal [normal?] relation of the two races produced the inevitable consequence of strife and bloody conflict," Barksdale concluded. "It was worse than folly to suppose that the negro who had through all the ages shown his utter incapacity for self-government could be elevated from a state of slavery into the rulership of the race which history teaches . . . has never bent the suppliant knee to an inferior race." Similar language and similar themes can be found in the works of other Mississippi historians of the late nineteenth and early twentieth centuries. Much the same kind of interpretation can also be found in general histories by Northern historians of that time, historians such as James Ford Rhodes.[4]

That view of Mississippi Reconstruction, the Conservative view, may be summarized as follows: the Negroes, for racial reasons, were incapable of taking care of themselves, to say nothing of governing themselves. They needed to be guided and controlled; and the Black Code, which the legislature adopted in 1865, before the beginning of Radical Reconstruction, was a fair and appropriate means of providing the necessary control. Once enfranchised by the Reconstruction Acts of 1867, the Negroes sought to govern for their own benefit; they drew the color line against most of the whites. Those white men who aided and abetted Negro rule—the carpet-baggers and the scalawags—were contemptible, low-class, self-seeking, unprincipled types. The carpetbaggers were penniless adventurers who, as soon as the vote had been given to the Negroes, swarmed down from the North like a "Vandal horde" to exploit that vote, win office, and get rich. The "renegade scalawags, with white skin and black hearts," were Southern poor whites, the dregs of antebellum society, who seized the opportunity to better themselves at the expense of the more respectable folk. Together, these motley Republicans gave Mississippi for several years a regime of unbelievable extravagance and corruption. The constructive achievements of which they boasted, such as the establishment of public schools, were paltry in comparison with the ruinous taxes they imposed and the fantastic debt they ran up. The final overthrow of the Negroes and carpetbaggers, in the state election of 1875, was due to a virtuous though violent uprising of

Mississippi whites. To some degree, the overthrow was facilitated by internecine quarrels within the Republican party and by the Democrats' positive appeal to Negro voters. The Democrats rallied practically all native white men, including those who formerly had cooperated with the Negroes and carpetbaggers, and even attracted many Negroes who were disgusted with the excesses of the dominant Republican faction.

Such, in brief, was the Conservative view, but there was also a Radical interpretation which traversed it at every major point. Just as the one version originated with Democratic politicians who had taken an active part in Reconstruction history, so the other originated with carpetbaggers and Negroes who had opposed them. Albert T. Morgan, who had come from Wisconsin to Mississippi and had become sheriff of Yazoo County, presented his case in his book *Yazoo* (1884). John R. Lynch, at one time a Negro congressman from Mississippi, disputed the Democratic charges in his book *The Facts of Reconstruction* (1913). Morgan praised the Mississippi Negroes as "the superiors of their former masters in physical strength, in manly courage, in political sagacity, and in love of country, and not inferior in any of the elements of good citizenship— general intelligence alone excepted." He condemned the mass of Mississippi white men as "a race once civilized but now reduced, by the inherent concupiscence of African slavery, to lecherous savages." Lynch described the Southern white Republicans, the so-called scalawags, as a group that numbered some of the "best and most substantial white men" of the state. Both writers defended the Republican program as a democratic attempt to provide for the general welfare of Mississippians, black and white. Both argued that the effort was largely frustrated, and the Republicans finally driven from power, by the terroristic tactics of their opponents.[5]

Besides the original Conservative and Radical versions of Mississippi Reconstruction, there is also a Revisionist interpretation, which has been developed by historians who were born too late to have taken part in the events of which they have written. The pioneer among the Revisionists, DuBois, though he did not devote himself specifically to Mississippi history, cast some light upon it in a brief article and a very long book. Donald took a new look at the Mississippi scalawags and the election of 1875, and Wharton left a significant volume whose scope was broader than its title, *The Negro in Mississippi, 1865–1890* (1947). In recent years the Revisionist trend in Reconstruction historiography has been greatly stimulated by the civil rights movement. The Revisionist interpretation, though more refined and better documented, is in spirit quite close to the Radical view—much closer to it than to the Conservative view. For instance, Donald confirmed and elaborated upon the Lynch thesis that a considerable number of respectable and well-to-do white Mississippians (possibly as many as 25 or 35 percent of all the white voters in 1873) were temporarily Republicans. Most of these native whites, according to Donald, were former Whigs, and the Whigs had constituted "the wealthiest and best educated element in the state" before the war. Wharton, who was markedly free from racism, believed that Mississippi had been "extremely fortunate in the character of her most important Negro Republican leaders."[6]

There are, altogether, four schools of Reconstruction historiography, whether considering Mississippi alone or the South as a whole (and there are, of course, differences regarding details among writers within each school). These are the Radical, the Revisionist, the Conservative, and the Dunningite, the last of which is, in the case of Mississippi, represented by Garner. The Revisionist view, as has been seen, is essentially a refinement and elaboration of the Radical view. The Dunning interpretation is, in the same way, closely related to the Conservative interpretation. Is Garner, whose book has won Revisionist praise and Conservative condemnation, to be classified as essentially a Revisionist?

As he indicated in the preface to his book, Garner had begun his study with a determination to do a thorough and impartial

job. He not only looked into a large number of newspapers and
state and federal documents; he also corresponded with former participants in Mississippi Reconstruction and sought
letters from them. One of those to whom he wrote was Adelbert Ames, a native of Maine who had been the leading carpetbagger in Mississippi. He sent Ames a list of questions. What,
for example, did Ames think were "some of the merits" of his
administration as Mississippi governor? The elderly Ames replied to Garner, at that time a twenty-eight-year-old faculty
member at Bradley Polytechnic Institute, "My dear Professor,
when you appear before St. Peter at the gates of Heaven, what
can you say in reply to his query as to 'the merits' of your
earthly career?" Ames added, "To say that I acted conscien-
tiously to the best of my ability does not seem to be sufficient." In this interchange, the old veteran comes off somewhat
better than the eager but rather callow and bumptious scholar.
Ames, feeling that he had nothing to hide, generously offered
his personal papers to Garner. "My hope is," Ames wrote,
"that as a young man, as I understand you to be, you will be
free from the animosities and prejudices of those days." By
the time Garner had completed his study, he was confident
that, having felt "keenly his own prejudices" and having made,
"an earnest effort to divest himself" of them, he had succeeded
reasonably well in presenting an unbiased account.[7]

It is true that having not yet reached his fourth birthday at
the time of the 1875 election, Garner was too young to remember from his own experience the events about which he
wrote. And there is no reason to doubt that he made a sincere
attempt to recognize and counteract the Mississippi outlook
with which he had been raised and educated. How well he
succeeded, and how close he came to the later Revisionist
point of view, can be seen from a sampling of his and others'
views on certain key issues of Mississippi Reconstruction.

"Even now," Garner said (1901), "the negro is not a model of
industry, frugality, and foresight. He was much farther from it
in 1866." This was but one of a number of deprecatory refer-

ences that Garner made to Negroes in general. One group of them he called "poor deluded creatures." He took it for granted that Negroes were, by nature, inferior to whites and incapable of self-government. Indeed, he criticized Governor Ames on the grounds, among others, that Ames had "had an overconfi-dence in the mental and moral ability of the black race, so far as their ability to govern themselves was concerned," and that he had failed to realize "a superior race will not submit to the government of an inferior one." Even when Garner singled out an individual Negro, John R. Lynch, for commendation, he paid him the racist compliment that he was "distinctly Caucasian in his habits." In this assumption of Negro inferiority, Garner was much closer to the Conservative historians than to later Revisionists such as Wharton, who conceded that the whites had constituted the "dominant race" but assumed that they had been dominant because of "tradition, education, and superior economic and legal advantages," not because of an innate mental and moral superiority.[8]

Like the Conservative historians, Garner defended the Black Code, which had been designed to make dependent laborers of the former slaves, even depriving them of the right to buy or lease farms of their own. This and other features of the law, he admitted, were "unwise" because they gave Republicans in Congress a "pretext" for Radical Reconstruction; but such provisions were probably necessary. "The condition of things seemed to demand the immediate adoption of measures to check the demoralization of the freedmen, and compel them to labor." According to Wharton, however, the Black Code was an "entirely natural" but "almost entirely unnecessary product of its time and of the forces at work," and it "complicated rather than simplified the relations of the races."[9]

Garner implied that the Negroes, once in office, had discriminated against the whites. "In the first reconstruction legislature," he said, "the colored members consented to have a white man preside over their deliberations, but afterward, as long as they were in power, with a temporary exception in

1873, a black skin was an indispensable qualification for the office of speaker, another illustration of their greed for power." This charge of discrimination, as Wharton was to point out, had originated with the Democrats, who undertook to unite all native whites in opposition to the blacks and justified this by contending that "the color line had already been drawn by the Negro." Wharton commented that the Democrats "ignored the fact that the Negroes had from the beginning welcomed the leadership of almost any white who would serve with them." Garner, too, ignored this fact. His view of the Negroes was very different from that of Wharton, who also pointed out: "Those in the legislature sought no special advantage for their race, and in one of their very first acts they petitioned Congress to remove all political disabilities from the whites." [10]

In his treatment of carpetbaggers, Garner differed from Conservative authors in taking a dispassionate and at times even a somewhat sympathetic approach, yet he did not break away completely from the Conservatives' stereotype. He accepted their definition of the carpetbagger as a Northerner who had gone south to take advantage of the political opportunities that the Reconstruction Acts of 1867, by enfranchising the Negroes, had opened to him. Garner noted, however, that most of the Northerners active in Mississippi politics after 1867 had arrived in the state before that year and had come originally as planters and businessmen, not as politicians. "It is incorrect, therefore, to call them 'carpet baggers,'" he remarked. "They did not go South to get offices, for there were no offices for them to fill. The causes which led them to settle there were purely economic, and not political. The genuine 'carpet baggers' who came after the adoption of the reconstruction policy were comparatively few in number." Here Garner was on the verge of drastically revising the carpetbagger concept, but he stopped short of doing so. Forgetting his own admonition, he proceeded to apply the term indiscriminately to all white Republicans from the North, including the great majority whom he had said the word did not fit. Albert T. Morgan, for example, had arrived in Mississippi in 1865 and had invested (and lost) some $50,000 in planting and lumbering enterprises before going into politics. Yet Garner referred to him as "the well-known 'carpet-bagger,' Colonel A. T. Morgan."

Garner tried to be fair to Morgan and others like him. He wrote, "Morgan's correspondence shows that he is a man of education, and his political opponents testify that as an officer [sheriff] he was able and faithful." Nevertheless, when relating events in which Morgan had taken part, Garner followed the hostile reports of those political opponents much more closely than he did Morgan's own account. Similarly, he recounted Ames's Mississippi career in a basically antagonistic spirit even though he grudgingly praised Ames for his "personal integrity," "courteous demeanor," and "education and refinement." He said Ames failed as governor because of his prejudice against Southern whites as well as his overestimation of Southern Negroes and also because of "the circumstances surrounding his advent into Mississippi." But Garner admitted that Ames was innocent of peculation, as indeed were many other carpetbaggers. "The charge sometimes made that they were all thieves and plunderers has no foundation in fact." This relatively charitable judgment set Garner apart from his Conservative predecessors, and it was one of the main reasons for the complaints of his Conservative critics.[11]

Garner described and analyzed the carpetbaggers much more thoroughly than he did the scalawags. This word he used seldom, and only to refer to certain men as a group, not to individuals. Thus, with regard to the constitutional convention of 1868, he wrote: "There were twenty-nine native white Republicans, derisively called 'Scalawags.' Four of the Northern born Republicans had lived in the South before the war, and two of them had served in the Confederate army." These Northern-born Republicans he apparently excluded from the scalawag category, limiting it by implication to native white

Republicans. In doing so, he made the term more restrictive than most people had done during Reconstruction and most historians have done since. By both popular and scholarly usage, it applies not only to native but also to Northern-born white Republicans in cases where these men had settled in the South before 1861 and had remained there during the war, giving active or merely passive support to the Confederacy. Garner's implied definition would leave out the man who, by common consent, was the greatest of Mississippi scalawags— James Lusk Alcorn. Born in Illinois and brought up in Kentucky, Alcorn had moved to Mississippi in 1844, when about thirty-three years old. During the war he served briefly and unenthusiastically as an officer of Confederate troops. Garner referred to him, erroneously, as a "native Republican," but never as a scalawag. Garner also refrained from using the term when mentioning specific white Republicans, such as R. W. Flournoy and J. L. Wofford, who actually had been born in the South.

In dealing with men who are generally known as scalawags, Garner was considerably more restrained but not much more sympathetic or understanding than were the writers of the Conservative school. He recognized Alcorn as a rich and respectable planter and a well-meaning politician: "He seems to have been sincere in his professions." He dismissed Colonel Flournoy, however, as "the most extreme and obnoxious radical in the state," even though Flournoy was the wealthiest and most distinguished man of his own county, a man whom the county historian, a Democrat, afterwards described as "highly respected and beloved." Garner did not even approach a sophisticated conception of the scalawags' identity, character, and role in Mississippi politics; it remained for the Radical Lynch and the Revisionists Wharton and Donald to throw some revealing light on these matters (and it remains for others to provide still more illumination).[12]

Garner accused the Republicans of levying burdensome and even confiscatory taxes. On this subject he agreed, in the

main, with Conservative writers, yet he pointed out that, as of
1874, the local taxes in the thirty-nine counties with Democratic administrations seemed to be, on the whole, no higher
than those in the thirty-four counties with Republican administrations. He did not entirely agree with Conservative
writers on the question of governmental extravagance. Some
of them charged that the Republicans had left a state debt of
$20 million, and this figure came to be widely accepted. Garner
concluded that Governor Ames, who had insisted that the
debt amounted to no more than $500,000, was substantially
correct. And, though he too complained of excessive government spending, Garner revealed that annual state expendi-
tures under the Republicans from 1870 to 1875 had averaged
less than under the Democrats in 1865 and 1866. Wharton
later concurred with Garner by saying there seemed to be "no
correlation at all between the rate of taxation and the political or racial character of the counties," and he went beyond
Garner by concluding that the Republicans had given Mississippi "a government of greatly expanded functions at a cost
that was low in comparison with that of almost any other
state."[13]

On the issue of fraud and corruption, Garner broke completely with the Conservatives, who had written in emotional
if rather vague language about "the most corrupt and colossal
schemes of public robbery ever devised by a band of plunderers." Referring to the legislature that met in 1876, after the
overthrow of the Republicans, Garner said the "majority of
the Democratic members honesty believed that much official
corruption" had existed, and the "most seaching investigation
was instituted in every department, with the confident expectation of unearthing numerous frauds." The Democrats found
little, however, and Garner himself could verify only a few of
the charges, and none involving more than comparatively tri-
fling sums. "The only large case of embezzlement among the
state officers during the postbellum period," he concluded,
"was that of the Democratic state treasurer in 1866. The

amount of the shortage was $61,962." Garner could have added, as both Lynch and Wharton later did, that the next important defaulter was also a Democratic state treasurer, the one who was elected in 1875. "His shortage," said Wharton, "was $315,612.19." Lynch maintained that, "when the insurrectionists [the Democrats] took charge of the government, every dollar of public money had been faithfully and honestly accounted for."[14]

Nevertheless, Garner's bitterest critic, the Conservative historian McNeily, repeated the theme of Republican corruption and accused Garner of falsifying the facts. McNeily indicated that Garner had confused the Democratic treasurer of 1866 with a much earlier state treasurer, Richard S. Graves, whose spectacular case was well known in Mississippi; he had been convicted of embezzlement and had escaped from jail by walking out in his wife's clothing after a visit from her. "The grossness of the perversion of history," McNeily protested, "in the misstatement of the time of the notorious Graves defalcation which occurred before the war, in 1843, can only be looked on as culpable carelessness." McNeily insisted that Garner was naïve as well as careless. "As there were no public funds whose amounts would have made 'great embezzlements' possible," McNeily explained, "this implication of freedom from corrupt practice is exceedingly thin. The game of graft was not played that way. It consisted in a general practice of scrip speculation and warrant shaving, of falsified tax rolls, etc." McNeily's refutation itself was rather thin, and he presented no evidence to sustain it.[15]

Regarding public education, Garner credited the Republicans with a larger contribution than Conservatives did but with a smaller one than Revisionists were to do. "Did the Reconstruction regime give Mississippi her public schools?" one Conservative writer asked, and she came up with an essentially negative answer to the question. The Republican educational authorities had been so prejudiced and so corrupt, she argued, that "certainly Mississippians would have been justified in condemning the public school system." Instead of abandoning it upon the fall of the Negroes and carpetbaggers, however, the white Mississippians had taken it over and brought "success out of failure." Garner, too, felt that the system under the Republicans had serious faults, such as an administration that was "needlessly expensive" and that put the "entire management of the schools" in the control of the "non-tax-paying class." He minimized the white Mississippians' resistance to the establishment of schools; it did not appear, he said, that "there was any opposition by the more intelligent whites to an economical scheme of negro education." Yet he was fairly generous to the Republicans in his conclusion: "When the reconstructionists surrendered the government to the democracy, in 1876, the public school system which they had fathered had become firmly established, its efficiency increased, and its administration made somewhat less expensive than at first." Wharton was still more favorable to the Republicans. He gave them credit for setting up and maintaining a school system which "was an amazing advance beyond anything the state had known before." He showed that the Democrats, in denouncing the schools, had raised the cry "that the new system involved an enormous expenditure, that the greater part of this was for the benefit of the Negroes, and that all of it came from the pockets of the whites." He blamed the Democratic leaders for the widespread burning of school buildings and of churches used as schools—a topic that Garner barely touched upon.[16]

To what extent was the Democratic victory of 1875 due to intimidation and fraud? Such things went unmentioned in the Conservative kind of history that was taught to Mississippi school children. "In this contest," they were told, "thousands of the colored voters all over the State came boldly out on the side of the taxpayers, and with their assistance the Democratic Conservative ticket swept the State." Writing for adults, however, some of the Conservative historians frankly acknowledged the importance of violent and fraudulent techniques, justifying these on the ground that they had been absolutely necessary for redeeming the state from the "blighting curse of negro rule." The Conservative McNeily wrote, "A few negroes voted the Democratic ticket; a good many, from fear of bodily injury, or the policy declared in some counties of refusing employment to those who voted the radical ticket, remaining away from the polls. In some counties the ballot boxes were manipulated and the vote as polled changed. It was either that or a more violent recourse, for the decree had been registered that the carpetbagger must go." The carpetbagger Morgan agreed that murder and threats of it had formed the essence of the so-called Mississippi Plan of 1875. "Throughout that period the Republicans were as helpless as babes," Morgan said. "There was never any resistance at all by them to the violence of the enemy." He thought of the Democratic campaign as a renewal of the rebellion. Similarly, the one-time Negro leader Lynch looked upon the Democratic party as a "reorganization of that part of the Confederate army" that resided in Mississippi, and he saw the Democratic campaign as an "insurrection" against the legitimate government of the state.

Garner took a different view. "In regard to the Republican charge of intimidation," he said, "it is undoubtedly true, as alleged, that intimidation was successfully practised by the whites, but, in most cases, it was resorted to before election day." All that, in any case, was a secondary factor. "A more important reason for the overthrow of the Republicans was the schism in their own ranks." Donald came to essentially the same conclusion in his 1944 article on Mississippi scalawags. "The triumph of the Democratic color-line policies, known as the Mississippi Plan of 1875, would seem to be due to the successful union of all southern whites into one party rather than to the intimidation of the Negro." But Wharton disagreed. In his account of the events of 1875, he made it clear that, in his opinion, the Democrats' use of "economic pressure" and, still more, their resort to "threats and actual violence" had played a decisive role. And Donald, in a later work, modified the judgment he had given in 1944. He presented, in 1960, the following appraisal of the Mississippi Plan: "One part of the scheme had to do with arousing enthusiasm among the Democratic masses and with coercing the few remaining scalawags into leaving the Republican party. Its principal purpose, however, was to intimidate the Negroes."[17]

To sum up, Garner departed a long way from Conservative interpretations and anticipated Revisionist views on certain topics, but he remained in essential agreement with the Conservatives on others, though he eschewed the Conservatives' emotional and vituperative language. He showed the greatest originality and independence in his treatment of carpetbaggers and of Republican finances. In handling the scalawags, he was less successful, viewing them on the whole objectively but largely ignoring their background and significance. He gave the Republicans much more credit than the Conservatives had done, but somewhat less than Revisionists were to do, for the establishment of public schools. On the election of 1875, however, he differed more from the Radicals and Revisionists than from most of the Conservatives; certainly, he was with the Conservatives in spirit, hailing the 1875 campaign of the Democrats as a "most exciting" one that would "compare favorably with any political struggle that ever occurred on American soil."[18] Basically, he was no different from the Conservative writers—or from his fellow historians of the Dunning school—in his attitude toward Negroes. No one held more firmly than he to the conviction that Negroes were innately inferior, that they needed to be kept under strict control, that they abused the power which had been thrust upon them, and that they had to be turned out of office at almost any cost. He assumed that, throughout the Reconstruction conflicts in Mississippi, the Democrats and their allies were fundamentally right and the Republicans fundamentally wrong.

All historians, whether they recognize them or not, hold

basic assumptions of one kind or another. In the case of Garner, it is not strange that he reflected, to the extent that he
did, the deep convictions with which he had been brought up.
The remarkable thing is that he succeeded so well in breaking
away from many of them. His book was, for 1901, an amaz-
ingly well-researched, accurate, and objective account of a
portion of Mississippi history by a white Mississippian. No
mere historiographical curiosity, this volume remains indispensable for the modern student of the subject. The student
may take an antidote for some of its biases by reading, along
with it, Vernon L. Wharton's book *The Negro in Mississippi,
1865–1900*, which treats much of the same material from a
different point of view. In the future, other scholars can be expected to come forth with new facts and new interpretations
at various phases of the story. The next historian to produce a
comprehensive study of Reconstruction in Mississippi will do
extremely well if he proves himself as thorough in his research, as accurate in his statements of fact, and as nearly
self-liberated from his prejudices as Garner was over two generations ago.

Chapter 8. Carpetbaggers Reconsidered

The story of the postbellum South is often told as if it were a morality play or a television melodrama. The characters personify Good or Evil, and they are so clearly identified that there is no mistaking the "good guys" and the "bad guys." One of the villains, who deserves the boos and hisses he is sure to get, is the carpetbagger. As usually portrayed, this contemptible Yankee possesses as little honor or intelligence as he does property, and he possesses so little property that he can, quite literally, carry all of it with him in a carpetbag. He is attracted southward by the chance for power and plunder that he sees when the vote is given to Southern Negroes and taken from some of the Southern whites by the Reconstruction Acts of 1867. Going south in 1867 or after, he meddles in the politics of places where, as a mere roving adventurer, he has no true interest. For a time he and his kind run the Southern states. At last, when the drama ends, Good has triumphed over Evil, and the carpetbagger has got his comeuppance. But he leaves behind him a trail of corruption, misgovernment, and lastingly disturbed race relations.

That picture may seem an exaggeration, a caricature. If so, it nevertheless has passed for a long time as a true, historical likeness, and it continues to pass as such. A standard dictionary defines *carpetbagger* as a term of contempt for Northern men who went south "to seek private gain under the often corrupt reconstruction governments."[1] Another dictionary, based on "historical principles," contains this definition: "One of the poor northern adventurers who, carrying all their belongings in carpetbags, went south to profit from the social and political upheaval after the Civil War."[2] A recent textbook refers to "the Radical carpetbaggers who had poured into the defeated section after the passage of the First Reconstruction Act of March, 1867."[3] The prevailing conception, then, is that these men were late arrivals who waited till the Negro was given the suffrage and who then went off with their carpetbags, cynically, to take advantage of the colored vote.

Even those who hold that view concede that "a few were men of substance, bent on settling in the South,"[4] and that some of them took up residence there before the passage of the Reconstruction Acts. With respect to men of this kind, however, the question has been raised whether they should be considered carpetbaggers at all. Many of the Northerners active in Mississippi politics after 1867, a historian of Reconstruction in that state observes, had arrived as would-be planters before 1867. "It is incorrect, therefore, to call them 'carpet baggers,'" this historian remarks. "They did not go South to get offices, for there were no offices for them to fill. The causes which led them to settle there were purely economic, and not political."[5] Thus the brothers Albert T. and Charles Morgan, when they moved from Wisconsin to Mississippi, "came not as carpetbaggers," for they brought with them some $50,000, which they invested in planting and lumbering enterprises (and lost).[6] And the much better known figure Albion W. Tourgée, who moved from Ohio to North Carolina, was perhaps no carpetbagger, either, for he took with him $5,000, which he put into a nursery business (and also lost).[7]

Now, suppose it could be demonstrated that, among the Northern politicians in the South during Reconstruction, men essentially like the Morgans and Tourgée were not the few but the many, not exceptional but fairly typical. Suppose that the majority moved to the South before 1867, before the establishment of the "corrupt reconstruction governments," and hence for reasons other than to seek private gain or political power under such governments. One of two conclusions must follow. Either we must say that true carpetbaggers were much fewer and less significant than has been commonly supposed, or we must seek a new definition of the word.

In redefining it, we should consider the actual usage on the part of Southerners during the Reconstruction period. We may learn something of its denotation as well as its connotation if we look at the way they applied it to a specific person: the one-time Union army officer Willard Warner, of Ohio and Alabama.

Warner might seem, at first glance, to exemplify the latecomer rising immediately in Southern politics, for he completed his term in the Ohio legislature and was elected to the United States Senate from Alabama in the same year, 1868. But he was not really a new arrival. He had visited Alabama and, with a partner, had leased a plantation there in the fall of 1865. He bought land in the state the next year, and he spent most of the spring and summer of 1866 and most of the autumn and winter of 1867–68 on his Alabama land. He intended to make an economic career in the South (and indeed he was eventually to do so).[8]

At first, Warner had no trouble with his Alabama neighbors. "A Northern man, who is not a fool, or foolish fanatic," he wrote from his plantation in the spring of 1866, "may live pleasantly in Alabama, without abating one jot of his self-respect, or independence."[9] At one time or another, as he was to testify later, the leading Democrats of the state, among them the ex-Confederate General James H. Clanton, came to him and said, "General, when we talk about carpetbaggers we want you to understand that we don't mean you; you have come here and invested what means you had in property here, and you have the same interest here that we have."[10]

The Alabamans changed their attitude toward Warner when he was elected to office with Negro support. Afterwards (1871) General Clanton himself explained,

If a man should come here and invest $100,000, and in the next year should seek the highest offices, by appealing to the basest prejudices of an ignorant race, we would call him a political carpet-bagger. But if he followed his legitimate business, took his chances with the rest, behaved himself, and did not stir up strife, we would call him a gentleman. General Warner bought land; I fixed some titles for him, and I assured him that when men came there to take their chances with us for life, we would take them by the hand. But we found out his designs. Before his seat in Ohio got cold, he was running the negro machine among us to put himself in office.[11]

Another Alabama Democrat, from Huntsville, elaborated further upon the same theme in testifying before a congressional committee, as follows:

Question: You have used the epithets "carpet-bagger" and "scalawag" repeatedly . . . give us an accurate definition. . . .
Answer: Well, sir, the term carpet-bagger is not applied to northern men who come here to settle in the South, but a carpet-bagger is generally understood to be a man who comes here for office sake, of an ignorant or bad character, and who seeks to array the negroes against the whites; who is a kind of political dry-nurse for the negro population, in order to get office through them.
Question: Then it does not necessarily suppose that he should be a northern man?
Answer: Yes, sir; it does suppose that he is to be a northern man, but it does not apply to all northern men that come here.
Question: If he is an intelligent, educated man, and comes here for office, then he is not a carpet-bagger, I understand?
Answer: No, sir; we do not generally call them carpet-baggers.
Question: If he is a northern man possessed of good character and seeks office he is not a carpet-bagger?
Answer: Mr. Chairman, there are so few northern men who come here of intelligence and character, that join the republican party and look for office alone to the negroes, that we have never made a class for them. . . . They stand *sui generis.* . . . But the term "carpet-bagger" was applied to the office-seeker from the North who comes here seeking office by the negroes, by arraying their political passions and prejudices against the white people of the community.
Question: The man in addition to that, under your definition, must be an ignorant man and of bad character?
Answer: Yes, sir; he is generally of that description. We regard any man as a man of bad character who seeks to create hostility between the races. . . .
Question: Having given a definition of the carpet-bagger, you may now define scalawag.

Answer: A scalawag is his subservient tool and accomplice, who is a native of the country.[12]

So far as these two Alabamans were concerned, it obviously made no difference whether a Northerner came before 1867 or after, whether he brought with him and invested thousands of dollars or was penniless, whether he was well educated or illiterate, or whether he was of good or bad character in the ordinary sense. He was, by definition, a carpetbagger and a man of ignorant and bad character if he, at any time, encouraged political activity on the part of the Negroes and thus arrayed the blacks against the whites, that is, the Republicans against the Democrats. He was not a carpetbagger if he steered entirely clear of politics or if he consistently talked and voted as a Democrat or Conservative.

This usage was not confined to Alabama; it prevailed throughout the South.[13] To speak of "economic carpetbaggers," as historians sometimes do, is therefore rather hard to justify on a historical basis. Politics—Republican politics— was the distinguishing mark of the man whom the Democrats and Conservatives after 1867 dubbed a carpetbagger, and they called him by that name whether or not he had gone south originally for economic rather than political reasons. To speak of "Negro carpetbaggers" is also something of an anachronism. Colored men from the North did go south and enter politics, of course, but in the Reconstruction lexicon (with its distinction among carpetbaggers, scalawags, and Negroes) they were put in a category of their own. Northern-born or Southern-born, the Negro was a Negro to the Southern Conservatives, and they did not ordinarily refer to him as a carpetbagger. From contemporary usage, then, we derive the following as a nonvaluational definition: the men called carpetbaggers were *white Northerners who went south after the beginning of the Civil War and, sooner or later, became active in politics as Republicans.*

With this definition at hand, we can proceed to make at least a rudimentary survey of the so-called carpetbaggers as a group, in order to find out how well they fit the traditional concept with respect to their background. Let us consider first the state and local officeholders. There were hundreds of these people, and many of them left too few traces for us now to track them down. Studies have touched upon the subject in some of the states, and though fragmentary, these studies at least suggest that most of the men under consideration do not conform to the stereotype.

In Arkansas the carpetbag governor (1868–1872) Powell Clayton had owned and lived on a plantation since 1865. Many years later he was to gather data showing that the overwhelming majority of the so-called carpetbaggers, who were in office when he was, had arrived in Arkansas before 1867, and that the small minority who came as late as 1867 "did so when the Democrats were in full power, and before the officers to be elected or appointed, together with their salaries and emoluments, had been fixed by the [reconstructed] State Constitution." Clayton adds,

With a very few exceptions, the Northern men who settled in Arkansas came there with the Federal Army, and . . . were so much impressed with its genial climate and great natural resources as to cause them . . . to make it their future home. A number, like myself and my brother William, had contracted matrimonial ties. Many of them had been away from home so long as practically to have lost their identity in the States [from which they had come]. . . . These were the reasons that influenced their settlement in Arkansas rather than the existence of any political expectations.[14]

That, of course, is *ex parte* testimony, from one of the carpetbaggers himself. Still, he supports his conclusion with ample and specific evidence.

And, with respect to some of the other states, Southern historians have tended toward similar conclusions. In Alabama, says one of these historians, "Many of the carpet-bag politicians were northern men who had failed at cotton planting."[15] In Florida, says another, about a third of the forty-six delegates elected in 1867 to the state constitutional conventional were white Republicans from the North. "Most of the

Northerners had been in the state for a year or more and were *bona fide* citizens of the commonwealth." "As a class," they were "intellectually the best men among the delegates."[16] In Mississippi, says a third, "The genuine 'carpet baggers' who came after the adoption of the reconstruction policy were comparatively few in number." The vast majority of the so-called carpetbaggers in Mississippi were men who had arrived earlier as planters.[17]

Information is not available regarding all the carpetbag officeholders in all the reconstructed states. What is needed, then, is information about a representative sample of such officeholders. A sample could be made of the carpetbag governors, of whom the total was ten. Nine of the ten arrived in the South before 1867. Two were officers of the Freedmen's Bureau, two were civilian officials of the federal government, and five were private enterprisers—two of them planters, one a lawyer, one a civil engineer, and the other a minister of the gospel. The single late-comer, Adelbert Ames of Massachusetts and Mississippi, first appeared in Mississippi as a regular army officer and as a military governor, not as an adventurer in search of a political job.[18]

A larger sample consists of the entire body of white Northerners who during the Reconstruction period were elected as Republicans to represent Southern constituencies in either branch of Congress. Altogether, there were about sixty-two of these men, seventeen in the Senate and forty-five in the House of Representatives. It is impossible to be absolutely precise in listing these congressional carpetbaggers. There were a few borderline cases where, for example, a man was born in the South but raised or educated in the North, and it is hard to know whether he should be classified as a Northerner or not.

Of the sixty-two senators and congressmen, practically all were veterans of the Union army. That is rather surprising, since, according to the stereotype, they were late arrivals seeking to exploit the victory that the soldiers had already won. Also surprising, in view of the carpetbagger's reputation

for "ignorant or bad character," is the fact that a large proportion were well educated. About two-thirds of the group (forty-
three of the sixty-two) had studied law, medicine, or engineering enough to practice the profession, or had attended one or
more years of college, or had been school teachers. Of the
senators alone, approximately half were college graduates.
Seemingly the academic and intellectual attainments of the
carpetbaggers in Congress were, on the whole, at least as high
as those of the other members of Congress, whether from the
North or from the South.

Still more significant is the fact that nearly five-sixths of
the entire carpetbag group (fifty of the sixty-two) had arrived
in the South before 1867, before the passage of the Reconstruction Acts, before the granting of political rights to the
Negro. Of the fifty early arrivals, only fifteen appeared on the
Southern scene as Treasury Department employees, Freedman's Bureau officials, or members of the postwar occupation
forces (and at least a few of these fifteen soon left the government service and went into private enterprise). Thirty-five of
the fifty were engaged in farming or business or the professions from the time of their arrival or soon after.

As for those other twelve of the sixty-two—the twelve who
did not begin to live in the South until 1867 or later—more
than half (at least seven) took up some private occupation before getting public office. Their comparatively late arrival
does not, in itself, signify that they moved south merely for
"office sake." [19]

If, then, the sixty-two carpetbag congressmen and senators
make up a representative sample, we must conclude that a
majority of the carpetbaggers, taken as a whole, do not conform to the traditional view, at least so far as their backgrounds are concerned. With comparatively few exceptions,
the so-called carpetbaggers had moved south for reasons other
than a lust for offices newly made available by the passage of
the Reconstruction Acts. These men were, in fact, a part of
the multitude of Union officers and soldiers who, during or

soon after the war, chose to remain in or return to the land they had helped to conquer.

To thousands of the young men in blue, at and after the war's end, the South beckoned as a land of wondrous charm, a place of almost magical opportunity. "Northern men are going to do well in every part of the South. The Southern men are too indolent to work and the Yankees are bound to win." So, for example, a cavalry sergeant wrote from Texas to his sister back home in Ohio in 1866. "I have some idea that I will not remain in Ohio long, and maybe I will locate in the sunny South," he continued. "What think you of roses blooming in open air in November, and the gardens glorious with flowers."[20]

Here, in the South, was a new frontier, another and a better West. Some men compared the two frontiers before choosing the Southern one, as did the Morgan brothers, who first looked over Kansas and then decided upon Mississippi. Albert T. Morgan afterwards wrote that the former cry, "Go West, young man," had been changed to "Go South, young man," and in 1865 the change was "already quite apparent, in the purpose of those of the North who were seeking new homes."[21] Many years later Albion W. Tourgée recalled the hopes and dreams with which, in the fall of 1865, he had settled as a badly wounded veteran in Greensboro, North Carolina:

He expected the future to be as bright and busy within the conquered territory as it had been along the ever-advancing frontier of the West. . . . He expected the whole region to be transformed by the power of commerce, manufactures, and the incursion of Northern life, thought, capital, industry, and enterprise. . . . Because he thought he bore a shattered life he sought a milder clime. He took his young wife with him, and they builded their first home-nest almost before the smoke of battle disappeared. . . . His first object was restored health; his next desire, to share the general prosperity.[22]

Once they had been released from the army, thousands of other Union soldiers and officers returned to the South with similar dreams of prosperity and a pleasant life. For the moment, land was cheap and cotton dear. Labor was abundant, and the Negroes were expected to work more willingly for their liberators than for their late masters. So the veterans turned south. At the end of 1865 a newsman from the North learned that, in Alabama alone, there were already five thousand of them "engaged in planting and trading." Even more than the uplands of Alabama, Tennessee, and Georgia, the Mississippi Valley was proving an "attraction to the adventurous capital," this traveling reporter found. "Men from the Middle States and the great West were everywhere, buying and leasing plantations, hiring freedmen, and setting thousands of ploughs in motion."[23] No impecunious wanderers were these, but bringers of "adventurous capital." They paid cash for lands or leases, for wages, for supplies. At a time when the South was languishing for want of money, these newcomers provided it, put it into circulation, and thus gave the economy a lift.[24]

Most of those who thus adventured with their capital were to lose it. They failed for several reasons. At cotton planting the Yankees were novices, unused to local conditions and deluded in their expectations of the Negro as a free worker, or so the Southerners said.[25] Actually, the Southerners as well as the Yankees ran into economic difficulties during the first few years after the war. "Various causes have arisen to prostrate the people, leaving them nearly ruined," a contemporary observed early in 1867, "among which I may more especially mention the following, which could not have been foreseen or provided against: The too great drouth at one season, which destroyed and blasted their corn; too much rain at another season, which injured their cotton; and then the army worm, which came out of the ground in vast numbers, destroyed what was left." There was, besides, the federal cotton tax, which both Northern and Southern planters denounced as ruinous.[26]

Often, whether as planters or as businessmen, the Northerners faced a special disadvantage—the hostility of the people around them. "The rebels will not buy from a Galvanized Yankee, or Loyal Unionist, nor from a Yankee either," a unionist Virginian complained late in 1865, "the result being that loyal or Northern merchants are failing all over the South."[27] In many places the Yankees were boycotted if they sympathized with or voted for Republicans. "Only one hundred and one men were found base enough to vote for the Radical ticket," a Memphis newspaper reported in April 1866. "We have held up the names of a portion of these men and written small pox over their doors in order that our people might shun them."[28]

Discouraged and disillusioned after a year or two in their new homes, large numbers of the Yankees abandoned them and returned to the North. Others, of whom some were successful and some were not, remained in the South. Of those who remained, many turned to state and local politics as Republicans in 1867 or after. These comprised the majority of that class of men who eventually came to be known as carpetbaggers.

Before 1867 the Northerners in the South possessed only limited opportunities in politics. As Republicans, they could not hope to be elected to office. As newcomers, they often found it difficult even to vote, because of the residence requirements. The Georgia constitution, as remade after the war, extended the residence requirement in that state from six months to two years. "Now it is generally admitted," a Northern settler in Georgia protested, "that this change . . . has been effected to prevent loyal men who were obliged to leave here during the war and those who have come here since the war from having any voice in choosing the officers of the State and representatives to Congress."[29] Of course, the newcomers could seek federal jobs, and many of them did so, but again they faced something of a handicap, for they understood that President Johnson preferred "Southern citizens" when "suitable persons" among them could be found.[30]

To the Northern settlers remaining in the South the congressional acts of 1867 suddenly brought political opportunity and also, as some of them saw it, political responsibility. Tour-

gée, for one, sought election to the new constitutional convention in North Carolina because, having failed in business
and lost the savings he had brought, he needed the money he
would be paid as a delegate. But he sought election also because he was concerned about Negro rights and wished to do
what he could to protect them.[31] A more prosperous settler, a
planter of Carroll Parish, Louisiana, who once had been an
Ohio school superintendent, took an active interest in Southern politics for reasons that he explained, in April 1867, to
Senator John Sherman:

> On the closing of my services as a Soldier, I became a member of the
> firm of Lynch, Ruggles & Co., which was organized in Circleville,
> Ohio, for the purpose of buying lands in the South and planting. We
> have located at this point, which is 40 miles above Vicksburg, have
> purchased lands, have organized most efficient labor forces, & our in-
> vestment now is on a scale which makes us on *that* account deeply
> interested in every effort made to bring peace to the South. . . .
>   I . . . respectfully ask your advice as to the proper course to be pur-
> sued by Northern men in the South who sympathize with Congress
> in the present crisis. . . . I have never held a civil office and never in-
> tended to, if I can avoid it; but we have a large force at work, have
> their confidence, and now as they are voters, they look to our advice,
> and I want to give it as wisely as possible. Other Northern men are
> similarly situated.[32]

The position of some of these other Northern men was later
recalled by C. M. Hamilton, a Pennsylvanian who had gone to
Florida in 1864, as a Freedmen's Bureau agent and had become,
after 1867, one of the most prominent carpetbaggers of that
state. In 1871 he told a congressional committee investigating
the Ku Klux Klan,

> . . . when the reconstruction acts first passed Congress, the Yankees,
> as we are called, most of us soldiers who were in the South, rather
> stood back, did not really feel at that time that they [we] had any par-
> ticular right to interfere in politics, or to take part in them. But the
> reconstruction laws were passed; reconstruction was necessary; . . .
> the democratic party of the South adopted the policy of masterly in-
> activity . . . ; there was a new element here that had been enfran-
> chised who were without leaders. The northern men in the South,
> and there were but a handful of them in this State, who had been in

the Army, took hold of this matter of reconstruction, and they have perfected it so far as it has been accomplished.[33]

These Northerners, already in the South in 1867, felt they had a right and a duty to be where they were and to do what they did. They were Americans. They had fought a war to keep the nation one. South as well as North, it was *their* country. They had chosen to live in the Southern part of it. This was now their home, and they had a stake in its future as well as the future of the country as a whole. Their attitude should be quite understandable—as understandable as the feeling of the majority of Southern whites.

Naturally, the native Conservatives and Democrats resented the Northern Republicans and reviled them with such epithets as "aliens," "birds of passage," and "carpetbaggers." As applied to most of the men, however, these were not objective and descriptive terms. The Union veterans who settled in the South were impelled by a variety of motives: restlessness, patriotic idealism, the desire to get ahead, and what not. But so were the pioneers at other times and places in the United States. So were the Southerners themselves who moved westward or northward during the Reconstruction period. At that time the newer states of the Southwest (such as Alabama, Mississippi, and especially Arkansas) were filled with fairly recent arrivals from the older states of the Southeast. And at that time there were more Southerners residing in the North than Northerners in the South.[34] The latter were no more "birds of passage" than the former. Perhaps the frontiersman has been too much idealized for his propensity to rove. Certainly the carpetbagger has been too much condemned for the mere act of moving from one part of the country to another.

Even if all this be conceded, there remain of course the other elements of the carpetbagger stereotype—the charges of misgovernment, corruption, and racial disturbance.

With regard to the charge of misgovernment and corruption, it is hard to generalize about the carpetbaggers as a class.

Nevertheless, a few tentative observations may be made. First, the extent and duration of "carpetbag rule" has been exaggerated. In six of the eleven ex-Confederate states (Texas, Tennessee, Alabama, Georgia, Virginia, North Carolina) there was never a carpetbag governor; there was never a majority of carpetbaggers among the Republicans in or out of office; certainly there was never anything approaching carpetbagger domination of state politics. In all those states the Republicans held power only briefly if at all, and they held it, to the extent that they did so, by means of their strength among Negroes and scalawags. In the other five states (Arkansas, Mississippi, Louisiana, Florida, South Carolina) there were carpetbag governors part of the time, but even in these states the carpetbaggers could maintain themselves only with Negro and native white support. Second, the extent of illegal and illegitimate spending by the carpetbag governments has been exaggerated—if spending for schools, transportation, and other social and economic services be considered legitimate.[35] Third, the improper spending, the private use of public funds, was by no means the work of carpetbaggers alone, nor were they the only beneficiaries: heavily involved also were native whites, including Conservatives and Democrats as well as scalawags.[36] Fourth, probably the great majority of the carpetbaggers were no more corrupt than the great majority of contemporary officeholders throughout the United States.[37]

Consider the carpetbag governors, who are generally mentioned as the most conspicuous examples of dishonesty. One of them, Joseph Brooks of Arkansas, did not succeed in exercising uncontested power, for either good or evil, and was soon ousted. Two of the governors, R. K. Scott of South Carolina and W. P. Kellogg of Louisiana, are rather difficult to defend. Four others—Powell Clayton of Arkansas, Harrison Reed and M. L. Stearns of Florida, and H. C. Warmoth of Louisiana—were loudly accused but never really proved guilty of misusing their offices for private profit.[38] Only one of the four, Warmoth, seems actually to have made much money while in

Reconstruction politics, and he made a fortune. While governor, he admitted that there was "a frightful amount of corruption" in Louisiana. He explained, however, that the temptation came from the business interests who offered bribes, and he insisted that the Republicans, black as well as white, had resisted bribery as well as had the Democrats.[39] It might be more true to say that Louisiana corrupted Warmoth (if indeed he was corrupted) than to say that Warmoth corrupted Louisiana. The other two carpetbag governors, Adelbert Ames of Mississippi and D. H. Chamberlain of South Carolina, were economy-minded and strictly honest.[40]

There remains the charge that the carpetbaggers disturbed the relations between the races of the South. Of course, the carpetbaggers did so. Their doing so was the basic cause of the animus against them. This is the reason why the honest ones among them, the men like Ames and Chamberlain and Warner, were as thoroughly hated and as strongly opposed as were any of the Yankee scoundrels. Most of the Southern whites opposed the granting of political rights to the former slaves. The carpetbaggers encouraged the Negroes to exercise such rights. Thus the carpetbaggers upset the pattern of race relationships, the pattern of Negro passivity, which most white Southerners considered ideal.

The party struggle in the postwar South amounted to something more than ordinary politics. In some of its aspects it was equivalent to a continuation, or a renewal, of the Civil War.

On the one hand, Southern Conservatives thought of themselves as still fighting for home rule and white supremacy—in essence much the same war aims as the Confederacy had pursued. Carpetbaggers, on the other hand, saw their own basic objective as the reunification of the country, which had been incompletely won at Appomattox, and as the emancipation of the Negroes, who had been but partially freed by the adoption of the Thirteenth Amendment.

On both sides the methods frequently were those of actual, though irregular, warfare. The Ku Klux Klan, the White

League, the Red Shirts, and the various kinds of rifle companies were military or semimilitary organizations. So, too, were the state militias, the Union Leagues and Loyal Leagues, and the other partisan institutions of the carpetbaggers and their Negro allies. The carpetbaggers served, so to speak, as officers of front-line troops, deep in enemy territory, "on the picket line of freedom in the South." The embattled Republicans undoubtedly suffered much heavier casualties than did their foes.

True, the Republicans had the advantage of support by the regular United States army, but often that support was more a potentiality than a fact, and at critical moments it failed to materialize. As for the warriors of white supremacy, they had the backing of Northern sympathizers in strength and numbers that would have gladdened the heart of Jefferson Davis in that earlier wartime when he was angling for the aid of the Knights of the Golden Circle. The carpetbaggers were divided and weakened by the Republican party schism of 1872, by personal rivalries among themselves, and by jealousies between them and their Negro and scalawag associates. Finally, as some of the carpetbaggers saw it, they were stabbed in the back—abandoned by the government and the people at the North.[41]

The history of this losing campaign has been written almost exclusively from the Southern, or Democratic, or disillusioned Republican point of view: the story of the carpetbaggers has been told mainly by their enemies. Historical scholarship has given its sanction to the propaganda of the victorious side in the Reconstruction war. That propaganda, like most, has its elements of truth, and like most, its elements of distortion and downright falsehood. Not that the carpetbaggers were invariably the apostles of righteousness and truth. We would make little progress toward historical understanding if we merely took the same old morality play and switched the labels of Evil and Good. But surely the time has long since passed when we can, uncritically, accept the "carpetbagger" stereotype.

No doubt men can be found who fit it. No doubt there were political tramps who went south to make cynical use of the Negro vote and who contrived to win both office and illicit gain. But such men were few and comparatively unimportant. Far more numerous and more significant were those energetic and ambitious men who, with or without carpetbags, brought their savings or their borrowings to invest, who eventually got into politics for idealistic as well as selfish reasons, and who in office behaved no better and no worse than most of their contemporaries. Some of these men, like some others of their time, proved corrupt. It would be interesting to know whether, as peculators, the carpetbaggers took out more than a small fraction of the money that, as speculators, they had brought in.

Chapter 9. Neo-Calhounism and Minority Rights

"Judged by later times and his meaning for them, Calhoun stands in the first rank of men America has produced," one of his biographers concluded a hundred years after his death. "For as a thinker and prophet he was more important for later times than his own."[1]

A number of present-day Americans share this view of John C. Calhoun. They consider him as somehow more relevant to the twentieth century than any of his political contemporaries, including his great rivals Daniel Webster and Henry Clay. His admirers look upon him as a defender of minority rights and an inventor of democratic techniques.

If the neo-Calhounites are to be believed—if Calhoun speaks for the democratic-minded citizens or for the minorities of today—then he is, indeed, more important for our times than for his. Not only that. He must also have a rather different significance now than a century and more ago.[2]

Calhoun's theory of government, together with its application to the United States of his time, may be summarized as follows:

Human nature is the starting point for governmental theory. Human beings are alike in having both individual (selfish) and social (unselfish) feelings, the former strong, the latter weak. In other respects, however, human beings are not alike. Certainly they are not equal except in a limited, legal sense;

they are endowed with widely varying capacities for self-development. Their nature is such that, with insignificant exceptions, they can live only in society and under government.

Government must be strong enough to protect the people not only from outside enemies but also from one another, for their self-interest leads to continual conflicts between individuals and between groups. Yet the people must be allowed the greatest possible liberty, so that they may realize to the fullest their individual potentialities. Since these potentialities vary, the more liberty there is, the more inequality there will be, which is desirable and, indeed, essential for progress. Thus liberty and equality do *not* go together. The proper balancing of security and liberty—or, in other words, of power and liberty—is the central problem of government. Imbalance usually comes from too much power rather than too little; for, like all human beings, rulers, even elected ones, are prone to self-aggrandizement.

A *constitution* is the governmental arrangement by which rulers are checked and power is limited. To be effective, the constitution must pit power against power—negative against positive. The right to vote is essential to constitutional government, but the right to vote is, by itself, insufficient. It results in rule by the numerical majority, that is, rule by the largest group or combination of groups. The rest, the minority or minorities, remain unprotected. They, too, must be provided with a negative power if there is to be a truly limited or constitutional government.

The *concurrent majority*, in addition to the numerical majority, must have a voice. The concurrent majority is the majority of every important group (or interest) taken separately. Under a true constitution, governmental action requires the approval of all the separate majorities as well as the approval of a majority of the people as a whole. Each group, then, must have a veto on governmental action.

Nullification, or state interposition, is, in the United States, a device for providing such a veto. (Nullification thus assumes that important interests are more or less identified with various states, and certainly the slaveholding interest is important to each of the slave states.) Through a special convention, the people of a state can nullify a federal law that they deem unconstitutional. In that state the law then becomes null and void. It remains so unless and until three-fourths of the states ratify a constitutional amendment specifically authorizing the nullified law.

Secession is a possible recourse on the part of the people of the nullifying state if, in their judgment, the new amendment is itself unconstitutional, that is, inconsistent with the original purpose and spirit of the Constitution. The rights of nullification and secession follow inevitably from the nature of sovereignty and of the constitutional compact.

Sovereignty, the ultimate and supreme power within a body politic, is not to be confused with governmental powers. The one is the source for the others. Governmental powers, which are derived from sovereignty, may be delegated and divided; sovereignty itself cannot be. In the United States, sovereignty resides in the people of each of the separate states.

The *constitutional compact* (the American Constitution) is an agreement among the several states as sovereign communities. It is, in effect, the set of instructions that these communities, as the principals, have given to the federal government as their agent or trustee. By the agreement they have delegated certain specified powers but have yielded no sovereignty. The people of each state must decide for themselves whether, in any of its actions, the federal government is exceeding its delegated powers. If the people of one state disagree with those of other states, with regard to the interpretation of the compact, the difference of opinion can be resolved by the amending process. By this process, the federal government is decisively adjudged to have exceeded its powers if one more than one-fourth of all the states agree that it has done so.

Slavery occupies a special place in the constitutional compact. A number of the sovereign communities would never have agreed to the compact without guarantees for slavery. These guarantees form part of the bargain. So far as its legitimate powers go, the federal government, as a trustee for the states, must protect and promote the interests of all of them—and especially the interests of slavery, since human chattels are the only kind of property specifically mentioned in the compact. In the conduct of foreign affairs, in the regulation of interstate commerce, in the management of federal property, in the making of rules for the territories, the federal government cannot use its own discretion but must merely give effect to state laws creating property in slaves.

The *class struggle* is the most serious and most important of all the group conflicts in civilized societies. This struggle arises from the fact that, in all such societies, one class exploits another. In the society of the Southern states, however, the exploitation is unusually mild, and the slave owner combines in himself the interests of capital and labor; therefore the class struggle does not develop. In the society of the Northern states, as in all modern industrial societies, the conflict between capital and labor grows more and more intense; it must eventuate in a revolutionary crisis. The only way to prevent revolution, and at the same time to permit extension of the suffrage, is to put into effect the principle of the concurrent majority. This will enable the planters and the capitalists, whose interests are fundamentally the same, to adjust their differences and collaborate against their common foe, the rising proletariat. If, however, Northern property owners persist in refusing to see the only means of their own salvation, the Southern slave owners will have to take increasingly drastic measures to save themselves.

The *dual presidency*, in addition to nullification, is one possibility for giving the slave owners an absolute veto. They would have as their tribune a second president, representing the South. Failing such a guarantee, secession may become necessary as a last resort.

*

After the Civil War the reputation of Calhoun declined. True, Jefferson Davis praised him, and Alexander H. Stephens declared that his works would live forever, but these men were really looking backward, not forward. In his own state, Calhoun became something of a folk hero. Carolina cotton farmers were heard to say, years after Appomattox, that the South would have won the war if he had been still living when it was fought.[3] He experienced a kind of resurrection when, in 1884, his iron coffin was moved from the temporary grave to a relatively imposing sarcophagus, for which the state finally had appropriated funds.[4] Yet, South as well as North, Calhoun personified the slave states at war, and those states had been defeated. His theories, it seemed, had been put to the test of battle, and they had failed the test. For Northerners, his name continued to glow with a "lurid intensity,"[5] but it was a light from the dead past, a name with evil yet quaint and antiquarian connotations. For Southerners, it was a symbol of defeat.

By the beginning of the twentieth century, Calhoun had lost practically all relevance for living Americans. In 1911 the historian William E. Dodd, himself a Southerner, could write, "No political party looks back to Calhoun as its founder or rejuvenator, no group of public men proclaim allegiance to his doctrines, no considerable group of individuals outside of South Carolina profess any love for his name and ideals."[6]

Suddenly, nearly a hundred years after his death, his reputation recovered and took on new aspects. By the middle of the twentieth century a Calhoun revival was under way. He and his theory seemed timely again.

New biographies came out: a three-volume, nearly definitive life; a "humanized" portrait that won a Pulitzer Prize; and a brief and critical "reappraisal."[7] A book-length study of his political philosophy appeared.[8] His *Disquisition on Government* was reissued again and again, in various editions. A project for publishing his complete writings, in twelve to fifteen volumes, was announced.[9] He was made the subject of dozens of essays, and these were given space not only in learned journals but also in popular periodicals, among them *Harper's Magazine*, *Time*, and the *Saturday Evening Post*.

More remarkable than the quantity of this writing was the theme of much of it. The authors treated Calhoun as no antiquarian curiosity but a political philosopher with an enduring message and a unique relevance for their time.

The *Harper's* article (1948) asserted, strange though it might seem, that his theory "came through the Civil War stronger than ever." True, Calhoun had been concerned with a veto to protect the interests of slaveholders, but "by implication he would have given a similar veto to every other special interest, whether it be labor, management, the Catholic church, old-age pensioners, the silver miners, or the corn-growers of the Middle West." In a "somewhat elusive sense," the American people actually had adopted this concept of group veto and had put it into practice. "But elusive and subtle as it may be, it remains the basic rule of the game of politics in this country—and in this country alone." In short, Calhoun was the author of the "unwritten rules of American politics" as currently carried on.[10]

Time magazine took up the same theme in reporting the news (1952) that Senator Richard Russell, of Georgia, had announced himself as a contender for the presidential nomination on the Democratic ticket. According to *Time*, Russell thus implied a "latent threat of revolt" which Southern Democrats were using to bargain with their Northern partisans. Here, in operation, was the "concurrent majority" principle of Calhoun. "He meant that every essential group in the nation had a veto on policies directly affecting it." Of course, his veto in the form of nullification was buried with him. "But Calhounism survives in a far more subtle and resilient form than legal nullification," said *Time*. "It was built into the structure of the American party system." It could be found in the give and take of the national nominating convention—"in a great and much maligned American institution, the smoke-filled room."[11]

Herbert Ravenel Sass, identified as a "hopping-mad Charlestonian," pursued a similar argument in a *Saturday Evening Post* article (1954), in which he complained that Northern writers did less than justice to the history and culture of the South. Sass mentioned Calhoun as a neglected figure of nineteenth-century intellectual history, and the *Disquisition* and *Discourse* as neglected classics. Calhoun's "brilliantly original" exposition of the concurrent majority was "the most revolutionary contribution to political science made by an American," according to Sass, and it was "also the blueprint by which our republic largely operates today." Calhoun had recognized that a free society could not exist as a mass of undifferentiated individuals. It was made up of groups with conflicting interests, and these groups had to have some means of protection against one another. Bringing the theory up to date, Sass explained,

The groups to which Calhoun wished to give formal voice—the labor group, the management group, the farm group, the Southern group and various others—have learned to protect themselves against one another and against the numerical majority and to maintain themselves as separate political elements whose concurrence with the numerical majority must be had in the shaping of legislation. Today the Washington lobbies of the principal interests which make up the republic have become a fully accepted part of the American political mechanism because both the soundness and the indispensability of the principle are tacitly recognized.[12]

Writing in the *New York Times,* Senator Paul H. Douglas, of Illinois, reflected the new interpretation of Calhoun. It is "almost impossible to force through measures that are deeply resented and opposed by any large minority of the population," Douglas noted, in discussing the presidency. "This means that Calhoun's theory of requiring majorities of each significant group in the country to concur before a measure can be passed, while rejected in theory, has nevertheless been largely realized on important matters in practice."[13]

These writers themselves had not rediscovered Calhoun; they were merely paraphrasing others, among them a political scientist, Peter F. Drucker, who had elaborated upon "Calhoun's pluralism" as a "key to American politics" in a professional journal (1948). Drucker contended that "for the constitutional veto power of the states over national legislation, by means of which Calhoun proposed to formalize the principle of sectional and interest compromise, was substituted in actual practice the much more powerful and much more elastic but extra-constitutional veto power of sections, interests, and pressure groups."

According to Drucker, this new veto power, the modern version of the concurrent majority, operated within Congress, the administration, the national nominating convention, and, above all, the political party. In Congress there were blocs, such as the farm bloc, that could negative measures adversely affecting the groups they represented; and there were lobbies that could check legislation opposed by any of the major interests. In the administration, some of the cabinet members, such as the secretaries of labor, agriculture, and commerce, looked out for the welfare of special groups. In the selection of a presidential candidate (and also of other candidates) availability or eligibility had to be taken into account: "Eligibility simply means that a candidate must not be unacceptable to any major interest, religious or regional group within the electorate; it is primarily a negative qualification." In the party—which "(rather than the states) has become the instrument to realize Calhoun's 'rule of the concurrent majority'"—the working of the veto was most in evidence: "It [the party] must, by definition, be acceptable equally to the right and the left, the rich and the poor, the farmer and the worker, the Protestant and the Catholic, the native and the foreign-born."[14]

Though he made the most elaborate presentation of the new Calhounism, Drucker did not originate it. Before him, Charles M. Wiltse had put forth the thesis in a couple of published essays (1937 and 1941). Even earlier, V. L. Parrington had suggested the idea. Among the new interpreters, only

Wiltse could claim a close acquaintance with Calhoun's career and works. He became the author of the most scholarly and most exhaustive of all Calhoun biographies.

Wiltse maintained that when, in Calhoun's scheme, a state insisted upon its sovereignty, the state was really acting as an economic rather than a geographical unit. Nullification was an assertion of the sovereignty of the interest group, not the state. "To Calhoun they were the same." In his day the negative took the form of state interposition to restrain the enforcement of a federal law. "In terms of the unlocalized economic interests of today, its expressions are strikes, lockouts, injunctions, and the political activities of pressure groups." Congress in the middle of the twentieth century could make no law objectionable to agriculture or industry without these interests finding some way, generally, to modify or nullify the law. So the country had come to have, in fact, a kind of "functional representation." This operated on a principle essentially the same as the concurrent majority of Calhoun. "Today it means that economic legislation should have the approval of labor as well as capital, of consumer as well as producer, of farmer as well as manufacturer."[15]

One of the most extreme statements of Calhoun's relevance for the present was that of another of his biographers, Margaret L. Coit (1950). She averred that Calhoun was the author of "perhaps the most powerful defense of minority rights in a democracy ever written."[16] She had taken her cue from Arthur M. Schlesinger, Jr. "In the end his theory was not a lawyer's brief, adroitly constructed to advance the pretensions of slavery," Schlesinger had written (1945), "but a brilliant and penetrating study of modern society, whose insights remain vital for any minority."[17]

Schlesinger viewed himself as a liberal; among his contemporaries he stood at the opposite extreme from Russell Kirk, a self-styled conservative. The liberal and the conservative could join, however, in admiration of Calhoun. Kirk praised him for his "devotion to freedom" and rated him, along with John

Adams, as "one of the two most eminent American political writers."[18]

Wiltse had been cautious enough to say, "Whether or not Calhoun would have conceded that the great unlocalized interests of today fulfill his definition can only be guessed."[19] Indeed, this is more than doubtful, and equally dubious is the description of present-day politics and policymaking that Wiltse and the other neo-Calhounites give. In appraising the new interpretation, then, two questions might be asked. First, does it, with reference to the "veto," accurately describe the political practices of the present? Second, does it really reflect the teachings of Calhoun a century and more ago?

The illustrations the neo-Calhounites use to demonstrate the "veto" by each interest or each minority today are plausible but unconvincing. Here is one: "For sixteen years [1932–1948] the Republicans lost much of their standing as a truly national party because they had made themselves unacceptable to labor."[20] Thus labor's "veto" did seem to have some effect during those years, but it failed to operate against the Taft-Hartley Act (1947), which the Republican Congress passed despite the last-ditch opposition of labor leaders, who denounced it as a "slave-labor law." And what had happened to labor's "veto" during the preceding twelve years of Republican supremacy? Another example: "Similarly, the Democrats during the middle stage of the New Deal incurred the wrath of the business interests."[21] What became of the *business* "veto" during those sixteen (ultimately twenty) years that the New Dealers were in power? The explanation is offered that President Franklin D. Roosevelt had set aside the "veto" by his appeal to the needs of the "temporary emergency" that the depression had brought. But what does a "veto" amount to if it can be charmed away by a couple of magic words, such as "temporary emergency"? Surely this is not the kind of negative power that Calhoun had in mind!

A third illustration, which the neo-Calhounites use to support their argument, does further damage to their own case.

"By 1946 . . . labor troubles could be resolved only on a basis acceptable to both labor and employer: higher wages *and* higher prices."[22] Now, this may illustrate a "veto" by labor and by employer, but it also shows the lack, in this instance, of a "veto" by consumer or by farmer. What the wage-price agreement here amounts to, in fact, is a deal between two interests at the expense of the rest of the community. It is not an agreement arrived at through consultation of all interests.

No doubt this sort of bargaining *is* fairly typical of what actually goes on in the United States. Together with the other examples mentioned, it demonstrates the fact that politicians and pressure groups normally do not appease every minority (not even every big one), do not allow each interest a "veto," do not arrive at action on the basis of unanimity. Instead, they construct a working majority through the combination of several (but not necessarily all) minorities. When, to form the combination, the support of a particular group is needed, the demands of that group, the positive or negative demands, are respected. To an extent, then, any interest or minority can get concessions from other interests or minorities in the process of forming the majority; to that extent the "veto" of the interest or minority is effective. But only to that extent. The process is familiar enough, and so is the word for it—"logrolling."

This practice is far from new in the history of American politics. In Calhoun's own time there were blocs, lobbies, and factions, and there was logrolling among them. Calhoun himself was aware, painfully aware, of the concessions that both Whig and Democratic politicians were prone to make to tariff lobbyists or to the antislavery or free-soil bloc. He knew from bitter experience what "availability" meant in the choosing of a presidential candidate. He was acquainted with the struggle, essentially the same then as now, by which contending groups sought to get control of the government. "If no one interest be strong enough, of itself, to obtain it," he wrote, "a combination will be formed between those whose interests are most alike—each conceding something to the others, until a sufficient number is obtained to make a majority."[23] That was the essence of the process in his day, and it remains the essence of the process in ours.

But this was not and is not what Calhoun advocated. Quite the contrary. He condemned that kind, the familiar kind, of politics. He thought that by its inevitable tendency "principle and policy would lose all influence in the elections; then cunning, falsehood, deception, slander, fraud, and gross appeals to the appetites of the lowest and most worthless portions of the community would take the place of sound reason and wise debate."[24] Certainly he had no use for the kind of trading that went on at party conventions. He opposed allowing minorities, such as the abolitionists, to exercise any kind of veto on presidential nominations. For example, as he looked forward, in 1847, to the election of the following year, he thought there was a scheme by which slaveholders and abolitionists would be "coerced into nominating and supporting the same candidate" on the Democratic ticket.

> Should it succeed—should the party machinery for President-making prove strong enough to force the slaveholding States to join in a convention to nominate and support a candidate who will be acceptable to the abolitionists, they will have committed the most suicidal act that a people ever perpetrated. I say acceptable; for it is clear that the non-slaveholding States will outnumber in convention the slaveholding, and that no one who is not acceptable to the abolitionists can receive their votes; and, of course, the votes of the States where they hold the balance; and that no other will be nominated, or, if nominated, be elected.

Calhoun went on to denounce all nominating conventions as "irresponsible bodies" that were unknown to the Constitution. He urged Southerners to renounce the forthcoming Democratic convention of 1848 and to unite in a strictly Southern party. The election of the president, he added, ought to be left strictly to the electoral college, as the framers of the Constitution had intended.[25] He refused to be satisfied with the combination of interests upon policy unless *all* interests (that is, all property-owning interests, and, in particular, the slavery interest) were consulted and their approval gained. "I am," he declared, "in favor of the government of the whole; the only really and truly popular government—a government based on the concurrent majority—the joint assent of all the parts, through their respective majority of the whole."[26] He insisted upon essential *unanimity* as the condition for governmental action.

This requirement, for all the assertions of the neo-Calhounites, does not exist today. It did not exist when Calhoun was alive. He looked for some means of imposing it; he found the means, constitutionally, in his theory of state's rights and, politically, in his plan for creating a sectional party or at least a sectional faction—the solid South. Except when his own presidential hopes were active and his own chances appeared to be good, he was inclined to turn away from the game of politics as it was customarily played—and still is.

In sum, the new interpreters of Calhoun have been careless in their reading of his philosophy and superficial in their description of current politics. They have attributed to him the very political principles and practices which he detested and for which he sought quite different alternatives. Without realizing it, they have misused the term "concurrent majority" so as to make it mean essentially what he himself meant by the term "numerical majority," that is, a combination of the majorities of many or even most *but not all* interests.

It might, or might not, be a good thing if the United States actually had institutions to give effect to the kind of "political pluralism" that the neo-Calhounites admire. It might be desirable, for instance, to set up a third house as a supplement to Congress, a third house in which economic, sectional, religious, racial, and other groups would be represented as such; and in which each of them could exercise a veto. Possibly this would work, and possibly it could be considered as a Calhounian situation—but only if certain passages are isolated from his works, unrestrained inferences are drawn from these passages, and the rest of his writings and his career itself are ignored.

On the whole, he seems to have taken a dualist, not a pluralist, view of politics. Though he mentioned the existence of various interests in society, he made no attempt to list and describe them, and certainly he never specified racial or religious minorities, or the working class, as deserving of the veto power. Generally he ignored the variety of possible groupings. When he got down to theorizing, he really thought about only two groups at a time, not several. On occasion he dealt with the duality of capital and labor. Most often he had in mind the twofold grouping of North Against South, free states against slave states. These were, to him, the majority and the minority, and this was the minority he sought to protect—the minority of slaveholders.

It is farfetched to say that his "insights remain vital for any minority." This might be remotely true if his theory were abstracted enough, but the theory would have to be stretched to the point where it had only the most tenuous connection with what Calhoun actually thought and said. The assumption would have to be made that, somehow, the case for the onetime master has been, or at least can be, converted into a case for the onetime slave. This assumption has yet to be proved. Perhaps the National Association for the Advancement of Colored People ought to peruse Calhoun's works for means of protecting Negro rights. If the NAACP should do so, the news would be startling, and if the search were successful, the news would be amazing.

Surely the spirit of Calhoun is not to be found in the meetings of today's minority groups, of whatever creed or color. Nor is it to be discovered in all the political bargaining of the lobby, the congressional bloc, the executive department, or the smoke-filled room. We of the twentieth century must look elsewhere if we are to find the genuine ghost of the Great Nullifier.

Wherever a White Citizens' Council meets in Mississippi, or a similar group in another of the Southern states, *there* is to be sought, nowadays, the true spirit of Calhoun. It is to be sought in the activities of conservative—or reactionary— Southern whites. The way *they* use the lobby, the bloc, the party convention, and other political devices can be considered as essentially Calhounian.

These white Southerners now face a problem quite similar to the one that Calhoun faced more than a hundred years ago. They talk of maintaining white supremacy and he talked of protecting slavery. The problem remains that of defending, against external attack, institutions based upon a belief in human inequality.

Chapter 10. Fiction as History: Vidal, Haley, Styron

Historical journals seldom carry reviews of novels, yet novelists may have a much greater influence than historians do on popular conceptions of the past. Even the author of a widely adopted textbook is unlikely to reach as large a readership as does a leading writer of fiction—a Gore Vidal, an Alex Haley, or a William Styron. And the textbook will probably leave no such lasting impression as will the novel, especially if the novel is dramatized for cinema or television.

There is less reason to be concerned about historical fiction than about fictional history. *Historical fiction* presents imaginary characters and events against a background of presumed historical facts. A few examples are the American Winston Churchill's *The Crisis* (1901), Thomas Dixon, Jr.'s *The Clansman* (1905), Walter Dumaux Edmond's *Erie Water* (1933), and Margaret Mitchell's *Gone with the Wind* (1936).[1] Historians no longer share the views of Reconstruction that either Dixon or Mitchell took, but neither of the two authors made his or her view up; each adopted what was a standard interpretation. Mitchell created a Scarlett O'Hara and a Rhett Butler; she did not attempt to re-create Jefferson Davis or Robert E. Lee. Dixon took Thaddeus Stevens as the model for his villain but gave him a new name (Austin Stoneman) and a new persona as the father of a heroic son and a lovely daughter.

Fictional history, in contrast with historical fiction, pretends to deal with real persons and events but actually reshapes them—and thus rewrites the past. The author may claim to be offering literal, documented facts, as David Balsiger and Charles E. Sellers, Jr., do in *The Lincoln Conspiracy* (1977), a tissue of preposterous fabrications about the Lincoln murder.[2] Or the author may admit to having embellished the facts and yet insist on having told the quintessential truth. This is the stand of Gore Vidal in *Lincoln: A Novel* (1984), Alex Haley in *Roots* (1976), and William Styron in *The Confessions of Nat Turner* (1967).[3] Fictional history of the Vidal kind and historical fiction of the Dixon sort are not quite mutually exclusive. Dixon brought Lincoln onstage and put words in his mouth; Vidal introduces admittedly fictitious along with ostensibly factual characters.

A best seller, unstintingly praised by journalistic reviewers and literary critics, Vidal's *Lincoln* calls for appraisal on historical as well as literary grounds. The book comes with the imprimatur of David Herbert Donald, whom Vidal thanks "for his patient reading—and correction—of the manuscript." Vidal professes to have written from primary sources the way any conscientious scholar would do. "As for Lincoln and the other historical figures," he says, "I have reconstructed them from letters, journals, newspapers, diaries, etc."[4] Indeed, he claims to be a better historian than any of the academic writers on Lincoln ("hagiographers," he calls them) with the implied exception of "Donald, who is the leading authority on this period, on Lincoln, [and on] the Civil War," and who "regards this as one of the best books ever written about Lincoln, particularly in its historical assessment."[5] Vidal is less complimentary to Stephen B. Oates, author of *With Malice Toward None* (1977), a book experts generally consider a first-rate biography. By denying there is any real basis for Vidal's intimation that Lincoln had syphilis, Oates "shows," according to Vidal, "that . . . Mr. Oat[e]s is not as good a historian as Mr. Vidal . . . ."[6]

For a good historian, Vidal has unexpected difficulty in finding the historically appropriate word. He seems slightly off key when, writing on a subject so distinctly American, he affects British usages such as "practise" (p. 104), for "practice," "jewellery" (p. 5) for "jewelry," and "in" (p. 416) Fourteenth Street for "on" Fourteenth Street.[7] Again and again he betrays a lack of feeling for the idiomatic. George B. Mc Clellan had not "seen action" (p. 241) in the Crimea; he had only observed action there. Elihu B. Washburne could not have referred to the Capital's horsecars as "trolleys" (p. 7); no one called streetcars that until they were electrified. After obtaining the resignations of William H. Seward and Salmon P. Chase, Lincoln did not say he felt like the farmer on horseback who had "put the second pumpkin in his saddlebag" (p. 411). Two pumpkins in one saddlebag would not have helped with the farmer's, or with Lincoln's, balance. What Lincoln is supposed to have said is this: "I have got a pumpkin in each end of my bag"—not the usual saddlebag but a large sack. When Lincoln was going to Gettysburg to dedicate the cemetery, Ben Wade did not say, "Let the politically dead bury the dead" (p. 487). Thaddeus Stevens reportedly said, "Let the dead bury the dead"—without the weakening modifier.[8]

When it comes to the accurate and telling detail, Vidal shows a similar lack of touch. Seward's pastime was whist, not "poker" (p. 26). Charles Sumner was attacked with a heavy cane, not with a "stick" (p. 81). Stevens was never a member of the Joint Congressional Committee on the Conduct of the War (p. 231). After recovering a scuttled Union ship, the Confederates renamed it the *Virginia*, not the *Merrimack* (p. 318). Ulysses S. Grant had not failed in "the saddlery business" (p. 346). Prostitutes were called "hookers" before the war; they did not get that name because General Joseph Hooker was "so addicted . . . to the flesh" (p. 429). Only the states could authorize their troops "to vote in the field" (p. 468); Secretary of War Edwin M. Stanton could hardly arrange for them to vote.

Of course, one expects to find little errors in factual history too, though perhaps not so many as in Vidal's *Lincoln*. What most sharply distinguishes this book from historical works is not the unintentional but the deliberate inclusion of things that never happened. These things fall into two categories: the pseudohistorical and the avowedly fictional. "All of the principal characters really existed," Vidal declares, "and they said and did pretty much what I have them saying and doing, with the exception of the Surratts and David Herold . . ."⁹—who figure in a story paralleling Lincoln's; both stories culminate in the assassination plot. It is stretching the phrase to assert that Lincoln and other principal characters said and did "pretty much" what Vidal has them saying and doing.

Like the novelist he is, Vidal has made up many scenes and conversations. In one of them (pp. 41–43) Lincoln and his wife, Mary, are retiring for the night at Willard's Hotel, where they await inauguration day. Lincoln, so constipated "that he seldom move[s] his bowels more than once a week" (p. 9), goes to the bathroom, where the commode is, and from there talks with Mary, already in bed, about cabinet appointments. His remarks accord well enough with the record of what he was thinking at the time, but the occasion itself cannot be documented, nor can the frequency of his bowel movements.

Imagined situations like this one no doubt hold the attention of most readers much better than would a mere summary of Lincoln's recorded thoughts. Perhaps, then, a critic ought to judge such scenes and conversations not by their faithfulness to documented detail but only by their consistency with the general record. Even by this lenient standard Vidal's *Lincoln* does rather poorly. At many points it is hard to know whether his version of Lincoln's life and times is an outright invention, a dubious interpretation, or simply a mistake.

Consider the following contentions: As early as April 1861 Lincoln was thinking of emancipation as possibly justifiable as "a military necessity" (p. 141). He excluded Union-held areas from the Emancipation Proclamation "as a favor" to "pro-Union" (p. 414) slaveholders. As late as April 1865 he was still planning to colonize freed slaves outside the United States (p. 635). He was familiar with Karl von Clausewitz's famous work *On War*, John Hay having translated it from the German for him (p. 248). Unfortunately, there is no convincing historical evidence for any of these assertions, and there is conclusive evidence against most of them.

Vidal pictures Lincoln as an ignoramus in regard to public finance. He makes him so stupid as to think Secretary of the Treasury Chase personally signed every greenback (p. 294), and so uninformed as to have "no idea what the greenbacks actually represented . . ." (p. 295). In truth, it is Vidal who is ignorant of the subject. He even confuses greenbacks with national banknotes, as when he says, "Chase had then asked Congress to set up a national banking system so that the government might issue its own paper currency. . ." (p. 229). Unlike Vidal, the historical Lincoln had an excellent understanding of the principles of money and banking.[10]

According to Vidal, Lincoln often assumed the "inherent powers" (p. 233) of the presidency and badly abused those powers. In April 1861 he "ordered every U.S. marshal in the country to seize the original of every telegram that has been sent and a copy of every telegram that has been received in the last twelve months" (p. 126). At the time of the 1862 elections he declared, "I have suspended *habeas corpus* throughout the Union . . ." (p. 383). These are figments of Vidal's mind.

Vidal leaves the impression that Lincoln "was unshaken in his belief that the colored race was inferior to the white" (p. 356) and that he "had no great sympathy for those who felt that external circumstances had held them back" (p. 356). In fact, Lincoln clearly stated his conviction that blacks were inferior to whites *only* to the extent that they had lacked the opportunities of whites. He once said "he favored *assigning* the superior position to . . . whites." He never suggested that they were naturally superior.[11]

So Vidal is wrong on big as well as little matters. He grossly distorts Lincoln's character and role in history by picturing him as ignorant of economics, disregardful of the Constitution, and unconcerned with the rights of blacks.

Vidal's book is a potpourri of his own inventions and bits and pieces he has picked up from other authors. He gathers in old and long discredited views—the supposition, for example, that Lincoln destroyed Stephen A. Douglas and the Democratic party by the question he put at Freeport (p. 100). Vidal also hints at most of the newer misconceptions. He implies that Lincoln, in his 1838 speech to the Young Men's Lyceum of Springfield, Illinois, identified with the very tyrant against whom he warned, the one who would someday demolish and then "re-create the republic" (p. 111). Vidal goes along with the authors of *The Lincoln Conspiracy* in resurrecting the Eisenschiml thesis—the innuendo that Stanton masterminded the assassination (p. 655)—and in intimating that "there was a *second* plot afoot" (p. 655) involving Radical Republicans in Congress.[12] But Vidal gives few if any signs of the extensive research in those "letters, journals, newspapers, diaries, etc.," on which he says he has relied.

One authority on whom he has relied, as many Lincoln biographers have done, is Lincoln's law partner William H. Herndon. Long after the supposed event, Herndon recalled or thought he recalled that Lincoln had once told him of having, as a youth, contracted syphilis from a whore. Vidal has Herndon hobnobbing with John Hay in a Washington bar and recounting the story to him (p. 290). (It is a favorite technique of Vidal's thus to comment on Lincoln through the voices of other characters in the book.) Before the book was published Vidal made known his belief that Lincoln was syphilitic, and Stephen B. Oates provoked Vidal's scorn by casting doubt on the story. Vidal knew it was true because Herndon had said so.[13] This trust in Herndon is curiously naïve for a person of Vidal's reputed sophistication. David Donald himself, an authority on Herndon as well as on the Civil War, has pointed out that Herndon is important largely because of "the errors that he spread."[14]

The Library of Congress classifies Vidal's *Lincoln*, appropriately enough, as fiction. A reviewer would hardly be justified in pointing out inaccuracies in the book if its author had not claimed to be writing authentic history but, instead, had prefaced his story with the kind of disclaimer that some novelists make to the effect that any similarity between the novel's characters and real persons, living or dead, is purely coincidental. The Library of Congress classifies Alex Haley's *Roots* not as fiction but as family history. Still, one may question whether Haley's book is any more reliable as genealogy than Vidal's is as biography.

In a touching conclusion to an often deeply moving narrative, Haley tells how he came to write *Roots*. As a boy, he reports, he listened to his grandmother and other "graying ladies" talk of their ancestry and his. According to their account, an African ancestor was brought to "'Naplis" (Annapolis) and sold to John Waller, a Virginia planter. Waller named him Toby, but the African insisted to fellow slaves that his real name was Kin-tay. Eventually Toby's daughter Kizzy, at sixteen, was sold to a North Carolina planter, Tom Lea, who proceeded to rape her and thus become a white forefather of Haley's. After serving in the Navy during World War II, Haley was inspired to look for the reality behind the story of Kin-tay, alias Toby, and his descendants. Going to Africa, Haley heard from a Mandingo *griot*, or oral historian, an account of Kunta Kinte (Kin-tay) and his capture by slavers. Looking into British shipping records and Virginia court documents, Haley ascertained that a slave ship, the *Lord Ligonier*, had docked in Annapolis in 1767 and that John Waller soon afterward was the owner of a slave named Toby. Sure enough, Toby must have been Kunta Kinte! It only remained for Haley to trace the rest of the family tree down to his own generation.[15]

All this, he says, took a long time and a lot of work, but the effort paid off in verification. "In the twelve years . . . I have traveled half a million miles, I suppose, searching, sifting, checking, crosschecking, finding out more and more about the people whose respective oral histories had proved not only to be correct, but even to connect on both sides of the ocean" (p. 583). The question is raised, "how much of *Roots* is fact and how much is fiction?" (p. 584). In reply Haley avers that "every lineage statement" is from either his "African or American families' carefully preserved oral history, much of which" he has been able "to corroborate with documents . . ." after his "years of intensive research in fifty-odd libraries, archives, and other repositories on three continents" (p. 584). So much for the genealogy itself. But *Roots* reads like a novel, and the author concedes that he has exercised a great deal of imagination: "by far most of the dialogue and most of the incidents are of necessity a novelized amalgam of what I *know* took place together with what my researching led me to plausibly *feel* took place" (p. 584).

Haley's book sold more than 1.5 million copies the first year. It was translated into dozens of languages, and it was converted into a six-part television spectacular that reached as many as 100 million viewers. The TV show won an award as the season's best, and the book itself was given a special Pulitzer Prize for the blend of fact and fiction that Haley denominated "faction."[16] Never had a literary work received such immediate and widespread popular acclaim.

At first its reception among professional historians also was favorable, though in some cases qualified. One critical reviewer, Willie Lee Rose, exposed a number of inaccuracies and anachronisms in Haley's story. For instance, Haley has cotton in Spotsylvania County extending "until the fields as far as Kunta could see were vast seas of whiteness" (p. 199) at a time when no cotton was grown in that part of Virginia. But on the whole the experts seemed unimpressed by the frequency of historical errors. "Any knowledgeable historian can go through the work and point out a lot of mistakes," Robert W.

Fogel was quoted as saying. "I never applied to it the standards I would have if it had been written by C. Vann Woodward or Oscar Handlin."[17] And according to report, Edmund S. Morgan remarked that *Roots* was a "statement of someone's search for an identity" and should be evaluated as such. It "would seem to me," Morgan is quoted as saying, "to retain a good deal of impact no matter how many mistakes the man has made. In any genealogy there are bound to be a number of mistakes."[18]

Practitioners of oral history hailed *Roots* as a beautiful demonstration of what could be done with word-of-mouth evidence, and students of black history and culture welcomed it as one of the greatest contributions ever made to the field. It was widely adopted as a textbook for school and college courses. Indeed, it became a model for the study and teaching of the black experience.[19] As applied to such a highly praised kind of composition, "faction" would seem to be a peculiarly unfortunate coinage, since the word has a quite different and much more familiar meaning, with an unpleasant connotation. According to *Webster's New International Dictionary*, second edition, the word carries "the suggestion of contentiousness, self-seeking, or recklessness of the common good."

In any case, doubt gradually accumulated as to whether *Roots* was based on exhaustive research and reflected the real past. As "faction," the book began to appear more factitious than factual. Novelists sued Haley for plagiarism, and he admitted that bits of fiction from other writers had got mixed in with his account. He blamed this on "his research assistants,"[20] whose role he does not mention in the pages of *Roots*, where he tells of his twelve years of research in fifty-odd places on three continents. Africanists, checking his oral sources in Africa, concluded that he had made improper use of them. "Haley's first error was to tell his story in great detail to nearly everyone he met in Gambia," Donald R. Wright charges, "since in doing so he made it all too clear just what he hoped to hear in return."[21] After looking into his presumed documentary sources in the United States, historian Gary B. Mills and genealogist Elizabeth Shown Mills give this verdict: "In truth, those same plantation records, wills, and censuses cited by Mr. Haley not only *fail to document* his story, but they *contradict* each and every pre-Civil War statement of Afro-American lineage in *Roots!*"[22]

Little seems to be left of Haley's family history after these critics have disposed of it. Apparently the North Carolina slave owner Tom Lea was not an ancestor of his, or at least has not been established as one. Worse still, "Toby Waller was not Kunta Kinte," which means that Kunta Kinte was not an ancestor of Haley's either. The records show that Toby was a slave of John Waller's at least four years before the *Lord Ligonier* presumably brought Kunta Kinte to Annapolis in September 1767.[23] "But did a Kunta Kinte exist at all?" Donald R. Wright asks. "It seems likely" that he was "either a wholly fictitious figure" or "a person who lived . . . much more recently than the middle of the eighteenth century and . . . about whom details of a story were made up or significantly embellished to meet the needs of a visitor from America in search of his origins."[24]

Haley has responded to adverse critiques by attributing them to racism. He says the faultfinders have "clearly sought to impugn the dignity of black Americans' African heritage"[25] (though one might wonder whether he could enhance that dignity by misrepresenting his own African heritage). "Yes," Gary and Elizabeth Mills concede, "*Roots* filled a need that Black America has long felt, a yearning for a literary hero with whom it could identify."[26] Some black reviewers have denounced William Styron's *The Confessions of Nat Turner* for essentially the same fault that Haley has found in some white critics of *Roots*. "Black people today must not permit themselves to be divested of their historical revolutionary leaders," one black writer has declared. "It is perfectly clear why Styron's book would be a hit on the American market: it confirms white America's racist feelings."[27]

In an "author's note" prefacing his book Styron says with some exaggeration that Nat Turner's 1831 uprising in Southampton County, Virginia, was "the only effective, sustained revolt in the annals of American Negro slavery." Parts of the recorded confessions of Turner, Styron adds, he has incorporated in his story. ". . . I have rarely departed from the *known* facts," he avers. "However, in those areas where there is little knowledge in regard to Nat, his early life, and the motivation for the revolt (and such knowledge is lacking most of the time), I have allowed myself the utmost freedom of imagination in reconstructing events—yet . . . remaining within the bounds of . . . history. . . ." His intention, he explains, is "to try to re-create a man and his era, and to produce a work that is less an 'historical novel' in conventional terms than a meditation on history."[28]

White historians have differed among themselves on the historical merits of Styron's book. "It seems to me," C. Vann Woodward has commented, "to be faithful in its respect for history, not only in its consideration of events—facts—but in the way it views the time and place in which these events happened. In that respect I think it is above criticism."[29] But Henry Irving Tragle, revealing important sources that Styron never looked into, has indicated that Styron also distorted many of the "*known* facts."[30] Herbert Aptheker is still more denunciatory. "History's potency is mighty," he writes. "The oppressed need it for identity and inspiration; oppressors for justification, rationalization and legitimacy." In Aptheker's opinion the Styron book is obviously a tool of the oppressors.[31]

One of the black critics, Lerone Bennett, Jr., accuses Styron of trying to prove the U. B. Phillips and Stanley Elkins thesis that Sambo was the "dominant plantation type" and of "emasculating Nat Turner" and making him a "white man in blackface." Bennett goes on to say, "Instead of following the traditional technique of the historical novelist, who works within the tension of accepted facts, Styron forces history to move within the narrow grooves of his preconceived ideas."[32] Certainly, Styron has produced fictional history rather than historical fiction. His Turner—weak, indecisive, masturbating to fantasies of sex with white women—is his own creation, not history's.

Having imagined the man, Styron might well have imagined the name and given the book some such title as *The Confessions of Joe Doakes.* He then would have been relatively immune to criticism on historical grounds. More than a century earlier a novelist did take Nat Turner as the inspiration for a fictional character, a rebellious slave whom the author gave the name Dred. That novelist was Harriet Beecher Stowe, and the book was *Dred* (1856).[33] Stowe's novel does not hold the reader's interest as Styron's does, but his might have been no less exciting if he had followed her example to the extent of writing historical fiction instead of fictional history.

Black critics have endorsed Aptheker's contention that history (or a historian) must serve the needs of either the oppressors or the oppressed. Though that may be good Marxism, it may also represent the fallacy of the excluded middle. Surely there are historians who try, not wholly in vain, to write and teach for the sake of neither oppressors nor oppressed but for the sake of historical truth.

Though aiming at objectivity and authenticity, a historian or a biographer sometimes misses because distracted by thoughts of literary effectiveness. Such thoughts present no problem if the only consideration is to write with clarity and force rather than with the vagueness and flabbiness of dissertationese. But there may be a temptation to emulate the novelist to the extent of presenting occasional scenes in lifelike detail. For each detail, perhaps no more than a single source can be found, and to depend on that one source is to violate the historiographical requirement of two or more independent and competent witnesses. This requirement accounts for much of the dry-as-dust quality that the work of academic historians is presumed to have: they are constrained to write what amounts to the lowest common denominator of the widest variety of sources.

The academic historian or biographer is not likely to imagine scenes or to invent dialogue—unless retracting them in footnotes—but may describe events and quote participants on the basis of inadequate evidence. Vidal is certainly not the first writer on Lincoln to take Herndon's word as gospel. Albert J. Beveridge and many another biographer have accepted anything and everything that happened to strike them as truly Lincolnian in the Herndon lore. Even Oates (whose biography, according to the jacket blurb, "has the appeal of a good novel") has Lincoln saying a number of things for which there is no word-for-word source. Oates has not originated these remarks but has fashioned them from the coarse materials that have come to hand.[34]

Psychobiographers have strayed much farther from the evidence than Vidal has done. George B. Forgie and Dwight G. Anderson, taking their cue from the literary critic and fiction writer Edmund Wilson, describe Lincoln as consciously or unconsciously harboring oedipal ambitions to slay the Founding Fathers, remake the republic they established, and rule as dictator of it. Anderson acknowledges his debt to Sigmund Freud and to Erik H. Erikson.[35] Erikson, the model for many psychobiographers, sets standards more psychoanalytical than historiographical for the criticism of evidence. He says "the making of legend is as much part of the scholarly rewriting of history as it is part of the original facts used in the work of scholars. We are thus obliged to accept half-legend as half-history, provided only that a reported episode does not contradict other well-established facts; persists in having a ring of truth; and yields a meaning consistent with psychological theory."[36] Such are the requirements for "half-history"; those for whole history are somewhat more strict.

To give Vidal his due, he does not get quite so far from documented reality as do some of Lincoln's psychobiographers, though he does include a hint of their thesis when he implies that Lincoln identified with the anticipated tyrant who would destroy and then "re-create the republic" (p. 111). Nor is Vidal's Lincoln quite so lacking in historicity as is Styron's Nat Turner or Haley's Kunta Kinte. Vidal has mastered a much larger amount of information (as well as misinformation) about Lincoln, his associates, and his times than has any other author of fiction in which Lincoln appears as the protagonist. Norman L. Corwin's play *The Rivalry* (1959) conforms much more closely to the historical record but confines itself to Lincoln's rivalry with Douglas. In comparison with Vidal's *Lincoln: A Novel*, John Drinkwater's *Abraham Lincoln: A Play* (1918) and Robert E. Sherwood's *Abe Lincoln in Illinois* (1938) are rather simplistic.[37] Vidal's story has the makings of at least an equally effective drama and, as was to be expected, a television miniseries based on it reportedly is on the way.

Even when basing a docudrama on some nonfiction work, a television producer usually takes liberties with the facts or, at best, selects those that have the greatest visual effect. Television no doubt has special credibility for most viewers because it is for them a bringer of news as well as of entertainment. They see with their own eyes what is going on in the world around them, and they see with equal verisimilitude what must have gone on in the past. Few who have watched *The Web of Conspiracy*, a repeatedly shown dramatization of falsehoods, are likely to doubt that Stanton was veritably the master plotter of Lincoln's death.

Of course, docudrama producers, like fiction writers, have a right to present whatever view of the past they wish to. They can always point to the example of William Shakespeare, who certainly responded to histrionic rather than to historiographic demands. "Dramas based on fact are a part of literature and the theatre," Donald Wear, vice president of the Columbia Broadcasting System, has recently said, "and if television is going to be a vital and contemporary medium, they have to be a part of TV, too."[38] But David Shaw, media critic for the *Los Angeles Times*, declares, "I think it's wrong—an unconscionable perversion of reality—for moviemakers to appropri-

ate real names, real events and real places and then reshape
them to suit their own dramatic (or political) objectives."³⁹
Then Lewis H. Lapham, editor of *Harper's Magazine*, makes a
sarcastic retort to Shaw. "Shaw observes that docudrama is not
history, which is like saying that art is not orange soda or that
New York is not Los Angeles," Lapham writes. "The statement is correct but not especially interesting."⁴⁰

What the publisher of Vidal's *Lincoln* says of the book, the
producer may even more convincingly say of the forthcoming
television show. Here is a portrait that "will become for this
and future generations the living Lincoln of the war years."
Probably so. Past reality and present fantasy blend more and
more into an inseparable mix. Apparently few people care except us historians—and not even all of us.

Chapter 11. The "New Ethnicity" and American History

In one way or another, I suppose, historiography is bound to reflect the spirit of its own time. So we have little cause for wonder that the writing and teaching of American history today should reflect the divisive tendencies within our contemporary society. Still, there is perhaps room to doubt whether we, as historians, ought to endorse and encourage all the current historiographical trends. For us, in interpreting our history, the question is not primarily what is good for particular groups within the country, or even what is good for the country as a whole. The question is, more immediately, whether the predilections now fashionable are likely to lead to clarity—or to distortion—in our understanding of the past. I have in mind the movement known as the "new ethnicity."

This "ethnic awakening" is a recent phenomenon. True, the First World War intensified the self-consciousness of various nationality groups in the United States, as the Old World ties of British-Americans, German-Americans, and other "hyphenated" Americans came into conflict. Little or nothing of lasting importance resulted, however, from the proposals at that time for the systematic preservation of immigrant inheritances and identities.[1]

The Second World War had no such traumatic effect as the First on ethnic relations in this country. During the 1940s, representatives of the more numerous groups joined on the Common Council for American Unity to foster cooperation, if not also assimilation. The council published the magazine *Common Ground.* "Never has it been so important," this magazine averred, "that we become intelligently aware of the ground Americans of various strains have in common . . . that we reawaken the old American Dream, the dream which, in its powerful emphasis on the fundamental worth and dignity of every human being, can be a bond of unity no totalitarian attack can break."[2]

During the postwar decades of booming prosperity, the once largely impecunious ethnic groups seemed to be rapidly realizing the American dream, at least insofar as the dream promised a chance for everyone to rise in the world. One researcher, the Reverend Andrew Greeley, a Roman Catholic of Irish extraction, produced some rather startling evidence in this regard. From responses to questionnaires, 1963–1974, Greeley deduced that, next to the Jews, the Irish Catholics enjoyed the highest average family income of any ethno-religious group in American society, and that Italian, German, and Polish Catholics were next in order, above any of the Protestant denominations of older stock. Greeley concluded, "The Jewish immigrants clearly have become immensely successful," and "considerable numbers of Catholics have 'made it' into the middle class and this must be counted, at least to some extent, a success for the American political, social, and economic experiment."[3]

Nevertheless, Greeley joined with a few other Catholic and a few Jewish intellectuals to renounce the American dream as an illusion and to promote in place of it a great variety of ideals, a different set of them for each ethnic group.[4] He founded and began to edit the periodical *Ethnicity,* which, quite unlike *Common Ground,* looks for and emphasizes signs of persisting ethnic distinctiveness.[5] But the classic exposition of the new ethnicity is to be found in Michael Novak's book *The Rise of the Unmeltable Ethnics* (1972). According to Novak, the melting pot would not work—and should not work—in the case of such peoples as his fellow Slovak-Americans. To him, as to other self-appointed leaders of the new movement, the villains in the American drama are and always have been the Protestants of British ancestry, the so-called White Anglo-Saxon Protestants, the WASPs.[6]

What Novak and the others denounce as "Americanization," they might more accurately refer to as "industrialization" or "modernization." It is a worldwide trend, though to be sure, it has gone the farthest in the United States. The broad and ineluctable sweep of events—far more than the narrow kind of Americanization that nativists once tried to impose—has given shape to the middle-class culture that now predominates among Americans, whatever their national origin. Against the new cosmopolitanism there has risen a reaction, also worldwide, that may be termed the new tribalism. It takes the form of Quebecois separatism in Canada, Scottish and Welsh nationalism in the United Kingdom, and other divisive movements in Europe, Asia, and Africa. It takes the form of ethnic chauvinism and exclusiveness in the United States. What Novak and others like him really object to is the growing universalism of the twentieth century. What they are actually calling for is a return to the imaginary virtues of nineteenth-century European peasant life.[7]

In this country the "white ethnic" campaign began as, in large part, a response to the Black Power movement, which also inspired other minorities. If Americans with African, aboriginal, Hispanic, or Oriental ancestors got special consideration, why should not Americans with European ancestors get the same kind of preferential treatment? If Black Studies in schools and colleges, why not also Irish, Italian, Polish, Hungarian, Slovak, and other such studies? Why not, indeed!

The ethnic agitators have undertaken to revolutionize public education in the United States, and they have made considerable headway. The Ford and Rockefeller foundations have provided generous grants for the cause. The federal government is giving moral and monetary support in accordance with the Ethnic Heritage Studies Programs Act of 1972, which calls for the training of teachers to "teach the importance of ethnicity" and for "the rewriting of American history as ethnic history." The educational establishment has added its approval, and pedagogical experts are busy refashioning the curriculum so as to feature ethnic studies.[8]

Now, let me hasten to say that I have no objection to ethnic studies as such. Far from it. I readily agree that, until quite recently, the role of immigration and of immigrants has been woefully neglected in the writing and teaching of American history. Much of the work now being done is of great scholarly value, and I have no quarrel with it. My doubts and criticisms apply only to the way in which some practitioners of ethnic studies make use of them—as propaganda to serve a present cause.

The ethnicity advocates describe and defend their programs under the rubric of *cultural pluralism*. This is an attractive, nice-sounding term, *cultural pluralism*, with its connotations of social harmony and respect for human diversity and individuality. But I do not see how harmony is likely to arise from telling each group that it is morally superior to other groups and especially to the WASPs (who, of course, do not constitute a single, homogeneous entity in any case). Nor do I see how individualism is to gain from the imposition of ethnic stereotypes, or how the kind of Slovakianization that Novak stands for can be considered an improvement on the kind of Americanization that the worst of the nativists once advocated. Still less do I see how cultural pluralism—in the sense of the new tribalism—will contribute much of value to historical scholarship.

An example of the sort of history I call into question is Lawrence J. McCaffrey's *The Irish Diaspora in America* (1976). In this account the Irish-Americans are good and are the source of practically all the good in the United States. Or, if they have any faults or do any wrong, the "Anglo-American" along with the "Anglo-Saxon" (that is, English) Protestants are to blame. The melting pot is nothing but a "myth," yet it has been all too effective in the case of the Irish, most of whom have lost their "Irish identity." In doing so, according to McCaffrey, they "probably gave up a great deal for very little; the American mainstream has the stench of an open sewer." All this, it seems to me, is essentially the old-fashioned style of immigrant history that critics used to dispose of as "filiopietism."[9]

McCaffrey and other ethnic partisans subscribe to certain historical propositions the validity of which I doubt. One is that racism has been peculiarly a disease of the Americans of British ancestry, and to the extent that "white ethnics" have shown symptoms of it, they have somehow caught the contagion from the WASPs. Thus, according to McCaffrey, the Irish-Americans of the 1860s were, along with the blacks, "victims of bigotry. But since they knew that Anglo-Saxon Protestants considered them something of a human subgroup, perhaps the Irish expressed some sort of ego-defense through feeling and acting superior to another persecuted group."[10]

A second claim is that the foreign-born, particularly the Germans and the Irish, contributed far beyond their numbers to the Union victory in the Civil War. Older immigrant historians, doubtless in the interest of acceptance and assimilation, stressed the wartime loyalty and sacrifice of their respective nationalities. Albert B. Faust, for example, contended that, in Union army enlistments, the "foreigners" provided more than "the number that would naturally be expected of them," but "the native American stock fell short of its due proportion," and the Germans "in their proportionate share surpassed both the native and the Irish elements." McCaffrey contends that, by 1863, the Irish "had already contributed more than their fair share to the combatants and casualties."[11]

A third thesis is that Americanization has been "really Waspification"; that assimilation, to the extent it has succeeded, has forced non-British immigrants into "Anglo-conformity"; and that, for them, the process has amounted to "cultural genocide." This theme recurs in the writings of Novak and other ethnicity-minded scholars and curriculum experts.[12]

A fourth contention is that the melting pot is not only a myth but a comparatively recent one—either the invention of WASP historians, as an ex post facto rationalization for WASP dominance, or the invention of a Jewish immigrant who happened at the moment to be in an assimilationist phase. We have high pedagogical authority for each of these views. The president of the American Association of Colleges for Teacher Education has charged that "historians and educators have either omitted or distorted the facts regarding American cultural diversity." He asserts, "The melting pot concept was an historians' invention, a way of looking at society as some men *wished* to see it." Two educationists at the University of Wisconsin-Milwaukee have dated the idea from 1909 and have explained, "The concept *melting pot* was drawn from the title of a play by Israel Zangwill."[13]

Now, I propose to test these four generalizations by reference to the history of Wisconsin. On the whole, Wisconsin would seem to provide a pretty good test case. At one time, early in its history, this state contained a greater variety and proportionately a larger number of European immigrants than practically any other. Of course, the very presence of so many immigrants means that Wisconsin was to some extent atypical, obviously different from states with far fewer of the foreign-born. Also, the particular mix of peoples, the timing of their arrivals, and other variables in historical development require the caution that Wisconsin may not be exactly representative of other ethnically diverse states, even in the Midwest. With these caveats in mind, let us proceed to consider each of the four propositions in the light of Wisconsin history.

(1) Were the native Protestants, in nineteenth-century Wisconsin, preeminently the racists?

Though the state's black population was infinitesimal (less than 0.2 percent of the total in 1860), the Negro was a topic of frequent and fervid controversy among Wisconsinites during the 1860s. The big issues were emancipation, in-migration, and the suffrage. On each of these questions a majority of the Republicans—the members of what was essentially the native Protestant party—took the side of the blacks. The Democrats, including the German and Irish Catholics among them, aligned themselves in opposition.

On the question of emancipation the American Protestant churches and the Roman Catholic hierarchy made their respective positions clear. Early in the war the state Baptist, Methodist, and Presbyterian and Congregational conventions declared themselves in favor of a crusade to free the slaves. They heartily approved the Emancipation Proclamation once President Lincoln got around to issuing it. Quite different was the response of the Milwaukee *Seebote,* a German-language newspaper that served as the semiofficial organ of the Wisconsin hierarchy. The *Seebote* expressed horror that, under Lincoln's edict, European immigrants should be "used as fodder for cannons" in an abolitionist war and that the "Germans and Irish must be annihilated, to make room for the Negro."[14]

On the prospective migration of blacks into Wisconsin, the foreign-born Democrats were among the most outspoken. To the Irish the blacks were especially unwelcome. The only lynching of a black in Wisconsin's history was the work of an Irish mob in Milwaukee in 1861; this lynching led to considerable out-migration of blacks. When some Wisconsin whites began to fear a new influx in consequence of emancipation, the *Seebote* editor, as a member of the legislature, took the lead in demanding a law to prohibit persons of African descent from settling in the state.

On Negro suffrage the Republicans were cautiously affirmative, the Democrats unequivocally negative. The state constitution did not give blacks the ballot but said they might have it if the qualified voters should approve. The voters turned down the proposal in 1849, 1857, and 1865. Each time, it received the strongest support in the predominantly Republican counties, especially those in the southeast that had been settled mainly by people from New England and New York. It got the least support in the Democratic counties, especially those stretching from Milwaukee northward, an area of heavy German settlement. Protestant churchmen in Wisconsin endorsed Radical Reconstruction, which conferred the vote on Negroes in the South and then in the nation as a whole. The *Seebote* deplored the Radical program, and the German head of a Milwaukee seminary for priests, writing to a missionary society in Munich, denounced the "depraved" congressmen who wanted to "torment the South in an unnatural manner."[15]

(2) Did the foreign-born win the war for the North?

We must continue to bear in mind that, at the time, most of the immigrants and practically all of the German and Irish Catholics were Democrats. The Republican party repelled them with its various isms—not only nativism but also sabbatarianism, prohibitionism, and abolitionism. Few if any of the German or Irish Catholics in Wisconsin voted for the Republican presidential candidate in 1860, despite the persisting delusion that Lincoln owed his election to the foreign-born in the Old Northwest, to the Germans above all.[16] In the circumstances, it would have been surprising indeed if these anti-Lincoln groups had shown an excess of enthusiasm for Mr. Lincoln's war.

Certainly they did not do so in Wisconsin. To be sure, thousands of immigrants, including Catholics, served as willingly and as heroically as any of the Protestants of Yankee stock. But that is beside the point. The point is that, statistically, the foreign-born fell far behind the natives in their promptness to volunteer, in the average length of their service, and in the extent of their exposure to battle. During the first several months of the war the American-born enlisted at about three times the rate of the foreign-born. The latter, in the first thirteen Wisconsin regiments, constituted only a little more than a fourth (26.6 percent) of the total. After the beginning of the draft the proportion of immigrants among Wisconsin troops increased, and by the end of the war, when fifty-three regiments had been raised, it stood at 40 percent. This, however, was still comparatively quite low, since the foreign-born made up about 55 percent of the state's men of military age.

The immigrants, particularly the Catholics, also showed their distaste for war service in other ways besides their reluctance to volunteer. German, Belgian, Luxembourger, and Irish Catholics forcibly resisted the draft, many of them resorting to mob violence. All in all, the evidence points to the conclusion that, among Wisconsinites at least, the (Catholic) Germans and Irish contributed somewhat more than their due share of antiwar rioters, draft dodgers, conscripts, and deserters and somewhat less than their full share of willing, fighting soldiers.[17]

(3) Did the melting pot, in its actual operation, cast off the non-British cultural elements as so much slag? Was assimilation merely a process of reducing the variegated cultures of Europe to a dull, gray "Anglo-conformity"? Did Americanization really mean no more than "Waspification"?

It is true that, among the New Englanders who were earliest upon the scene, there were zealots who aspired to transform the Wisconsin wilderness into a Puritan Zion. It is also true that there were German immigrants who wanted to found a German state, and there were Catholic clergymen who hoped and expected to make Wisconsin a religious province of Rome. The presence of a variety of peoples, with differing religious and moral values, resulted in a fairly long period of cultural conflict. One of the recurring nineteenth-century disputes concerned the proper observance of the Seventh Day. Evangelical Protestants—Norwegian, Dutch, and German as well

as American—insisted that all groups conform to the requirements of the Puritan Sabbath, a day of rest, prayer, and con-
templation, of complete abstention from both pleasure and
work. Others demanded the right to enjoy what may be called
the German Sunday or the Catholic Sunday, an occasion for
after-church drinking, dancing, target shooting, bowling, and
other games.

The merging of cultures and the abatement of conflicts took
a long time even for these earlier immigrants, the Germans,
Norwegians, Irish, Dutch, Swiss, Belgians, and French. A contemporary might have concluded that they, too, were "unmeltable ethnics." (Then, as now, there were clergymen, journalists,
professors, politicians, and others who had a vested interest in
the maintenance of ethnic self-consciousness.) The later immigrants—such as the Poles, Italians, Greeks, and Slovaks—
could be expected to take as long, or longer, to melt.

Though pockets of ethnicity remain, Wisconsin as a whole
has come to have a fairly widely shared culture. Assimilation
has not meant Americanization in the old, one-way sense in
which nativists advocated it. Wisconsin today is not the Puritan Zion that pioneer Yankee evangelists once desired. Neither is it a German state. Culturally, it is a blend of native and
foreign ingredients, mainly Yankee and Teutonic. The German
Sunday prevails among the people of British and Norwegian as
well as those of German descent. Characteristic of Wisconsin
are, among other things, beer, brandy, and "brots" (bratwurst).
Wisconsinites consume more per capita of each of these than
do the people of any other state. And not one of these things
did the WASPs impose on the rest of the groups.[18]

(4) Was the melting pot a tardily fabricated myth, a notion
that historians concocted and assimilationists used as an ex
post facto rationalization?

By no means a figment of some recent WASP historian's
imagination, this concept represents the aspirations of immigrants themselves, and it dates back far beyond 1909, at least

as far as 1782, back to the very birth of the American republic. In 1782 Michel de Crevecoeur, born in France, a resident of New York, published his book *Letters from an American Farmer* (under the pseudonym J. Hector St. John). "Here," Crevecoeur wrote of his adopted country, "individuals of all nations are melted into a new race of men, whose labor and posterity will one day cause great changes in the world."[19]

Some early Wisconsin settlers, both from New England and from the Old World, shared Crevecoeur's belief and hope. In 1850, just two years after the state's admittance to the Union, the Milwaukee Sons of the Pilgrims, at their annual banquet celebrating the historic landing on Plymouth Rock, applauded the following toast: "Our adopted state. She has gathered her sons from many lands and given them all a home amid her bounty and her beauty. May the elements of strength and greatness peculiar to each be here transplanted and united to form a perfect commonwealth."[20]

In 1855 a Wisconsinite from Ireland, in a book on *The Industrial Resources of Wisconsin,* said the state's population was composed of "heterogeneous masses collected from every quarter of the globe." This Irish-American conceded that the "admixture of different habits, customs, passions and feelings" would generate a certain amount of "gaseous" discord. "But," he wrote, "though these elements may jar for a moment, like different metals in the furnace, yet the amalgamation of the races, by intermarriage, must produce the most perfect race of men that has ever appeared upon earth."[21]

The vision of a blending of nationalities to produce a new, distinctive, constantly improving American people and American civilization—this was widely shared long before Israel Zangwill, in 1909, brought out his famous play *The Melting Pot.* So-called cultural pluralists may sniff at it as a "myth." Well, one man's myth is another man's ideal. This ideal is an aspect of what we used to call the American dream. It no longer has any charm for some of the self-styled "ethnics" and some of the curriculum-making experts of today. They would prefer to shatter the American dream and idealize the fragments—the separate Polish, Italian, Irish, Greek, Slovak, and dozens of other tribalistic dreams. And they would rewrite American history in such a way as to falsify it while pursuing their divisionist aim.

Notes

1. An Imaginary Declaration of Independence, 1775–1975

1. William A. Graham, *The Address of the Hon. Wm. A. Graham on the Mecklenburg Declaration of Independence of the 20th of May, 1775* (New York, 1875), 54–56. The quotation of Murphey is from a letter of his to Joseph Graham, July 20, 1821. For further information on Murphey and a reproduction of the same letter, see William A. Graham's sketch of Murphey in W. J. Peele, ed., *Lives of Distinguished North Carolinians* (Raleigh, 1898), 111–127. Murphey did manage to put together some articles on the Mecklenburg Declaration of Independence; these were published in the *Hillsborough Recorder* between January and March 1821. See William H. Hoyt, *The Mecklenburg Declaration of Independence: A Study of Evidence Showing that the Alleged Early Declaration of Independence by Mecklenburg County, North Carolina, on May 20th, 1775, Is Spurious* (New York, 1907), 181–182. See also V. V. McNitt, *Chain of Error and the Mecklenburg Declarations of Independence: A New Study of Manuscripts: Their Use, Abuse, and Neglect* (Palmer, Mass., 1960), 75. For those who wish to consult manuscript sources concerning Murphey's viewpoint on the Mecklenburg Declaration, see the Archibald DeBow Murphey Papers, Southern Historical Collection, University of North Carolina Library, Chapel Hill.
2. On the "Rip Van Winkle State," see Guion Griffis Johnson, *Ante-Bellum North Carolina: A Social History* (Chapel Hill, 1937), 20–51, 827–831. For the Byrd quotations, see William K. Boyd, ed., *William Byrd's Histories of the Dividing Line betwixt Virginia and North Carolina* (Raleigh, 1929), 90, 92. The Virginian Edmund Ruffin put Byrd's century-old manuscript into print in 1841. Boyd, *Byrd's Histories of the Dividing Line*, xvi.
3. Hoyt, *Mecklenburg Declaration*, 1–5, 11–14.
4. Chalmers Davidson, "The Mecklenburg Celebrations," in *Cradle of Liberty: Historical Essays Concerning the Mecklenburg Declaration of Independence, Mecklenburg County, North Carolina, May 20, 1775*, ed. Archibald Henderson (Charlotte, 1955), 43–44. Graham, *Address of the Hon. Wm. A. Graham*, 7–8. Davidson quotes Thomas G. Polk to William Polk, 2 May 1822. Graham quotes the *Raleigh Register*, 7 June 1825, on the "immense concourse."
5. Jefferson to John Adams, 9 July 1819, in *The Adams-Jefferson Letters*, ed. Lester J. Cappon, 2 vols. (Chapel Hill, 1959), 1 : 543–544.
6. J. H. Wheeler to W. Q. Force, 7 August 1875, quoted in McNitt, *Chain of Error*, 84.

7. *The Declaration of Independence by the Citizens of Mecklenburg County, on the Twentieth Day of May, 1775, with Accompanying Documents* . . . (Raleigh, published by the Governor, under the Authority and Direction of the General Assembly of the State of North Carolina, 1831). The quotations are from p. 10.

8. Jo. Seawell Jones, *A Defence of the Revolutionary History of the State of North Carolina from the Aspersions of Mr. Jefferson* (Boston, Raleigh, 1834), 5–6.

9. The Whigs charged that Polk's grandfather Ezekiel Polk had been a tory in the Revolution. See Norman D. Brown, *Edward Stanly: Whiggery's Tarheel "Conqueror"* (University, Ala., 1974), 99.

10. See the sheet music of "The Old North State" as republished by the North Carolina Daughters of the American Revolution (1950). Written in 1835, this became the official state song by act of the General Assembly in 1927.

11. Davidson, "Mecklenburg Celebrations," 44; Graham, *Address of the Hon. Wm. A. Graham,* 8–9; William A. Graham, *General Joseph Graham and His Papers on North Carolina Revolutionary History* (Raleigh, 1904), 41–42.

12. Hoyt, *Mecklenburg Declaration,* 17–19, 23, 25. Compare McNitt, *Chain of Error,* 87.

13. William D. Cooke, ed., *Revolutionary History of North Carolina, in Three Lectures* (Raleigh, New York, 1853), 70, 88–89, 96–98. For the quotations from the *Raleigh Register,* 9 August 1851, and the *Fayetteville Observer,* 1 September 1856, see Johnson, *Ante-Bellum North Carolina,* 20–21.

14. Hoyt, *Mecklenburg Declaration,* 19–20.

15. McNitt, *Chain of Error,* 87–89, 99.

16. George Bancroft, *History of the United States of America, from the Discovery of the Continent,* 6 vols. (New York, 1882–1886), 4:196–198. Vol. 4 was copyrighted in 1858.

17. Hinton Rowan Helper, *The Impending Crisis of the South: How to Meet It* (New York, 1860 [c. 1857]), 217–220.

18. Kemp P. Battle, *The Legislation of the Convention of 1861,* James Sprunt Historical Monographs, vol. 1 (Chapel Hill, 1900), 111.

19. James C. Welling, "The Mecklenburg Declaration of Independence, May 20, 1775," *North American Review* 118 (April 1874): 256–293. The quotations are from pp. 262–263 and 291. On Welling, see James G. Wilson and John Fiske, eds., *Appleton's Cyclopaedia of American Biography,* 6 vols. (New York, 1887–1889), 6:427–428.

20. Graham, *Address of the Hon. Wm. A. Graham,* 3, 4, 10, 21, 76, 77, 103. On Graham, see Peele, *Distinguished North Carolinians,* 333–376.

21. Davidson, "Mecklenburg Celebrations," 45; McNitt, *Chain of Error,* 103.

22. There was during these years one exchange of polemics: C. M. Wilcox, "Mecklenburg Declaration of Independence, May 20, 1775," *Magazine of American History* 21 (January 1889): 31–45; and James C. Welling, "The Mecklenburg Declaration of Independence: President Welling's Reply to General Wilcox," in the same magazine 21 (March 1889): 221–233. According to Justin Winsor, *Narrative and Critical History of America,* 6 vols. (New York, 1905–1925), 3:161 n., "authorities are united in discrediting the so-called Mecklenburg Declaration of May 20, 1775." Vol. 3 was published in 1905.

23. W. R. Edmonds, *The North Carolina State Flag* (Raleigh, 1913), 1–15. For the act making May 20 a legal holiday, see *Laws of North Carolina*, 1881, c. 294.
24. Edward King, *The Great South* (Hartford, Conn., 1875), 515.
25. *North Carolina and Its Resources* (Raleigh, 1896), 13.
26. David Bennett Hill, "The Mecklenburg Declaration of Independence," *Southern Historical Society Papers* 20 (1892): 337, 339. The notion that the Battle of Alamance was the first battle of the American Revolution is another aspect of the "first in freedom" question and deserves separate study. As recently as 1951 an author upheld this contention in a national magazine. See Roger Butterfield, "The First Battle for American Freedom," *Saturday Evening Post*, 19 May 1951, 36–37.
27. Graham, *Address of the Hon. Wm. A. Graham*, 11; Davidson, "Mecklenburg Celebrations," 44–45.
28. George W. Graham, *The Mecklenburg Declaration of Independence, May 20, 1775, and Lives of Its Signers* (New York, 1905), 7–9, 36–37, 58–60, 82. Earlier advocates of the May 20 resolutions had conceded the genuineness of the May 31 resolutions. Graham, however, maintained the latter had never been officially adopted (though so reported in contemporary newspapers) but had been amended on May 20 so as to form a declaration of independence.
29. A. S. Salley, Jr., secretary of the South Carolina Historical Commission, and Worthington C. Ford, chief of the manuscripts division of the Library of Congress, justify their verdicts in "Dr. S. Millington Miller and the Mecklenburg Declaration," *American Historical Review* 11 (April 1906): 548–558. See also H. Addington Bruce, "New Light on the Mecklenburg Declaration of Independence," *North American Review* 183 (July 1906): 53n. Dr. Graham persisted in believing that the lost *Cape-Fear Mercury*, if ever found, would prove his point. See George W. Graham, "The Mecklenburg Declaration: What Did the Governor See?" *American Historical Review* 13 (January 1908): 394–397.
30. Hoyt, *Mecklenburg Declaration*, v–vi. On Hoyt, see McNitt, *Chain of Error*, 36.
31. See the reviews in the *Nation*, (29 August 1907): 187, and the *Outlook*, (29 August 1907), 128–130. In "The Mecklenburg Declaration: The Present Status of the Question," *American Historical Review* 13 (October 1907): 16–43, A. S. Salley, Jr., concludes that the Alexander manuscript (as published in the *Raleigh Register* in 1819) was a "fabrication," that Joseph McKnitt Alexander knew it was, and that he was guilty of deception if not downright forgery.
32. James H. Moore, *Defence of the Mecklenburg Declaration of Independence: An Exhaustive Review of and Answer to All Attacks on the Declaration* (Raleigh, 1908). Reviewing the Moore book in the *American Historical Review* 14 (1909): 386–387, the distinguished colonial historian C. H. Van Tyne said he had "little patience with the whole dispute." Even if the Mecklenburg Declaration could be verified, "it would not signify that North Carolina was the first colony to take up the idea of independence, for but one county and the radicals in it are concerned. Other colonies contained individuals who had the idea even earlier."
33. *Publications of the Southern History Association* 11 (July 1907): 261. The review is unsigned, but it may be safely, though conjecturally, attributed to Weeks, who was a member of both the publication committee

and the administrative council of the Southern History Association, with headquarters in Washington, D.C. For biographical sketches of Weeks, see Samuel A. Ashe and others, eds., *Biographical History of North Carolina: From Colonial Times to the Present*, 8 vols. (Greensboro, 1905–1917), 5:433–441; and Christopher Crittenden, William S. Powell, and Robert H. Woody, eds., *100 Years 100 Men* (Raleigh, 1971), 387–389. Hoyt in his preface, pages v–vii, acknowledges the assistance of Weeks along with A. S. Salley, Jr. and Reuben G. Thwaites, head of the State Historical Society of Wisconsin. Thwaites wrote, but never published, a monograph repudiating the Mecklenburg Declaration.

34. Samuel A'Court Ashe, *History of North Carolina*, vol. 1: *1584–1783* (Greensboro, 1908); vol. 2: *1783–1925* (Raleigh, 1925), 1:438–462. In his preface (1:vi), Ashe "makes acknowledgment to Stephen B. Weeks for valuable suggestions. . . . It is largely due to his critical acumen, to his scholarly taste and to his unsparing labor that this volume will be found so free from defects."

35. Stephen B. Weeks, "Sentiment versus History in North Carolina," *Nation*, April 1909, 330. The legislative history of the bill may be traced in the *Journal of the Senate of North Carolina, 1909*, 109, 268, 294, 316–317; and the *Journal of the House of Representatives of North Carolina, 1909*, 898, 913, 920–921.

36. R. D. W. Connor, "North Carolina's Priority in the Demand for Independence," *South Atlantic Quarterly* 8 (July 1909): 234–235.

37. Henderson, *Cradle of Liberty*, 9, 14. In "The Mecklenburg Declaration of Independence," *Mississippi Valley Historical Review* 5 (September 1918): 211, Henderson restated his contention: "If . . . it is proven that the news of the battle of Lexington first reached Charlotte on May 19, this fact completely demonstrates that the popular convention actually did take place on May 19 and 20, 1775."

38. Woodrow Wilson, *The New Democracy: Presidential Messages, Addresses, and Other Papers (1913–1917)*, eds. Ray Stannard Baker and William E. Dodd, 2 vols. (New York, 1926), 2:182. Wilson was the second president to honor one of the anniversaries with his presence. The first, in 1909, was William Howard Taft, who also talked of national affairs instead of local events. See Davidson, "Mecklenburg Celebrations," 46.

39. Henderson first announced his discovery in an article in the *Charlotte Observer*, which is reprinted in Henderson, *Cradle of Liberty*, 29–31. J. G. de Roulhac Hamilton, as director of the Southern Historical Collection, had come upon the Alexander manuscript in 1917, but it was left to Henderson to analyze the manuscript and discover its supposed significance. See McNitt, *Chain of Error*, 96–97.

40. Archibald Henderson, "Author and Editor of Volumes One and Two," *North Carolina: The Old North State and the New*, 5 vols. (Chicago, 1941), 1:viii. For Patton's review, Henderson's reply, and Patton's response, see the *Mississippi Valley Historical Review* 28 (December 1941): 445–446; and 29 (June 1942): 79–90.

41. French Strother, "North Carolina's Dreams Come True," *World's Work* 49 (November 1924), 72. On North Carolina's progressive image in the early twentieth century, see Richard N. Current, "Tarheels and Badgers: A Comparative History of Their Reputations," *Journal of Southern History* 42 (February 1976), 9–10, 16–19.

42. Jonathan Daniels, *Tar Heels: A Portrait of North Carolina* (New York: Dodd, Mead & Co., 1941), 12; Nell Battle Lewis, "North Carolina," *American Mercury* 8 (May 1926), 41; William E. Shea, "North Carolina Hugs a Delusion," *Independent* 120 (26 May 1928), 496–498.
43. Quoted in McNitt, *Chain of Error*, 114. On the observances, see Davidson, "Mecklenburg Celebrations," in Henderson, *Cradle of Liberty*, 46–47. The Mecklenburg Historical Association published *Cradle of Liberty*, containing four Henderson essays that had appeared in newspapers between 1916 and 1954, and Chalmers Davidson's account of the "Mecklenburg Celebrations," on the 180th anniversary, May 20, 1955.
44. *Greensboro Daily News*, 18, 20 May, 1975. Elisha P. Douglass had dismissed the "spurious 'Mecklenburg Declaration of Independence' of May 20" in his *Rebels and Democrats: The Struggle for Equal Political Rights and Majority Rule During the American Revolution* (Chapel Hill: University of North Carolina Press, 1955), 116. Curiously, Hugh Talmage Lefler and Albert Ray Newsome, *North Carolina: The History of a Southern State*, 3rd ed. (Chapel Hill, 1973), 205, continued to give equal treatment to both May 20 and May 31. The Charlotte newspaperman V. V. McNitt, in *Chain of Error*, elaborated on the Henderson thesis but also provided a good deal of new information on the history of the controversy.
45. *Greensboro Daily News*, 20, 21 May, 1975.
46. *Time*, 2 June 1975, 7, barely mentioned Ford's "speech at a Bicentennial celebration in Charlotte, N.C." *Newsweek*, 2 June 1975, 17, said merely that Ford "dashed down to Charlotte, N.C. for a quick speech hailing the South's patriotism and progress."

2. Who Started the War, Abraham Lincoln or Jefferson Davis?

1. J. G. Randall, *Lincoln the President: Springfield to Gettysburg*, 2 vols. (New York, 1945), 1:343; David R. Barber and Milledge L. Bonham, Jr., "Fort Sumter Again," *Mississippi Valley Historical Review* 28 (1941): 72–73; T. J. Pressly, *Americans Interpret Their Civil War* (Princeton, N.J., 1954), 65; A. H. Stephens, *A Constitutional View of the Late War between the States*, 2 vols. (Philadelphia, 1868–1870), 2:34–36, 349; Jefferson Davis, *The Rise and Fall of the Confederate Government*, 2 vols. (New York, 1881), 1:292, 294, 297.
2. T. M. Anderson, *The Political Conspiracies Preceding the Rebellion, or The True Stories of Sumter and Pickens* (New York, 1882), 57–58; J. G. Nicolay and John Hay, *Abraham Lincoln: A History*, 10 vols. (New York, 1890), 4:33, 44–45, 62–63; C. W. Ramsdell, "Lincoln and Fort Sumter," *Journal of Southern History* 3 (1937): 259–288; J. S. Tilley, *Lincoln Takes Command* (Chapel Hill, N.C., 1941), 139–148, 262, and passim.
3. J. G. Randall, "Lincoln's Sumter Dilemma," *Abraham Lincoln Quarterly* 1 (1940): 3–42, reproduced in Randall, *Lincoln the Liberal Statesman* (New York, 1947), 88–117; Randall, *Lincoln the President*, 1:311–350; D. M. Potter, *Lincoln and His Party in the Secession Crisis* (1942; softcover edition with new preface, New Haven, Conn., 1962), 315, 320, 326, 358–359, 363–367, 374–375; K. M. Stampp, "Lincoln and the Strategy of Defense in the Crisis of 1861," *Journal of Southern History* 11 (1945):

297–323; Stampp, *And the War Came: The North and the Secession Crisis* (Baton Rouge, La., 1950), 263–286.

4. Potter pointed out Tilley's error before 1947; see *Lincoln and His Party*, 333–335. See also Stampp, *And the War Came*, 264 n.

5. Randall, *Liberal Statesman*, 109.

6. Randall, *Lincoln the President*, 1:350.

7. Potter, *Lincoln and His Party*, 315, 363–367; Randall, *Liberal Statesman*, 98–101. Randall says in *Lincoln the President*, (1:316), "Pickens was susceptible of adjustment. Sumter, on the other hand, was packed with psychological dynamite." The evidence certainly does not bear out this view. Though Sumter received the greatest immediate attention from both North and South, Pickens was also packed with psychological dynamite, and the situation there, already explosive enough, would have remained explosive even if, somehow, the Sumter issue had been disposed of. Curiously, Nicolay and Hay, in *Lincoln* (3:427), accept the idea of the Sumter-for-Pickens alternative as Lincoln's, even though this is inconsistent with other evidence they present, if not indeed inconsistent with their overall treatment of the Sumter question.

8. Compare Ramsdell, "Lincoln and Fort Sumter," 278, and Stampp, *And the War Came*, 178, both of whom stress April 4 rather than April 6 as the crucial date.

9. Potter, *Lincoln and His Party*, 374–375. Both Potter and Randall read their own conclusions into Lincoln's inaugural. They give the impression that Lincoln promised to refrain from using force. Randall goes so far as to omit the qualifying phrase, "beyond what may be necessary for these objects," in quoting Lincoln's statement that he intended "no invasion, no using of force." *Liberal Statesman*, 115. See Stampp, *And the War Came*, 200.

10. W. E. Dodd, *Statesmen of the Old South* (New York, 1911), 220–221.

11. See also Richard N. Current, "The Confederates and the First Shot," *Civil War History* (December 1961): 368–369. Allan Nevins, *The Improvised War, 1861–1862*, vol. 1, of *The War for the Union* (New York, 1959), 67–74, redresses the balance. Nevins remarks (74 n.) that the efforts of the Ramsdell school may well be left "to fulfill their presumed purpose of comforting sensitive Southerners." Apparently the Ramsdell thesis meets an emotional need.

12. *The Collected Works of Abraham Lincoln*, eds. Roy P. Basler and others, 9 vols. (New Brunswick, N.J., 1953), 8:332.

3. The Myth of the Jealous Son

1. George B. Forgie, *Patricide in the House Divided: A Psychological Interpretation of Lincoln and His Age* (New York, 1979), 284 and passim. See my review of this book in the *Journal of Southern History* 46 (August 1980): 438–440.

2. Dwight G. Anderson, *Abraham Lincoln: The Quest for Immortality* (New York, 1982), 99. See my review of this book in the *Wisconsin Magazine of History* 66 (Winter 1982–1983): 154–155.

3. Robert K. Murray and Tim H. Blessing, "The Presidential Performance Study: A Progress Report," *Journal of American History* 70 (December 1983): 535–539.

4. This Herndon quotation and the preceding one are from William H. Herndon and Jesse W. Weik, *Herndon's Life of Lincoln*, ed. Paul M. Angle (Cleveland, 1949), xxxviii, 304.
5. *The Collected Works of Abraham Lincoln*, eds. Roy P. Basler and others, 8 vols. (New Brunswick, N.J., 1953), 1:108–115.
6. Edmund Wilson, *Patriotic Gore: Studies in the Literature of the American Civil War* (New York, 1962), 106–108, 129–130. Wilson's essay on Lincoln had been published earlier in his *Eight Essays* (New York, 1954).
7. Forgie, *Patricide*, 84–85.
8. Charles B. Strozier, *Lincoln's Quest for Union: Public and Private Meanings* (New York, 1982), pp. 31, 40, 50, 59–61, 123. After reading Strozier's study in manuscript, I endorsed it upon publication, and on the whole I still do.
9. Anderson, *Quest for Immortality*, 11–12, 79–80, 246–247. In a paper, "Abraham Lincoln's 'Lyceum' Speech Reconsidered," which he presented at the American Historical Association's annual meeting in San Francisco on 29 December 1983, Anderson reemphasized his claim that Lincoln had *consciously* identified with the tyrant. As a commentator, Forgie sharply criticized both Anderson's paper and his book. In reply, Anderson complained of being the victim of an "intellectual mugging," though Forgie in his comments was no more severe on him than he had been on Forgie in the passage from his book here quoted. When questioned by Kenneth M. Stampp from the floor, Anderson protested that his interpretation was only intended to be hypothetical, and he admitted that it could not be sustained by historical evidence.
10. Erik H. Erikson, *Young Man Luther: A Study in Psychoanalysis and History* (New York, paperback ed., 1962), 37.
11. For some sensible observations on the Lyceum speech, see Harry V. Jaffa, *Crisis of the House Divided: An Interpretation of the Issues in the Lincoln-Douglas Debates* (Garden City, N.Y., 1959), 222–224. Jaffa, 214–215, does concede this much to Wilson's claim that "Lincoln has projected himself into the role against which he is warning": "We believe this is true, in the sense that Lincoln envisaged himself playing the highest political role. But we do not believe he envisioned himself as the destroyer, except in so far as every true strategist imagines himself in the position of his enemy."
12. Basler and others, *Collected Works*, 4:316–318.
13. Herndon to J. E. Remsberg, September 1887, quoted by Angle, in Herndon and Weik, *Herndon's Life of Lincoln*, xxxix.
14. Speech at Clinton, Illinois, July 27, 1858, referring to Stephen A. Douglas's use of Lincoln's "house divided" phrase, in Basler and others, *Collected Works*, 2:525.

4. Lincoln Biographies: Old and New Myths

1. Stephen B. Oates, *With Malice Toward None: The Life of Abraham Lincoln* (New York, 1977); *Abraham Lincoln: The Man Behind the Myths* (New York, 1984).
2. Oscar Handlin and Lilian Handlin, *Abraham Lincoln and the Union* (Boston, 1980).
3. Ibid., ix–x.

4. Lord Charnwood, *Abraham Lincoln* (New York, 1917).

5. Nathaniel Wright Stephenson, *Lincoln: An Account of His Personal Life Especially of Its Springs of Action as Revealed and Deepened by the Ordeal of War* (Indianapolis, 1922).

6. Benjamin P. Thomas, *Abraham Lincoln: A Biography* (New York, 1952).

7. Reinhard H. Luthin, *The Real Abraham Lincoln: A Complete One Volume History of His Life and Times* (Englewood Cliffs, N.J., 1960).

8. Ibid., xiv.

9. Ibid., 96.

10. David Donald, *Charles Sumner and the Rights of Man* (New York, 1970); Harold M. Hyman, "Lincoln and Equal Rights for Negroes: The Irrelevancy of the 'Wadsworth Letter,'" *Civil War History* 12 (1966): 258–266; Hans L. Trefousse, *The Radical Republicans: Lincoln's Vanguard for Racial Justice* (New York, 1969); James M. McPherson, *The Struggle for Equality: Abolitionists and the Negro in the Civil War and Reconstruction* (Princeton, N.J., 1964); Herman Belz, *Reconstructing the Union: Theory and Practice During the Civil War* (Ithaca, N.Y., 1969); Peyton McCrary, *Abraham Lincoln and Reconstruction: The Louisiana Experiment* (Princeton, N.J., 1978); LaWanda Cox, *Lincoln and Black Freedom: A Study in Presidential Leadership* (Columbia, S.C., 1981).

11. Oates, *Man Behind the Myths,* 209.

12. Ibid., 106.

13. Ibid., 109.

14. Ibid., 111.

15. Lincoln to Orville H. Browning, 22 September 1861, in *The Collected Works of Abraham Lincoln,* Roy P. Basler and others, eds., 8 vols. (New Brunswick, N.J., 1953), 4:532.

16. Oates, *Man Behind the Myths,* 140.

17. Ibid., 144.

18. McCrary, *Abraham Lincoln and Reconstruction,* 288–289.

19. Oates, *Man Behind the Myths,* 137.

20. Lerone Bennett, Jr., "Was Abe Lincoln a White Supremacist?" *Ebony* 23 (February 1968): 35–42.

21. J. G. de Roulhac Hamilton, "Lincoln and the South," *Sewanee Review* 17 (April 1909): 134–138.

22. J. G. Randall, *Lincoln and the South* (Baton Rouge, 1946), 119–123.

23. McCrary, *Abraham Lincoln and Reconstruction,* 351.

24. James A. Reed, quoted in Richard N. Current, *The Lincoln Nobody Knows* (New York, 1958), 54.

6. *Love, Hate, and Thaddeus Stevens*

1. Thompson Powell to Stevens, 22 February 1866, in the Thaddeus Stevens Papers, Library of Congress.

2. E. B. Callender, *Thaddeus Stevens, Commoner* (Boston, 1882); James A. Woodburn, *The Life of Thaddeus Stevens . . .* (Indianapolis, 1913), 57–59; Thomas F. Woodley, *Great Leveler: The Life of Thaddeus Stevens* (New York, 1937); Elizabeth Lawson, *Thaddeus Stevens* (New York, 1942); Elsie Singmaster, *I Speak for Thaddeus Stevens* (Boston, 1947).

3. James F. Rhodes, *History of the United States from the Compromise of*

1850 . . . , 8 vols. (New York, 1893–1920), 5 : 544; William A. Dunning, *Reconstruction, Political and Economic, 1865–1877,* vol. 22 of *The American Nation: A History,* ed. Albert B. Hart (New York, 1907), 86; Claude G. Bowers, *The Tragic Era: The Revolution after Lincoln* (Boston, 1929), 69; Lloyd P. Stryker, *Andrew Johnson: A Study in Courage* (New York, 1929), 245–46; J. G. Randall, *The Civil War and Reconstruction* (Boston, 1937), 722–723. See also George F. Milton, *The Age of Hate: Andrew Johnson and the Radicals* (New York, 1930), 262–264.

4. W. E. Burghardt DuBois, *Black Reconstruction: An Essay toward a History of the Part Which Black Folk Played in the Attempt to Reconstruct Democracy in America, 1860–1880* (New York, 1935), 182, 265–266; James S. Allen, *Reconstruction: The Battle for Democracy (1865–1876)* (New York, 1937), 22; Howard K. Beale, "On Rewriting Reconstruction History," *American Historical Review* 45 (1940): 818–819; Louis M. Hacker, *The Triumph of American Capitalism* (New York, 1940), 340–341, 353, 373; "Professor Hacker v. Some Sons of Dixie," *Fortune* 36 (1947): 6, 9. See also Beale, *The Critical Year: A Study of Andrew Johnson and Reconstruction* (New York, 1930), passim, and "What Historians Have Said about the Causes of the Civil War," in *Theory and Practice in Historical Study: A Report of the Committee on Historiography,* Social Science Research Council Bulletin no. 54 (New York, 1946), 75. In the first of these two writings Beale does not emphasize Stevens's radicalism; in the second he says that some extremist Republicans were really economic conservatives but "Stevens and [George W.] Julian were thoroughgoing social and economic radicals."

5. Richard N. Current, *Old Thad Stevens: A Story of Ambition* (Madison, Wis., 1942), iii–iv.

6. Robert H. Woody, Review of *Old Thad Stevens, Journal of Southern History* 9 (1943): 274–275.

7. For a fascinating discussion of "idols and ideals" as used by politicians, see F. S. Oliver, *the Endless Adventure,* 2 vols. (London, 1931), 1 : 44–55.

8. See Richard N. Current, "Hamilton Fish," in *Public Men in and out of Office,* ed. J. T. Salter (Chapel Hill, 1946), 210–224.

9. In the state campaign of 1835, Stevens attacked both the Democratic candidates as enemies of the common man—Muhlenberg as an advocate of "ignorance" and Wolf as a member of the Masonic order. Philadelphia *American Advertiser,* 8 May, 27 July 1835; Harrisburg *Pennsylvania Reporter,* 2 October 1835.

10. Biddle to Stevens, 3 July 1838, in *Correspondence of Nicholas Biddle Dealing with National Affairs, 1768–1844,* ed. R. C. McGrane (Boston, 1919), 315.

11. Early in 1836, Stevens said there was "no other question than Masonry and Anti-Masonry." Stevens to the Literary Society of Lafayette College, 19 March, 1836, in the Edward McPherson Papers, Library of Congress. Later in the same year, after his reverse at the polls, he seemed convinced there was no other question than slavery and antislavery. Harrisburg *Pennsylvania Reporter,* 30 December 1836.

12. John Agg and others, reporters, *Proceedings and Debates of the Convention of the Commonwealth of Pennsylvania to Propose Amendments to the Constitution, Commenced and Held at Harrisburg on the Second Day of May, 1837,* 13 vols. (Harrisburg, 1837–1839), 1 : 208, 386–387,

390; 2:108–110, 340–344; 3:685–686, 693–696; 4:24, 245–247; 5: 302–303; 6:154–167.

13. See the *Pennsylvania House Journal*, 1838–39, vol. 2, part 2, 4–5, 7, 10, 78–79; Stevens to Samuel Evans, 5, 8 October 1854, manuscripts in the Pennsylvania State Library, Harrisburg; Stevens to Henry C. Carey, 24, 30 September 1856, Edward Carey Gardiner Collection, Historical Society of Pennsylvania, Philadelphia.

14. Philadelphia *National Enquirer*, 1 March 1838.

15. The issue between Stevens and Sumner was well stated in a letter that Stevens received from one of his correspondents and forwarded with his endorsement to Sumner. Chas. W. Wardwell to Stevens, 3 March 1866, Charles Sumner MSS, Harvard College Library.

When the Radical Republican convention met in Philadelphia in September 1866 Stevens disapproved the conspicuous attention which Theodore Tilton there gave the Negro abolitionist Frederick Douglass. "It does not become radicals like us to particularly object," Stevens wrote privately. "But it was certainly unfortunate at this time [with the crucial congressional elections in the offing]. The old prejudice, now revived, will lose us some votes." Stevens to William D. Kelley, 6 September 1866, in the Stevens Papers. Publicly, Old Thad did not object.

16. Stevens to McPherson, 16, 27 August 1867, and Stevens to M. G. D. Pfeiffer, 14, 18, 24 October 1867, in the Stevens Papers; *New York Herald*, 8, 9 November 1867; *New York Times*, 8, 10 January 1868.

17. "Sir: Take notice that before Tuesday night next you have all your things away from my house and that you do not yourself enter my House during my absence to sleep or for any other purpose, under the penalty of being considered a Housebreaker." Stevens to Isaac Smith, 9 November 1867, in the Edward McPherson Papers.

18. Stevens to Simon Stevens, 10, 11 July, 1863, in the Stevens Papers; *Lancaster Intelligencer*, 17 September 1863.

19. Stevens to Sumner, 17 August 1865, in the Sumner MSS; John W. Forney, *Anecdotes of Public Men*, 2 vols. (New York, 1873–1881), 1:38.

20. The report of this interview covered most of a page in the *New York Herald*, 8 July 1867.

21. *Congressional Globe*, 40th Cong., 2d sess., 1867–68, 2810–2811; obituary of Stevens in the *New York Tribune*, 18 August 1868; Buchanan to Stevens, 31 July, 10 August 1850, and W. B. Reed to Edward McPherson, 13 January 1869, in the Stevens Papers.

22. *New York Tribune*, 12 September 1865; *New York Herald*, 10, 11, 16 July 1867.

23. Undated manuscript in Stevens's handwriting in the Stevens Papers, vol. 16; *Congressional Globe*, 39th Cong., 1st sess., 1865–66, 72–75, 2459–2460, 2544, 3148; 39th Cong., 2nd sess., 1866–67, 1075–1076, 1167, 1213–1215; 40th Cong., 2nd sess., 1867–68, 2399–2464; *New York Times*, 9, 14 June 1866, 27 May, 23 June 1868; *New York Tribune*, 23, 29 June 1868.

24. *Congressional Globe*, 36th Cong., 2nd sess., 1860–61, 1188–1189; 39th Cong., 1st sess., 1865–66, 2239–2246; letter to Stevens from D. A. Baldwin, 2 May 1864; A. W. Moore, 20 June 1866; Josiah Perham, 19 July 1866; and John D. Perry, 24 June 1868, all in the Stevens Papers.

While Stevens succeeded pretty well in harmonizing the conflicting interests of ironmakers and railroad builders, he found it impossible to do the same for the interests of ironmakers and national bankers. When he demanded more greenbacks after the war, Jay Cooke lumped him with Ben Wade and Ben Butler as a dangerous economic radical. Jay to Henry Cooke, 9 October 1867, in Ellis P. Oberholtzer, *Jay Cooke: Financier of the Civil War*, 2 vols. (Philadelphia, 1907), 2 : 27–28. But Stevens was no radical, no "agrarian." He was merely responding to the urgent need of local ironmakers, bankers, and other businessmen in his part of the country who were suffering from a scarcity of money and were unable to get sufficient bank notes under the new National Banking System. R. A. Ahl to Stevens, 5 May 1866, in the Stevens Papers. This letter indicates that in the beginning the National Banking System discriminated not only against the West and the South (as is shown in Randall, *Civil War and Reconstruction*, 457–458), but also against certain rural areas of the East.

7. *Reconstruction in Mississippi*

1. James W. Garner, *Reconstruction in Mississippi* (New York, 1901); Wendell Holmes Stephenson, *Southern History in the Making: Pioneer Historians of the South* (Baton Rouge, 1964), 149; *Who Was Who in America, 1897–1942* (Chicago, 1942), 441; Garner obituary in *American Political Science Review* 23 (1939): 90–91.
2. *Nation* 73 (1901): 110; W. A. Dunning, *Reconstruction, Political and Economic, 1865–1877* (New York, 1907), 353; W. E. B. DuBois, *Black Reconstruction* (New York, 1935), 720; H. K. Beale, "On Rewriting Reconstruction History," *American Historical Review* 45 (1940): 808–809; J. G. Randall and David Donald, *The Civil War and Reconstruction* (Boston, 1961), 780; V. L. Wharton, "Reconstruction," in Arthur S. Link and Rembert W. Patrick (eds.), *Writing Southern History: Essays in Historiography in Honor of Fletcher M. Green*, (Baton Rouge, 1965), 300.
3. J. S. McNeily, "Climax and Collapse of Reconstruction in Mississippi, 1874–1876," *Publications of the Mississippi Historical Society* 12 (1912): 312, 457, 459. For a biographical sketch of McNeily, see the same journal, 6 (1902): 129 n.
4. H. A. Herbert, ed., *Why the Solid South? Or, Reconstruction and Its Results* (Baltimore, 1890), 333–338. See also Dunbar Rowland, "The Rise and Fall of Negro Rule in Mississippi," *Publications of the Mississippi Historical Society* 2 (1899): 188–199; Robert Bowman, "Reconstruction in Yazoo County," in the same journal, 7 (1903): 115–130; J. R. Lynch, "Some Historical Errors of James Ford Rhodes," *Journal of Negro History* 2 (1917): 345–368.
5. A. T. Morgan, *Yazoo: Or, on the Picket Line of Freedom in the South* (Washington, 1884), 273, 357; J. R. Lynch, *The Facts of Reconstruction* (New York, 1913); Lynch, "Historical Errors," 352.
6. W. E. B. DuBois, "Reconstruction and Its Benefits," *American Historical Review* 15 (1910): 781–799, and *Black Reconstruction*; David Donald, "The Scalawag in Mississippi Reconstruction," *Journal of Southern History* 10 (1944): 447–460 (especially 448–449); V. L. Wharton, *The Negro in Mississippi, 1865–1890* (Chapel Hill, 1947), 158.
7. Blanche Ames Ames, *Adelbert Ames, 1835–1933: General, Senator, Governor* (New York, 1964), 573; Garner, *Reconstruction*, vii–viii.

8. Garner, *Reconstruction,* 296, 336, 353, 408; Wharton, *Negro in Mississippi,* 198.
9. Garner, *Reconstruction,* 116–118; Wharton, *Negro in Mississippi,* 93.
10. Garner, *Reconstruction,* 295; Wharton, *Negro in Mississippi,* 179.
11. Garner, *Reconstruction,* 136, 309–310, 376 n., 408, 413–414; R. N. Current, "Carpetbaggers Reconsidered," in *A Festschrift for Frederick B. Artz* (Durham, 1964), 140–141 (also reprinted in this volume).
12. Garner, *Reconstruction,* 187, 237, 243, 270, 279–281, 349; Wharton, *Negro in Mississippi,* 158; F. L. Riley, "James Lusk Alcorn," *Dictionary of American Biography* (New York, 1928): 137–139. See also A. W. Trelease, "Who Were the Scalawags?" *Journal of Southern History* 29 (1963): 445–468.
13. Garner, *Reconstruction,* 312–313, 320–321; Wharton, *Negro in Mississippi,* 170, 180.
14. Garner, *Reconstruction,* 323, 412; Wharton, *Negro in Mississippi,* 179; J. R. Lynch, "A Letter on the Tragic Era," *Journal of Negro History* 16 (1931): 114.
15. McNeily, "Climax and Collapse," 457–459.
16. Elise Timberlane, "Did the Reconstruction Regime Give Mississippi Her Public Schools?" *Publications of the Mississippi Historical Society* 12 (1912): 89; Garner, *Reconstruction,* 356–357, 370; Wharton, *Negro in Mississippi,* 175, 245.
17. Robert Lowry and W. H. McCardle, *A History of Mississippi for Use in Schools* (New York and New Orleans, 1892), 232–233; Rowland, "Rise and Fall," 191; McNeily, "Climax and Collapse," 422; Morgan, *Yazoo,* 487; Lynch, "Tragic Era," 113; Garner, *Reconstruction,* 396–397; Donald, "Scalawag in Mississippi," 460; Wharton, *Negro in Mississippi,* 187, 190; Randall and Donald, *Civil War and Reconstruction,* 684–685.
18. Garner, *Reconstruction,* 372.

8. Carpetbaggers Reconsidered

This paper was presented, in an earlier form, at the annual dinner of the Mississippi Valley Historical Association in Chicago on December 28, 1959. Thanks are due to the Research Council of the University of North Carolina at Greensboro for a grant assisting part of the research on which the essay is based.

1. *Webster's New International Dictionary of the English Language* (Springfield, Mass., 1934), p. 410.
2. Mitford M. Mathews, ed., *A Dictionary of Americanisms on Historical Principles* (Chicago, 1951), p. 273.
3. Richard Hofstadter, William Miller, and Daniel Aaron, *The United States: The History of a Republic* (Englewood Cliffs, N.J., 1957), p. 404. The use of the carpetbagger stereotype in recent historical writing could be illustrated at length. Nash K. Burger and John K. Bettersworth, *South of Appomattox* (New York, 1959), 124, speak of Congress having instituted "military reconstruction" in 1867 and go on to say, "It was now that the era of carpetbag and Negro rule flourished unabated in the South. When carpetbaggers arrived from the North to control the Negro . . ." J. G. Randall, *The Civil War and Reconstruction* (Boston, 1937), 847, says the carpetbaggers went south to "make money and seize political power."

The revised edition of this work, by Randall and David Donald (Boston, 1961), omits this passage but substitutes no other definition or description of the carpetbaggers. In the preface to the best-selling novel by Harold Robbins, *The Carpetbaggers* (New York, 1961), there is an eloquent description, from the stereotyped view, of men who "came to plunder." The title is figurative, and the novel itself has nothing to do with Northerners in the postwar South.

4. William A. Dunning, *Reconstruction Political and Economic, 1865–1877* (New York, 1907), 121.
5. James W. Garner, *Reconstruction in Mississippi* (New York, 1901), 136. But Garner is inconsistent; see the next note.
6. Frank E. Smith, *The Yazoo River* (New York, 1954), 153, 156. Garner, forgetting his own words of caution, refers on pp. 309–310 to "the well-known 'carpet-bagger,' Colonel A. T. Morgan."
7. Ethel S. Arnett, *Greensboro, North Carolina* (Chapel Hill, 1955), 400 n.
8. Warner to John Sherman, 15 April, 21 June, 1866; 9, 19 December 1867; 10 January 1877, John Sherman MSS, Library of Congress.
9. Warner to Sherman, 15 April 1866.
10. *Testimony Taken by the Joint Select Committee to Enquire into the Condition of Affairs in the Late Insurrectionary States: Alabama,* 41st Cong., 2d sess., 1872 H. Rep. 22, pt. 8, 1:34.
11. Ibid., 233.
12. Testimony of William M. Lowe, ibid., 887–888.
13. In the text and footnotes of this paper more than seventy so-called carpetbaggers are mentioned by name. All are illustrations of this usage.
14. Powell Clayton, *The Aftermath of the Civil War in Arkansas* (New York, 1915), 298–306. These facts did not, and do not, exempt Clayton and his colleagues from the "carpetbagger" epithet. Thus, for example, Thomas S. Staples, *Reconstruction in Arkansas, 1862–1874* (New York, 1923), 276–277, writes of Clayton, "Though a carpetbagger, he claimed to be identified with local interests by virtue of the fact that he had purchased a plantation in Jefferson County and had decided to become a permanent resident of the state."
15. Walter L. Fleming, *Civil War and Reconstruction in Alabama* (New York, 1905), 718 n.
16. William W. Davis, *The Civil War and Reconstruction in Florida* (New York, 1913), 476–477.
17. Garner, *Reconstruction in Mississippi,* 136, 414 n.
18. R. K. Scott of South Carolina and M. L. Stearns of Florida were Freedmen's Bureau agents. Harrison Reed of Florida was a federal tax commissioner (1863) and a United States postal agent (1865). W. P. Kellogg of Louisiana was collector of the port of New Orleans. H. C. Warmoth of Louisiana was a lawyer, Joseph Brooks of Arkansas was a minister, and Powell Clayton of Arkansas and D. H. Chamberlain of South Carolina were planters. Ridgley C. Powers of Mississippi, who had an engineering background, also became a planter.
     Ames, a regular army officer, became provisional governor of Mississippi in 1868 and military commander of the district in 1869. He was elected United States Senator and served from 1870 to 1874; he was elected governor and served from 1874 to 1876. Though a late-comer to Mississippi, he at times considered establishing a permanent residence in the state. He wrote his wife, October 26, 1872, "I think I will get a house

and home for us on the Gulf at Pass Christian or some other point near there. And for business we will go into raising oranges." On November 9, 1872, he bought a house for $6,100 in Natchez, a town that had appealed to his wife. The dangerous and disagreeable aspects of life for a Republican Northerner in Mississippi caused him to change his mind about living permanently there, even before he lost out in politics. See *Chronicles from the Nineteenth Century: Family Letters of Blanche Butler and Adelbert Ames*, compiled by Blanche Butler Ames and privately issued by Jessie Ames Marshall (Clinton, Mass., 1957), 1:403, 416.

Rufus B. Bullock, governor of Georgia from 1868 to 1871, has been called a carpetbagger but does not fit in the category as defined according to the most common contemporary usage. Though a white Republican Northerner, Bullock had settled in the South before the war and had served in the Confederate army. See C. Mildred Thompson, *Reconstruction in Georgia: Economic, Social, Political, 1865–1872* (New York, 1915), 217.

19. Following is the list, by states, of the carpetbag congressmen and senators as defined and selected for this study (each senator is indicated by an asterisk): *Alabama*—A. E. Buck, C. W. Buckley, J. B. Callis, T. Haughey, F. W. Kellogg, B. W. Norris, G. E. Spencer*, W. Warner*. *Arkansas*—P. Clayton*, S. W. Dorsey*, J. Edwards, J. Hinds, A. McDonald, B. F. Rice*, L. H. Roots, W. W. Wilshire. *Florida*—H. Bisbee, S. B. Conover*, A. Gilbert*, C. M. Hamilton, T. W. Osburn*, W. J. Purman, A. S. Welch*. *Georgia*—J. W. Clift, C. H. Prince. *Louisiana*—C. B. Darrall, J. S. Harris*, W. P. Kellogg*, J. E. Leonard, J. McCleery, J. Mann, F. Morey, J. P. Newsham, L. A. Sheldon, G. A. Sheridan, G. L. Smith, J. H. Sypher, J. R. West*. *Mississippi*—A. Ames*, H. W. Barry, A. R. Howe, G. C. McKee, H. R. Pease*, L. W. Perce, G. W. Wells. *North Carolina*—J. C. Albott*, J. R. French, D. Heaton. *South Carolina*—C. W. Buttz, L. C. Carpenter, S. L. Hoge, J. J. Patterson*, F. A. Sawyer*, B. F. Whittemore. *Tennessee*—L. Barbour, W. F. Prosser. *Texas*—W. T. Clark. *Virginia*—R. S. Ayer, J. Jorgensen, J. H. Platt, C. H. Porter, W. H. H. Stowell.

There were also several Northerners elected as Democrats to represent Southern constituencies in Congress. These Democrats have not been included in the list. Information on the carpetbag congressmen and senators has been derived from the *Biographical Directory of the American Congress*, 81st Cong., 2d sess., 1950, H. Doc., 607, and from standard biographical encyclopedias and other sources.

See also C. Mildred Thompson, "Carpet-baggers in the United States Senate," *Studies in Southern History and Politics, Inscribed to William Archibald Dunning* (New York, 1914), 159–176. Miss Thompson does not undertake the same sort of analysis of backgrounds as is attempted here.

20. John A. Gillis, Victoria, Texas, to "Sister Hattie," 21 November 1866, Sherman MSS. There are, in the Sherman MSS, a number of other letters in which Northerners described the attractions of the South. See, for example, the letters to Sherman from W. P. Dumble, Nashville, 23 June 1865; J. Y. Cantwell, Decatur, Alabama, 11 December 1865 and 23 January 1866; J. Davis, Jr., Macon, Georgia, 31 January 1866; and John Friend, Fernandina, Florida, 12 March 1866.

21. Albert T. Morgan, *Yazoo; or, On the Picket Line of Freedom in the South* (Washington, 1884), 25.

22. Albion W. Tourgée, *An Appeal to Caesar* (New York, 1884), 55–67. The conception of the carpetbagger as a frontiersman is borne out by David

H. Overy, Jr., "The Wisconsin Carpetbagger: A Group Portrait," *Wisconsin Magazine of History* 44 (1960): 15–49. Overy writes, p. 15, "During the Civil War, Wisconsin soldiers on duty in the South discovered a new frontier."

23. John T. Trowbridge, *The South . . . A Journey through the Desolated States* (Hartford, 1866), 380, 448.

24. See, for example, Staples, *Reconstruction in Arkansas*, 86–87. Staples says that there was much suffering in Arkansas during the winter of 1865–1866 because of the money scarcity. Money came "for the most part" from partnerships of Southern merchants and planters with Northern capitalists. "New comers from the North brought in more or less cash, which was thrown into immediate circulation through the purchase of lands and initial supplies." Fleming, *Reconstruction in Alabama*, 717–718, says "Northern energy and capital flowed in" to that state in 1865 and 1866.

25. Fleming, *Reconstruction in Alabama*, 323–324.

26. James E. Yeatman, St. Louis, to John Sherman, 1 February 1867, Sherman MSS. Sherman received other letters from Northern planters in the South who protested against the federal cotton tax. See, for example, R. N. Barr, Claiborne, Alabama, to Sherman, 19 July 1867.

27. Augustus Watson, Fredericksburg, to Thaddeus Stevens, 9 December 1865, the Thaddeus Stevens Papers, Library of Congress.

28. Memphis *Avalanche*, 22 April 1866, clipping enclosed in letter of William Wilder to Stevens, Stevens Papers.

29. Frank S. Hesseltine, Savannah, to Stevens, 26 April 1866, Stevens Papers.

30. W. B. Woods, Mobile, to John Sherman, 28 January 1866, Sherman MSS. A. C. Bryant, Stevenson, Alabama, seeking Sherman's aid in obtaining a federal job, wrote, 15 June 1866, "It is hard for a Northern man to get a position here as the people feel naturally a strong prejudice against them & they are so poor themselves that they *go for everything in sight.*"

31. Roy F. Dibble, *Albion W. Tourgée* (New York, 1921), 34–41.

32. John Lynch to Sherman, 20 April 1867, Sherman MSS.

33. *Testimony Taken by the Joint Select Committee to Enquire into the Condition of Affairs in the Late Insurrectionary States: Florida*, 42d Cong., 2d sess., 1872, H. Rep. 22, pt. 13, 289.

34. Tourgée, *An Appeal to Caesar*, 150, 176–177. Tourgée's tables are taken from an article by E. W. Gilliam in the *Popular Science Monthly* for February 1883. They include in "the South" all fifteen of the prewar slave states and also West Virginia.

35. W. E. Burghardt DuBois, "Reconstruction and Its Benefits," *American Historical Review* 15 (1910): 781–799.

36. Jonathan Daniels, *Prince of Carpetbaggers* (Philadelphia, 1958), 23, 289–299, and passim, eloquently shows the involvement of others besides the Northerner Milton S. Littlefield in the fraudulent financing of North Carolina railroads. With regard to Mississippi, Garner writes, p. 323, "The only large case of embezzlement among the state officers during the postbellum period was that of the Democratic state treasurer in 1866."

37. The period of Reconstruction in the South, it must be remembered, was the time of scandals in the Grant administration, in the Shepherd government of Washington, D.C., in the Tweed Ring in New York City, and in state and local government elsewhere.

38. "It was never proved that he got any of the bonds," writes Dixon Y. Thomas

with regard to the charge that Powell Clayton stole Arkansas railroad securities. *Dictionary of American Biography* (New York, 1928–1958) 4: 187–188. "These charges were specific and definite enough, but the trial did not develop any substantial proof of the allegations," opines Davis with regard to embezzlement charges against Reed. *Reconstruction in Florida,* 631–634.

39. *New York Tribune,* 14 March 1872, clipping in the Warmoth MSS, Southern Historical Collection, University of North Carolina.

40. Garner, *Reconstruction in Mississippi,* 229–236, 297–305, 320–323, concedes that, as governor, Ames made many good appointments and on the whole administered the state honestly and economically. Chamberlain was attorney general of South Carolina before becoming governor. A letter attributed to him and written while he was attorney general might be viewed as incriminating him in corruption. However, a South Carolina Democrat has written, "No stolen money was ever traced to him, and he positively denied any participation in the proceeds of public rascality." As governor, he was not even accused of corruption or extravagance. See Henry T. Thompson, *Ousting the Carpetbagger from South Carolina* (Columbia, S.C., 1926), 36, 92–93, 101–102, and passim.

41. See, for example, Morgan, *Yazoo,* 487; Tourgée, *An Appeal to Caesar,* 68–69; Walter Allen, *Governor Chamberlain's Administration in South Carolina* (New York, 1888), 507–520.

9. *Neo-Calhounism and Minority Rights*

1. Margaret L. Coit, *John C. Calhoun: American Portrait* (Boston, 1950), 531.

2. Vernon L. Parrington seems to have originated the notion that Calhoun's theory of the concurrent majority has some special relevance for our times. In *The Romantic Revolution in America, Main Currents in American Thought,* (New York, 1926), 2:77, Parrington suggests that "Calhoun was face to face with a revolutionary conception—the conception of proportional economic representation." Charles M. Wiltse elaborates upon the idea in "Calhoun and the Modern State," *Virginia Quarterly Review* 13 (Summer 1937): 396–408, and in "Calhoun's Democracy," *Journal of Politics* 3 (May 1941): 210–223.

In his treatment of Calhoun, Arthur M. Schlesinger, Jr., *The Age of Jackson* (Boston, 1945), agrees with the neo-Calhounites. Schlesinger misconstrues Calhoun at several points, but worst of all in explaining Calhoun's decision to abandon his Whig allies and combine with the Democrats in 1837. Schlesinger says,

> The Southern dilemma was this: which was the greater menace to the plantation system—radical democracy or finance capital? Should the ruling class of the South ally itself to the upper class of the North, and thus to broad construction, capitalism and conservatism, or to the lower classes of the North, and thus to State rights, agrarianism and reform? Should the South join the Whigs in their fight against radicalism, or should it join the Democrats in their fight against business rule?
>
> In the end Calhoun could not but see the struggle in Jeffersonian terms, between landed capital and business capital—not, as the South-

ern Whigs saw it, in Federalist terms, between property, whether in land or business, and the propertyless. His decision showed how profoundly he inherited the Jeffersonian tradition. (p. 246)

Indeed, his fear of radical democracy, with its equalitarian and majoritarian tendencies, remained second only to his fear of capitalism itself. (p. 247)

Now, there is not a shred of evidence in Calhoun's writings to support that interpretation. The evidence, as I have tried to show in the preceding pages, leads to quite a different conclusion. To the end of his life Calhoun continued to believe that the property owners of the North were the natural allies of the property owners of the South. In politics, it is true, he aligned himself after 1837 with the party of the Northern "radicals," but he did so as a second choice, and for reasons of expediency, not principle.

Peter F. Drucker, "A Key to American Politics: Calhoun's Pluralism," *Review of Politics* 10 (October 1948): 412–426, develops most fully the neo-Calhounite misconceptions. John Fischer, "Unwritten Rules of American Politics" (*Harper's*, November 1948), 27–36, merely quotes and paraphrases the Drucker essay, published the preceding month. "The Negative Power," *Time*, 19 May 1952, 29–32, further popularizes the Wiltse-Drucker-Fischer view and applies it to current events. Herbert Ravenel Sass, "They Don't Tell the Truth about the South," *Saturday Evening Post*, 9 January 1954, 25, 67–68, makes use of the idea in a denunciation of Northerners and the North.

Richard N. Current, "John C. Calhoun, Philosopher of Reaction," *Antioch Review* 3 (Summer 1943): 223–234, calls attention to the place of the class-struggle concept in the thinking of Calhoun. I began this study in 1936, while a student of Professor William B. Hesseltine at the University of Wisconsin. I am much indebted to Professor Hesseltine for suggesting the topic as one worth exploring.

Richard Hofstadter carries further the conception of Calhoun as, in his words, "the Marx of the Master Class," in a chapter (pp. 67–91) of *The American Political Tradition and the Men Who Made It* (New York, 1948). Hofstadter discusses, with aptness and insight, the relation of Calhounism to current events in his essay, "From Calhoun to the Dixiecrats," *Social Research*, 16 (June 1949): 136–150.

3. William E. Dodd, *Statesmen of the Old South, or from Radicalism to Conservative Revolt* (New York, 1911), 166.
4. William M. Meigs, *The Life of John Caldwell Calhoun*, 2 vols. (New York, 1917), 2:466–467 n.
5. H. Von Holst, *John C. Calhoun* (Boston, 1882), 3–4.
6. Dodd, *Statesmen of the Old South*, 91.
7. Charles M. Wiltse, *John C. Calhoun*, 3 vols. (Indianapolis, 1944–1951); Coit, *John C. Calhoun*; Gerald M. Capers, *John C. Calhoun, Opportunist: A Reappraisal* (Gainesville, Fla., 1960).
8. August O. Spain, *The Political Theory of John C. Calhoun* (New York, 1951).
9. *New York Times*, 19 April 1953, sec. 1, p. 49, col. 1. The first volume of the *Papers of John C. Calhoun, 1801–1817*, was published by the University of South Carolina Press for the South Carolina Society in 1959.
10. Fischer, "Unwritten Rules," 27–36.
11. "The Negative Power," *Time*, 29–32.

12. Sass, "They Don't Tell the Truth," 25, 67–68.
13. Paul H. Douglas, review of *The American President*, by Sidney Hyman, *New York Times Book Review*, 14 February 1954, 6.
14. Drucker, "Key to American Politics," 412–426. The article by Fischer in *Harper's*, cited above, was based closely upon Drucker's essay.
15. Wiltse, "Calhoun and the Modern State," 396–408. For Parrington's earlier view, see his *The Romantic Revolution in America*, vol. 2 of *Main Currents in American Thought* (New York, 1926), 69–82.
16. Coit, *John C. Calhoun*, 518. Miss Coit entitled her concluding chapter "Minority Champion."
17. Schlesinger, *Age of Jackson*, 405.
18. Russell Kirk, *The Conservative Mind* (Chicago, 1953), 194, 208–209.
19. Wiltse, "Calhoun's Democracy," 219–220.
20. Fischer, "Unwritten Rules," 33.
21. Ibid.
22. Drucker, "Key to American Politics," 415.
23. *The Works of John C. Calhoun*, ed. Richard K. Crallé, 6 vols. (Charleston and New York, 1851–1856), 1:1, 16.
24. Quoted in Charles E. Merriam, "The Political Philosophy of John C. Calhoun," *Studies in Southern History and Politics, Inscribed to William Archibald Dunning . . . by His Former Pupils the Authors* (New York, 1914), 322–323.
25. Calhoun, *Works*, 4:393–394.
26. *Niles National Register*, 72, 8 May 1847, 148.

10. *Fiction as History: Vidal, Haley, Styron*

1. Winston Churchill, *The Crisis* (New York and London, 1901); Thomas Dixon, Jr., *The Clansman: An Historical Romance of the Ku Klux Klan* (New York, 1905); Walter Dumaux Edmonds, *Erie Water* (Boston, 1933); Margaret Mitchell, *Gone with the Wind* (New York, 1936).
2. David Balsiger and Charles E. Sellier, Jr., *The Lincoln Conspiracy* (Los Angeles, 1977).
3. Gore Vidal, *Lincoln: A Novel* (New York, 1984); Alex Haley, *Roots* (Garden City, N.Y., 1976); William Styron, *The Confessions of Nat Turner* (New York, 1967).
4. Vidal, *Lincoln*, "Afterword," 659.
5. Vidal interview, the Larry King Show, Mutual Broadcasting System, 19 June 1984, transcript by Burrelle's Radio Clips.
6. Ibid.; Stephen B. Oates, *With Malice Toward None: The Life of Abraham Lincoln* (New York and others, 1977).
7. Quotations obviously from Vidal's *Lincoln* will be cited parenthetically in the text.
8. Francis B. Carpenter, *Six Months at the White House with Abraham Lincoln* (New York, 1866), 38.
9. Vidal, *Lincoln*, 659.
10. See G. S. Boritt, *Lincoln and the Economics of the American Dream* (Memphis, 1978).
11. Richard N. Current, ed., *The Political Thought of Abraham Lincoln* (Indianapolis and New York, 1967), xx (quotation), 84–93, 104–111. In urg-

ing free blacks to take the lead in colonization, Lincoln (14 August 1862) drew a distinction between blacks yet to be freed, whose "intellects" were "clouded by Slavery," and freeborn blacks who, not having been "systematically oppressed," were as "capable of thinking as white men." *The Collected Works of Abraham Lincoln,* ed. Roy P. Basler, 9 vols. (New Brunswick, N.J., 1953–1955), 5:372–373.

12. The so-called Eisenschiml thesis is presented in Otto Eisenschiml, *Why Was Lincoln Murdered?* (Boston, 1937).

13. Vidal interview, the Larry King Show.

14. David Donald, *Lincoln's Herndon* (New York, 1948), 368.

15. Haley, *Roots,* 565–584 (quotations on p. 566). Subsequent quotations obviously from *Roots* will be cited parenthetically in the text.

16. *New York Times,* 19 April 1977, 1.

17. Gary B. and Elizabeth Shown Mills, "*Roots* and the New 'Faction': A Legitimate Tool for Clio?" *Virginia Magazine of History and Biography* 89 (January 1981): 4.

18. Ibid., 4 (first quotation), 7 (last two quotations).

19. Elizabeth Shown Mills and Gary B. Mills, "The Genealogist's Assessment of Alex Haley's *Roots,*" *National Genealogical Society Quarterly* 72 (March 1984): 35, 37, 43, 46–47.

20. Ibid., 46.

21. Donald R. Wright, "Uprooting Kunta Kinte: On the Perils of Relying on Encyclopedic Informants," *History in Africa* 8 (1981): 205–206, 209–210 (quotation on p. 210). I am indebted to Bennett H. Wall and Gary B. Mills for making available to me copies of the articles by the Millses and Wright.

22. Mills and Mills, "*Roots* and the New 'Faction,'" 6.

23. Ibid., 9.

24. Wright, "Uprooting Kunta Kinte," 214.

25. Quoted in Mills and Mills, "Genealogist's Assessment," 41.

26. Ibid., 47.

27. Charles V. Hamilton, "On Nat Turner and William Styron's Creation," in *William Styron's Nat Turner: Ten Black Writers Respond,* ed. John Henrik Clarke (Boston, 1968), 74 (first quotation), 77 (second quotation).

28. Styron, *Confessions,* ix.

29. Quoted in Henry Irving Tragle, *The Southampton Slave Revolt of 1831: A Compilation of Source Material* (Amherst, Mass., 1971), 398.

30. Ibid., 409.

31. Quoted by Clarke in "Introduction," *William Styron's Nat Turner,* vii.

32. Lerone Bennett, Jr., "Nat's Last White Man," in ibid., 7 (first quotation), 11 (second and third quotations), 4–5 (last quotation).

33. Harriet Beecher Stowe wrote in an appendix to *Dred: A Tale of the Great Dismal Swamp,* 2 vols. (Boston, 1856), 2:338, "As an illustration of the character and views ascribed to Dred, we make a few extracts from the Confessions of Nat Turner, as published by T. R. Gray, Esq., of Southampton, Virginia, in November, 1831."

34. "For example, Oates (*With Malice Toward None,* 207) quotes Lincoln as saying to [Orville H.] Browning in February 1861 that only 'the surrender of everything worth preserving' would satisfy the South. But what Browning recorded in his diary was this: 'He agreed with me no concessions by the free States short of a surrender of every thing worth preserv-

ing, and contending for would satisfy the South.' Thus the words and the thought actually came from Browning, and Lincoln merely acquiesced in them." Don E. Fehrenbacher, "The Words of Lincoln" (paper presented at Brown University, Providence, R.I., 8 June 1984), 7. The Albert J. Beveridge volumes are *Abraham Lincoln, 1809–1858*, 2 vols. (Boston and New York, 1928).

35. George B. Forgie, *Patricide in the House Divided: A Psychological Interpretation of Lincoln and His Age* (New York, 1979); Dwight G. Anderson, *Abraham Lincoln: The Quest for Immortality* (New York, 1982), 11–12.

36. Erik H. Erikson, *Young Man Luther: A Study in Psychoanalysis and History* (New York, 1958), 37. On Lincoln's psychobiographers, see Richard N. Current, "Lincoln After 175 Years: The Myth of the Jealous Son," *Papers of the Abraham Lincoln Association* 6 (1984), 15–24 (also reprinted in this volume).

37. Norman L. Corwin, *The Rivalry* (New York, 1959); John Drinkwater, *Abraham Lincoln: A Play* (London, 1918); Robert E. Sherwood, *Abe Lincoln in Illinois: A Play in Twelve Scenes* (New York, 1938).

38. Donald Wear, quoted in William A. Henry, III, "The Dangers of Docudrama," *Time*, 25 February 1985, 95.

39. David Shaw, "Danger! Please Don't Mix Facts with Fiction," *TV Guide*, 20 April 1985, 6.

40. Lewis H. Lapham, "Reality, Fantasy and News," *Chicago Tribune*, 25 April 1985, sec. 1, p. 23.

11. The "New Ethnicity" and American History

1. See Horace M. Kallen, "Democracy Versus the Melting Pot," *Nation*, 18, 25 February 1915, 190–194, 217–220; Randolph Bourne, "Transnational America," *Atlantic Monthly*, July 1916, 86–97; Julius Drachsler, *Democracy and Assimilation: The Blending of Immigrant Heritages in America* (New York, 1920).

Responding to the nativist Edward Alsworth Ross, *The Old World in the New* (New York, 1914), Kallen (219–220) proposed a "democracy of nationalities" in the United States, with a "harmony" instead of a "unison" of cultures. Bourne (96) wished to see a "trans-nationality" develop through the "weaving . . . of many threads of all sizes and colors." Drachsler (187) urged the experiment of "consciously creating a composite culture in America."

2. *Common Ground* 19 (Autumn 1949): 2, quoting the magazine's original prospectus.

3. Andrew M. Greeley, *Ethnicity, Denomination, and Inequality* (Beverley Hills, 1976), 5–12, 45–47, 71. Greeley also found that his own group, the Irish Catholics, was the "best educated Gentile group in American society," and the Italian and Polish Catholics were making the most rapid educational rise. Though, as Greeley himself realized, there were "limitations in the data" available to him, there seems little reason to doubt his basic conclusions.

4. As one member of the "coterie" recalled, "a small coterie of about twenty people gave birth to what was called the 'ethnic movement.'" Among them, in addition to Greeley and Michael Novak, were Monsignor Geno

Baroni, son of an Italian coal miner in Pennsylvania, and Irving Levine, a Jew of Polish and Lithuanian descent. Richard Krickus, *Pursuing the American Dream: White Ethnics and the New Populism* (Bloomington, Ind., 1976), xii–xiii.

5. The first issue of *Ethnicity: An Interdisciplinary Journal of the Study of Ethnic Relations* was dated April 1974. The *Journal of Ethnic Studies* had already begun publication with the Spring 1973 number. Neither of these periodicals confines itself to American subjects, but the *Journal of American Ethnic History*, scheduled to begin publication in the fall of 1981, does so. For Greeley's views, see also his *Ethnicity in the United States* (New York, 1974).

6. Michael Novak, *The Rise of the Unmeltable Ethnics: Politics and Culture in the Seventies* (New York, paperback edition, 1973), xvii–xviii, 65, 115. Novak himself has "made it" in the academic world, and his own family history involves amalgamation—he has dedicated his book (vii) to "the great-grandparents of our children," and these forebears include persons with such names as John Swenson and Dora Carver.

To Novak, as to other new ethnic theorists, ethnicity is largely something one makes up for oneself. He writes (56), "What is an ethnic group? It is a group with historical memory, real or *imaginary*. One belongs to an ethnic group in part involuntarily; in part *by choice*. Given a grandparent or two, *one chooses* to shape one's consciousness by one history rather than another." (Italics added.)

Novak pleads again for a "self-conscious and freely chosen ethnicity" in "Cultural Pluralism for Individuals: A Social Vision," in *Pluralism in a Democratic Society*, eds. Melvin M. Tumin and Walter Plotch (New York, 1977), 48.

There is no general agreement on the usage of the terms *ethnic, ethnicity*, and *ethnic group*, or of the term *minority*. One writer says the "largest minority is the so-called 'WASP-NN,' that is, White Anglo-Saxon Protestant Native-born of Native Parents," but it is "misleading" to think of them as constituting either a minority or an ethnic group. They should be considered, rather, as "natives, since they early became dominant and effectively pre-empted the crucial levers of political power." Perry L. Weed, *The White Ethnic Movement and Ethnic Politics* (New York, 1973), 7.

Others view the WASPs as belonging either to a single ethnic group or to one or another of several groupings. "Appalachian Americans" and "Welsh Americans," for example, are among the groups listed in Lois Buttlar and Lubomyr R. Wynar, *Building Ethnic Collections: An Annotated Guide for School Media Centers and Public Libraries* (Littleton, Colo., 1977), 11, 17, and passim.

7. For effective criticisms of the new ethnicity movement, see Howard F. Stein and Robert F. Hill, *The Ethnic Imperative: Examining the New White Ethnic Movement* (University Park, Pa., 1977); Orlando Patterson, *Ethnic Chauvinism: The Reactionary Impulse* (New York, 1977).

8. Stein and Hill, *Ethnic Imperative*, 195–196; Leon Hymovitz, "Multicultural Education in the Bicentennial . . . ," *Journal of Ethnic Studies* 3 (Winter 1976): 49–50. The American Association of Colleges of Teacher Education adopted a resolution endorsing the ethnic approach as "cultural pluralism" at its 1972 meeting.

For professional educationists' discussions of the ethnic approach, see

the *Journal of Teacher Education* (published by the American Associa-
tion of Colleges of Teacher Education) 24 (4) (Winter 1973); *Educational
Leadership: Journal of the Association for Supervision and Curriculum
Development* 33 (3) (December 1975). See also Nathan Glazer, "Cultural
Pluralism: The Social Aspect," in *Pluralism in a Democratic Society,*
12–18.

9. Lawrence J. McCaffrey, *The Irish Diaspora in America* (Bloomington,
Ind., 1976), 96–97, 172, 176, 178, and passim. See the adverse review by
Richard N. Current in *History: Reviews of New Books* 4 (September
1976): 216. See also the favorable reviews by Margaret J. Sullivan in the
Journal of American History 64 (June 1977): 145–146; and Jay P. Dolan
in *Reviews in American History* 5 (June 1977): 174–179. Sullivan char-
acterizes the book as a "solid, challenging contribution" and rejoices that
McCaffrey and other Irish-American scholars have at last "come to their
ancestors' defense."

10. McCaffrey, *Irish Diaspora,* 68. See also McCaffrey's discussion of "Anglo-
Saxon racism" on pp. 102–105.

11. Albert B. Faust, *The German Element in the United States, with Special
Reference to Its Political, Moral, Social, and Educational Influence,* 2
vols. (Boston, 1909), 1, 524–525; McCaffrey, *Irish Diaspora,* 68.

The exaggeration of the immigrant role did not, of course, begin with
ethnic historians. After the Civil War, ex-Confederates maintained that
they had not been defeated by the Yankees but had been overwhelmed by
alien hordes. The notion has received support from the neo-Confederate
historian Frank L. Owsley, who has estimated that "between 400,000 and
500,000 mercenary troops, the bulk of whom were from impoverished
Catholic countries, were by force of bounties and trickery induced into
the American [Union] Army." Owsley, *King Cotton Diplomacy: Foreign
Relations of the Confederate States of America* (Chicago, [1931], 2d ed.,
1959), 498. As many as 500,000 foreign "mercenaries" (not counting the
foreign-born who were willing volunteers) in a grand total of approximately 1,500,000 who served at one time or another in the Union armies!

12. Novak, *Unmeltable Ethnics,* 115; McCaffrey, *Irish Diaspora,* 178;
Thomas R. Lopez, Jr., "Cultural Pluralism: Political Hoax? Educational
Need?" and Carl J. Dolce, "Multicultural Education: Some Issues," *Jour-
nal of Teacher Education* 24 (4) (Winter 1973): 278, 284; Hymovitz,
"Multicultural Education," 50.

13. William A. Hunter, "Cultural Pluralism: The Whole *Is* Greater Than the
Sum of Its Parts," and Norman R. Bernier and Richard H. Davis, "Syn-
ergy: A Model for Implementing Multicultural Education," *Journal of
Teacher Education* 24 (4) (Winter 1973): 262, 264–265.

McCaffrey also sees the melting-pot idea as a WASP rationalization,
one originating in the 1880s and 1890s. He writes: "Since nativism could
not triumph in the face of the nation's rising labor needs, American leaders were forced to adopt a new vision of the country to accommodate the
immigrant newcomers. The melting pot thesis replaced nativism as the
new philosophy of the American spirit." *Irish Diaspora,* 96–97.

Like the terms *ethnic* and *cultural pluralism,* the term *melting pot* has
meant different things to different people. To nativists, and likewise to
new ethnicists, it has connoted forced Americanization along with com-

plete rejection of immigrant heritages. To true assimilationists, however, the melting pot has symbolized a mutual and syncretic process through which "native" and "foreign" elements are combined.

For a brilliant analysis—which reveals changes and ambiguities in the usage of such terms as *ethnicity, cultural pluralism,* and *melting pot*— see Philip Gleason, "American Identity and Americanization," in *The Harvard Encyclopedia of American Ethnic Groups,* eds. Oscar Handlin, Ann Orlov, and Stephen Thernstrom (Cambridge, Mass., 1980), 31–58.

14. Milwaukee *Seebote,* 25 October 1862, quoted in Mary D. Meyer, "The Germans in Wisconsin and the Civil War: Their Attitude Toward the Union, the Republicans, Slavery, and Lincoln" (master's thesis, Catholic University of America, 1937), 45–46.

15. On Wisconsin attitudes toward blacks, see Richard N. Current, *The History of Wisconsin: The Civil War Era, 1848–1873* (Madison, Wis., 1976), 313–314, 389–391, 585–586.

16. For a collection of the best scholarship on this topic, see Frederick C. Luebke, ed., *Ethnic Voters and the Election of Lincoln* (Lincoln, Neb., 1971). See especially the editor's preface, pp. xxv–xxxii.

17. Current, *Wisconsin: Civil War Era,* 306–309, 315–319, 324–325, 334–335, 353–355. Alan T. Nolan, *The Iron Brigade: A Military History* (New York, 1961), 32, exaggerates the number of the foreign-born in the early Wisconsin regiments; he has misread the 1861 annual report of the state adjutant general. Ella Lonn, *Foreigners in the Union Army and Navy* (Baton Rouge, La., 1951), 125, incorrectly describes the Eleventh Wisconsin Regiment as "chiefly Irish" and the Seventeenth as "completely Irish." See Current, *Wisconsin: Civil War Era,* 308 n. and 309 n.

18. See Richard N. Current, *Wisconsin: A Bicentennial History* (New York, 1977), 34–66, for a discussion of ethnic relations in the state.

Evidence of increasing amalgamation among the various Wisconsin groups appears abundantly in Richard M. Bernard, *The Melting Pot and the Altar: Marital Assimilation in Early Twentieth-Century Wisconsin* (Minneapolis, 1980). See especially the conclusions on pp. 118–119 and 125. Bernard finds that the proportion of exogamous marriages was much higher in 1910 than in 1880. By 1910 it was 70 percent or more for Swedes, Danes, Bohemians, and Austrians and nearly 50 percent for Germans and Norwegians. It was considerably less for Russians and Poles, but this could be explained largely by their more recent arrival and more heavily urban concentration. "The 'melting pot' concept," Bernard concludes, "needs more attention, not less."

19. J. Hector S. John, *Letters from an American Farmer* (New York, 1904), 54–55.

20. Current, *Wisconsin: Civil War Era,* 117.

21. John Gregory, *Industrial Resources of Wisconsin* (Milwaukee, 1855), 12–13, 22–25.

Index

Abe Lincoln in Illinois (Sherwood), 160
abolition, 67, 143
Abraham Lincoln: A Play (Drinkwater), 160
Abraham Lincoln: The Man Behind the Myths (Oates), 61, 63, 65
Abraham Lincoln Quarterly, 35–36
Abraham Lincoln: The Quest for Immortality (Anderson), 56–58
Adams, John, 59, 140–141
Alcorn, James Lusk, 108
Alexander, John McKnitt, 10–11, 24
Alexander, Joseph McKnitt, 10
Alexander, Moses, 26
Alexander, William, 10
Allen, James S., 84–85
American dream, 163, 172
Americanism, 86
Americanization, 164, 165, 166–167, 171
American Mercury, 29
American Revolution, 10
Ames, Adelbert, 104, 105, 107, 109, 121, 129
Anderson, Dwight G., 56–58, 159
Anderson, Robert, 32–33, 37, 42, 45, 51
And the War Came (Stampp), 36
Antimasons, 87, 88
Aptheker, Herbert, 157, 158
Arkansas, 120
army, Union, 166
Ashe, Samuel A., 24–25

Badeau, Adam, 73
Balsiger, David, 148

Bancroft, George, 16–17
banking system, 151
Baptists, 168
Barksdale, Ethelbert, 100–101
Beale, Howard K., 85, 99
Beauregard, P. G. T., 33, 45, 49
Belz, Herman, 64
Bennett, Lerone, Jr., 68, 157
Beveridge, Albert J., 159
Biddle, Nicholas, 88
black codes, 72, 81, 101, 105
black history, 4
Black Power movement, 164
blacks:
  Calhoun and, 145
  carpetbaggers and, 117–119, 123–124, 129–130
  ethnic groups and, 167–169
  fictional histories and, 156
  Garner on, 104–106
  Stevens and, 83–86, 95, 96
  violence against, 74
  in Wisconsin, 167–169
  see also racial attitudes; slavery; suffrage; Negro
Blair, Montgomery, 63
Blythe, LeGette, 29
Bowers, Claude G., 84, 86
Bright, John, 64
British-Americans, 162
Brooks, Joseph, 128
Browning, Orville H., 40
Buchanan, James, 38–39, 92–93
Butler, Ben, 93
Byrd, William, 10

Caesar, Julius, 59

Calhoun, John C., 7, 59, 132–146
    concurrent majority principle of,
        133, 137–138, 139, 140, 144
    Drucker on, 139
    dualist view taken by, 145
    interest groups and, 141–145
    new interpreters of, 139–144
    nominating conventions opposed
        by, 143
    as political philosopher, 136–138
    reputation of, 136–137
    Schlesinger on, 140
    sectional party proposed by, 143–
        144
    theory of government developed
        by, 132–135
    veto concept and, 141–142
    Wiltse on, 139–141
Cameron, Simon, 89, 92
Canada, 164
Cape-Fear Mercury, 22
capitalism, 85
carpetbaggers, 6–7, 80, 101–102,
        115–131
    in Arkansas, 120
    background of, 121–122
    capital provided by, 124
    corrupt governments and, 116–
        117, 127–129
    definition of, 119
    economic, 119
    economic failure of, 124–125
    examples of, 117–119
    Garner on, 106–107
    as governors, 128–129
    Negro, 119
    as officeholders, 120–123, 128–
        129
    race relations and, 129–130
    as Republicans, 119, 125, 127, 128,
        130
    Southern view of, 117–119, 124–
        125
    stereotype of, 115–116, 130–131
    survey of, 119–123
    as Union veterans, 121, 122–124,
        127
Catholics, 163, 168
    in Civil War, 169, 170
Chamberlain, D. H., 129

Chandler, Zachariah, 64
Channing, Edward, 20
Charnwood, Lord, 62
Chase, Salmon P., 38, 149, 151
Chestnut, James, 45
Churchill, Winston, 147
civil rights movement, 5, 70
Civil War:
    Dunning's view of, 78
    immigrants in, 166, 169–170
    Reconstruction as continuation
        of, 79–81
    revisionist view of, 3, 4–5
    see also Fort Sumter expedition
Clansman, The (Dixon), 147
Clanton, James H., 117–118
class struggle, 135
Clausewitz, Karl von, 151
Clay, Henry, 132
Clayton, Powell, 120, 128
Cobden, Richard, 64
Coit, Margaret L., 140
Colfax massacre, 75
Collier's Magazine, 22–23
Columbia Broadcasting System, 160
Common Council for American
        Unity, 162–163
Common Ground, 163
Communism, 86
concurrent majority principle, 133,
        137–138, 139, 140, 144
Confessions of Nat Turner, The
        (Styron), 148, 156–158
    black critics of, 158
    historians' evaluations of, 157
Congregationalists, 168
Congress, U.S.:
    carpetbaggers in, 121
    concurrent majority principle in,
        139, 140
    force acts passed by, 74
    New Deal legislation in, 141
    Reconstruction Acts and, 89–90
Connor, R. D. W., 25–26
Conservative historiography, 101–
        102, 103, 105, 106, 107, 109,
        110, 111–112, 113
Constitution, U.S., 66–67, 68
    Calhoun on, 134
Copperheads, 73, 94

corruption and fraud, government,
109–110, 111–112
carpetbaggers and, 116–117, 127–
129
Corwin, Norman L., 160
counterrevisionism, 3
Couohatta massacre, 75
Cox, LaWanda, 64
Crevecoeur, Michel de, 172
Crisis, The (Churchill), 147
cultural pluralism, 165, 172–173

Daniels, Jonathan, 28–29
Davidson, Chalmers, 30
Davidson, William, 10
Davie, William R., 15–16
Davis, Henry Winter, 93
Davis, Jefferson, 130, 136
Sumter expedition and, 32, 44–51
*Defence of the Revolutionary His-
tory of the State of North Caro-
lina, A* (Jones), 12
Democrats, 12–13, 69
Calhoun and, 143
carpetbaggers and, 119, 127
corruption and, 109–110, 111–
112
German-Americans as, 168, 169
Grant and, 75, 76, 77
Irish-Americans as, 168, 169
in Mississippi Plan of 1875, 112–
113
public education issue and, 111
in Reconstruction histories, 102
school issue and, 87–88
Stevens and, 94
in Wisconsin, 168–169
Disquisition on Government (Cal-
houn), 136, 138
Dixon, Thomas, Jr., 147, 148
docudramas, 7, 160–161
Dodd, William E., 136
Donald, David, 64, 99, 103, 108, 112,
113, 148, 152–153
Douglas, Paul H., 138
Douglas, Stephen A., 152
Douglass, Frederick, 62
Dred (Stowe), 158
Drinkwater, John, 160
Drucker, Peter F., 139

dual presidency, 135
DuBois, William E. B., 4, 84, 99, 103
Dunning, William A., 4, 6, 78–79,
84, 103
at Columbia, 97
Garner and, 97, 99
Dutch immigrants, 170, 171

Edmond, Walter Dumaux, 147
Eisenhower, Dwight D., 29
Eisenschiml, Otto, 152
elections of 1874, 75, 76
Elkins, Stanley, 157
Emancipation Proclamation, 65–67
in Vidal's *Lincoln*, 150–151
in Wisconsin, 168
Erie Water (Edmond), 147
Erikson, Erik, 4, 55–56, 58, 159
ethnic chauvinists, 7–8
ethnic groups:
in Civil War, 169–170
in 1940s, 162–163
race relations and, 167–169
"unmeltable," 171
in World War I, 162
see also new ethnicity movement
Ethnic Heritage Studies Programs
Act of 1972, 165
Ethnicity, 163
excluded middle, fallacy of, 158

faction, 154, 155
Facts of Reconstruction, The
(Lynch), 102
Faust, Albert B., 166
Fayetteville Observer, 15
Fessenden, W. P., 92
fictional history, 7, 147–161
defined, 147–148
Haley's *Roots* as, 147, 148, 153–
156
historical fiction vs., 147–148
Styron's *Turner* as, 147, 148, 156–
158
Vidal's *Lincoln* as, 148–153
Fifteenth Amendment, 73–74, 77–
78, 82, 90, 100
filiopietism, 166
Fish, Hamilton, 86
Flournoy, R. W., 108

Fogel, Robert W., 154–155
Force, Peter, 13, 14
Force, Samuel, 16
force acts, 74–75, 78
Ford, Gerald R., 30
Ford, Worthington C., 23
Ford Foundation, 164
Forgie, George B., 54–55, 56–57, 59, 159
Forney, John W., 92
Forrest, Nathan Bedford, 80
Fort Pickens, 36, 41–44, 47
Fort Sumter expedition, 31–51
   advance notice of, 34–35
   Buchanan's expedition and, 38–39
   cabinet position on, 38
   Davis and, 32, 44–46
   Fort Pickens landing and, 41–44, 47
   hunger crisis issue and, 36–37
   probable chain of events in, 46–51
   probable hostilities expectation in, 39–40
   Pryor's testimony on, 45
   Ramsdell thesis on, 33–41, 44–46
   war blame and, 31–33
Fourteenth Amendment, 74, 77–78, 82, 94
Fox, Gustavus Vasa, 39, 42, 45, 48, 49
Freedmen's Bureau, 121, 122
Frémont, John C., 66
Freud, Sigmund, 53, 56, 159

Garner, James W., 6, 97–114
   background of, 97–98
   Black Code defended by, 105
   on carpetbaggers, 106–107
   on corruption and fraud, 109–110, 111–112
   critics of, 98–100
   Dunning and, 97, 99
   McNeily and, 99–100, 110
   as prolific writer, 98
   racial views of, 104–106, 113
   as Revisionist, 103
   on scalawags, 107–108
   sources for, 104
   on taxes, 108–109
Gaston, William, 13

German-Americans, 162, 163, 166
   in Civil War, 169, 170
   as Democrats, 168, 169
   melting pot concept and, 170–171
   in Wisconsin, 168, 169
Gone with the Wind (Mitchell), 147
G. P. Putnam's Sons, 23
Graham, A. W., 25
Graham, George W., 22, 23
Graham, Joseph, 13, 19
Graham, William Alexander, 18–20, 21
Grant, Ulysses S., 5–6, 71–82
   Dunning's assessment of, 78, 82
   federal troops used by, 74–78
   historians' ranking of, 71, 82
   martial law under, 74–75
   Negro suffrage and, 72–73, 77
   Reconstruction under, 71–78, 81–82
   Southern policy of, 71–73, 75, 77–78
Graves, Richard S., 110
Greeley, Andrew, 163
Greeley, Horace, 94

Hacker, Louis M., 85
Haley, Alex, 7, 147, 148, 153–156
   see also Roots
Hamilton, C. M., 126
Hamilton, J. G. deRoulhac, 68–69
Hampton, Wade, 80
Handlin, Oscar, 61–62
Handlin, Lilian, 61
Harding, Warren G., 71
Harper's Magazine, 137, 161
Hawks, Francis L, 14–15
Hay, John, 33, 151, 152
Hayes, Rutherford B., 78
Helper, Hinton Rowan, 17
Henderson, Archibald, 26, 27–28
Herndon, William H., 53, 60, 70
   Vidal's use of, 152–153, 159
Hill, David Bennett, 21
historians:
   "half-history" and, 159
   literary effectiveness and, 158
   new ethnicity movement and, 162
   subjects' motives and, 86
   two or more sources rule for, 158

historical fiction:
    fictional history vs., 147–148
    Stowe's novel as, 158
History of North Carolina (Ashe),
    24–25
History of North Carolina (William-
    son), 9
History of the United States (Ban-
    croft), 16–17
Holshouser, James, 30
Hooker, Joseph, 149
Hoyt, William Henry, 23–24, 27
human nature, 132–133
Hunter, Humphrey, 11
Hurlbut, Stephen S., 39
Hyman, Harold, 64
hyphenated Americans, 162
    see also ethnic groups; *specific
    ethnic groups*

immigrants, *see* ethnic groups; new
    ethnicity movement
Impending Crisis (Helper), 17
industrialization, 164
*Industrial Resources of Wisconsin,
    The*, 172
interest groups, 141–145
Irish-Americans, 163, 165–166
    in Civil War, 169, 170
    as Democrats, 168, 169
    in Wisconsin, 168, 172
Irish Diaspora in America, The
    (McCaffrey), 165–166
Irving, Washington, 9
Italian-Americans, 163

Jack, James, 29
Jackson, Andrew, 59, 88
Jefferson, Thomas, 11, 12, 13, 22
Jews, 163
Johnson, Andrew, 72, 73, 79, 81,
    91–92
    impeachment of, 92, 95
    Stevens and, 91–92
Johnson, Lyndon B., 82
Johnston, Joseph E., 72
Jones, Joseph Seawell, 12
Journal of Southern History, 36

Kellogg, William Pitt, 75, 128

King, Edward, 20
Kirk, Russell, 140–141
Knights of the Golden Circle, 130
Ku Klux Klan, 72, 74, 78, 80, 126,
    129–130

labor unions, 141–142
Lapham, Lewis H., 161
Lee, Robert E., 72
Lefler, Hugh, 30
Letters from an American Farmer
    (Crevecoeur), 172
Liberal Republicans, 64, 75
Library of Congress, 153
Lincoln, Abraham, 79
    ambition of, 58–59
    Anderson's analysis of, 56–57, 58
    biographies of, 61–70
    emancipation and, 65–66
    fictional accounts of, 160
    Forgie's interpretation of, 54–
        57, 59
    Fort Sumter expedition and,
        31–51
    Handlin's treatment of, 61–62
    Herndon and, 53, 60, 70, 152–
        153, 159
    monotheism and, 56
    Negro suffrage and, 67
    Oates's biographies of, 61, 62–69
    Oedipus complex interpretation
        of, 5, 52–55
    popularity of, 53
    psychological interpretations of,
        51–60, 159
    public finance and, 151
    racial views of, 62, 68–69, 151
    Ramsdell on, 33–41, 44–46
    Reconstruction and, 67–68
    revisionist view of, 3, 4–5
    sociological law understood by,
        59–60
    Strozier's analysis of, 55–56,
        57–58
    syphilis thesis and, 148, 152
    Vidal's portrayal of, 148–153
    Wade-Davis bill vetoed by, 67
    as Whig, 59
    Wilson on, 53–55
Lincoln, Mary Todd, 53

*Lincoln and His Party in the Seces-
sion Crisis* (Potter), 36
Lincoln: A Novel (Vidal), 148–153
Lincoln Conspiracy, The (Balsiger
and Sellers), 148
Lincoln's Quest for Union (Stro-
zier), 55
Loco Focos, 88, 94
Lodge, Henry Cabot, 98
Lord Ligonier slave ship, 153, 156
Los Angeles Times, 160
Lovejoy, Elijah, 59
Loyal Leagues, 130
Luthin, Reinhard H., 62
Lynch, John R., 102, 105, 108, 110,
112
lynchings, 168

McCaffrey, Lawrence J., 165–166
McClellan, George B., 149
McCrary, Peyton, 64–65, 67, 69
McNeily, John S., 99–100, 110, 112
Macon, Nathaniel, 10
McPherson, Edward, 90
McPherson, James, 64
McPherson, John B., 88
martial law, 74–75
Marxists, 89, 158
Masons, 87, 88
Massachusetts, 10
Massachusetts Spy, 13
Mecklenburg Declaration, 9–30
annual celebrations of, 13, 20–21,
29–30
in Ashe's history, 24–25
Davie copy and, 27
Democrats' claim to, 12–13
earlier resolutions and, 13–16
first public readings of, 10–11
forged paper and, 22–23
George Graham's lecture on,
22–23
Hawks's lecture on, 14–15
Henderson's campaign for, 26–28
Hill's address on, 21
Historical Commission and,
25–26
Hoyt's monograph on, 23–24
independence proclaimed in, 20
Jefferson's correspondence on, 11–
12, 13, 22

Phillips's article on, 15–17, 18
promotional use of, 20–21
school teachings on, 28–29
"scientific" historians and, 24
secession and, 17
senate debate on, 25
Welling's article on, 18
William Graham's address on,
18–20
Melting Pot, The (Zangwill), 172
melting pot concept:
immigrants' aspirations and, 171–
172
Irish-Americans and, 166
Novak on, 163–164
as WASP invention, 167
Wisconsin experience and, 170–
172
Merrimack battleship, 149
Methodists, 168
Mexican War, 62
Miller, S. Millington, 23
Mills, Elizabeth Shown, 157
Mills, Gary B., 156
Milwaukee *Seebote*, 168, 169
Milwaukee Sons of the Pilgrims,
172
Mississippi, 99–114
Mississippi Plan of 1875, 112–113
Mitchell, Margaret, 147
monotheism, 56
Morgan, Albert T., 102, 107, 112,
116, 123
Morgan, Charles, 116
Morgan, Edmund S., 155
Murphey, Archibald D., 9, 24

Napoleon I, Emperor of France, 59
Nassau Literary Magazine, 16
Nation, 25, 99
National Association for the Ad-
vancement of Colored People
(NAACP), 145
nationalism, 7
nativists, 164, 165
*Negro in Mississippi, 1865–1890,
The* (Wharton), 103, 114
New Deal, 141
new ethnicity movement, 7–8, 162–
173
Americanization and, 166–167

cultural pluralism and, 165
divisive quality of, 172–173
generalizations in, 166–167
McCaffrey in, 165–166
melting pot concept in, 164, 166,
    167
Novak and, 163–164
public education and, 164–165
racial attitudes and, 166
Wisconsin experience and, 167–
    172
New York Herald, 92, 94
Nicolay, John G., 33
North American Review, 18, 19
North Carolina:
    as historyless, 9
    self-image and reputation of, 9–
        10, 28
    see also Mecklenburg Declaration
North Carolina (Henderson), 27–28
North Carolina Historical Commis-
    sion, 25–26
*North Carolina University Maga-
    zine*, 15–16
Northern Pacific railroad, 95
Norwegian immigrants, 170, 171
Novak, Michael, 163–164, 165, 167
nullification, 133–134, 140

Oates, Stephen B., 61, 62–69
    sources used by, 159
    Vidal and, 148, 152
On War (von Clausewitz), 151
oral history, 153, 155

Parrington, V. L., 139
Patricide in the House Divided
    (Forgie), 54–55
Patriotic Gore (Wilson), 53
Patton, James W., 28
Pennsylvania Anti-Slavery Soci-
    ety, 90
Perzel, Edward S., 30
Petersburg Express, 31
Phillips, Charles, 16–17, 18, 26, 27
Phillips, U. B., 157
Pierrepont, Edwards, 76
pluralism, 144–145
Polish-Americans, 163, 171
politicians, behavior of, 86–87
Polk, James K., 12–13

Polk, Thomas G., 11, 12
Polk, William, 11
Pollard, E. A., 31
Potter, David M., 36, 40, 41, 44
Powell, William, 30
Powhatan flagship, 49
Presbyterians, 168
presidential nominating conven-
    tions, 143
Protestants, 168
    Evangelical, 170–171
Pryor, Roger A., 45, 92
psychobiographies, 4, 5, 51–60, 159

racial attitudes, 62, 68–69, 81
    carpetbaggers and, 129–130
    of Lincoln, 62, 68–69, 151
    in new ethnicity movement, 166
    in Reconstruction historiography
        schools, 105, 113
    of Stevens, 83–86, 95, 96
    Vidal's presentation of, 151–152
Radical historiography, 102, 103,
    113
Radical Republicans, 6, 67, 68–70
    capitalism and, 85
    confiscation plan and, 93–94
    freedmen's rights and, 81
Raleigh Register, 10, 11, 12, 13–
    14, 15
Ramsdell, Charles W., 33–34, 35,
    36, 37, 40–41, 44–46
Randall, James G., 35–36, 40, 41,
    44, 69, 84
Reconstruction, 71–82
    Civil War continued in, 79–81
    Confederate veterans and, 80
    confiscation plan in, 93–94
    Conservative view of, 101–102,
        103, 105, 106, 107, 109, 110,
        111–112, 113
    Dunning school of, 78–79, 97, 99,
        103
    federal troops in, 74–78, 79, 80
    Garner's history of, 97–114
    Grant and, 71–78, 81–82
    Hayes and, 78
    in historical fiction, 147
    irregular warfare during, 79–80
    Johnson and, 72, 73
    Lincoln and, 67–68

Reconstruction (*continued*)
  in Mississippi, 99–114
  Radical interpretation of, 102, 103,
    113
  regional autonomy in, 80–81
  Revisionist interpretations of, 3–
    4, 102–103, 105, 108, 113
  Stevens and, 94–95
  see also carpetbaggers
Reconstruction, Political and Eco-
    nomic, 1865–1877 (Dunn-
    ing), 97
Reconstruction Acts of 1867, 72,
    101, 106, 115
  carpetbaggers and, 122, 125–126
Reconstruction in Mississippi (Gar-
    ner), 97, 98–114
Red Shirts, 74, 80, 130
Reed, Harrison, 128
Republicans:
  carpetbaggers as, 119, 125, 127,
    128, 130
  Fort Sumter expedition and, 34
  German-Americans and, 169
  Grant and, 75, 76
  Liberal, 64, 75
  in Mississippi, 103
  public education issue and, 110–
    111
  as scalawags, 107–108
  in Southern states, 77
  taxes levied by, 108–109
  in Wisconsin, 168–169
  see also Radical Republicans
Revisionist historiography, 3–5,
    102–103, 105, 108, 113
Rhodes, James Ford, 79, 84, 101
R. H. Shannon schooner, 38
rifle clubs, 74
*Rise and Fall of the Confederate
    Government, The* (Davis), 32
Rise of the Unmeltable Ethnics, The
    (Novak), 163–164
Rivalry, The (Corwin), 160
Robinson, Blackwell, 30
Rockefeller Foundation, 164
Roosevelt, Franklin D., 141
Roots (Haley), 148, 153–156
  critics of, 156
  historians' responses to, 154–155
  origins of, 153–154

  popular acclaim for, 154
  research for, 153–154, 155
  sources used in, 155–156
Rose, Willie Lee, 154
Russell, Richard, 137
Rutledge, Ann, 53

Sabbath observances, 170–171
Sass, Herbert Ravenal, 138
Saturday Evening Post, 137, 138
scalawags, 6, 101, 102
  Garner on, 107–108
Schlesinger, Arthur M., Jr., 71, 140
schools, public, 87–88, 110–111
  ethnic studies in, 164–165
Scotch-Irish Society of America, 22
Scott, R. K., 128
Scott, Winfield, 32
secession, 134, 135
Sellers, Charles E., Jr., 148
Sergeant, John, 90
Seward, William H., 32, 42, 43–44,
    48, 60, 149
Shakespeare, William, 160
Shaw, David, 160–161
Sheridan, Philip H., 72, 76
Sherman, John, 126
Sherman, William T., 72
Sherwood, Robert E., 160
Shout Freedom! (Blythe), 29
Singmaster, Elsie, 83–84
slave revolts, 156–158
slavery:
  Calhoun on, 134–135
  Emancipation Proclamation and,
    65–67
  Grant and, 73
  Reconstruction and, 81
  Thirteenth Amendment and, 67
Slovak-Americans, 163, 171
Smith, Lydia, 90, 91
South Carolina Gazette, 13
sovereignty, 134
Stampp, Kenneth M., 36
Stanton, Edwin M., 149
Stearns, M. L., 128
Stephens, Alexander H., 32, 81, 136
Stephenson, Nathaniel W., 62
Stevens, Thaddeus, 6, 68, 83–96,
    149
  biographers of, 83–84

Buchanan and, 92–93
Civil War historians and, 84–85
confiscation plan of, 93–94
democracy and aristocracy symbols used by, 87
Johnson and, 91–92
as leveler, 83, 88–89
love-hate thesis and, 83, 85–86,
89, 95–96
Masonry and, 87–88
Negro suffrage and, 89–90
as politician, 86–87, 89
public vs. private actions of, 87,
90–91, 93, 95
racial views of, 83–86, 95, 96
Reconstruction and, 94 95
in school issue, 87–88
Smith and, 90–91
Southerners and, 90–91
Stevenson, Adlai E., 21
Stowe, Harriet Beecher, 158
Strozier, Charles B., 55–56, 57–58
Stryker, Lloyd P., 84
Styron, William, 7, 147, 148, 156–158
suffrage, Negro:
Dunning's view of, 78
Grant and, 72–73, 77
Lincoln and, 67
Stevens and, 89–90
in Wisconsin, 168–169
Sumner, Charles, 64, 68, 90, 93, 149
Supreme Court, U.S., 79
Swain, David L., 13

Taft-Hartley Act (1947), 141
tariffs, 95
taxes, 108–109
television, 160–161
Thirteenth Amendment, 67, 94, 129
Thomas, Benjamin P., 62
Tilley, John S., 35, 36–37
Time, 137
Tourgée, Albion W., 116, 123, 125–
126
Tragle, Henry Irving, 157
Trefousse, Hans, 64
Turner, Nat, 7, 156–158

Union Leagues, 130
United Kingdom, 164
universalism, 164

veterans:
Confederate, 80
Union, 12, 122–124, 127
Vidal, Gore, 7, 147, 148–153, 159–
161
discredited views adopted by, 152
factual errors by, 148–149
fictional characters used by, 150
Herndon used by, 152–153, 159
historians and, 148
pseudohistorical events used by,
150
psychobiographical thesis used by,
159
racial attitudes portrayed by, 151–
152
sources used by, 148, 152
syphilis thesis promoted by, 148,
152
Vindictives, 6
Virginia, 10
Virginia battleship, 149

Wade, Benjamin F., 64, 92, 93, 149
Wade-Davis manifesto, 67
Walker, Leroy P., 45
Warmoth, H. C., 128–129
Warner, Willard, 117, 129
war powers, 66
Washburne, Elihu B., 149
Washington, George, 52–53, 59
Washington *Daily National Intelli-
gencer*, 13, 18
Wear, Donald, 160
Web of Conspiracy, The, 160
Webster, Daniel, 59, 132
*Webster's New International Dic-
tionary*, 155
Weeks, Stephen B., 24
Welles, Gideon, 38, 43
Welling, James C., 18, 21, 27
Wharton, Vernon L., 99, 103, 105,
106, 108, 109, 110, 111, 112,
114
Whigs, 12, 59, 87, 88, 103
White Anglo-Saxon Protestants
(WASPs), 164, 165, 166, 167
White Citizens' Councils, 146
white ethnic campaign, 164–165
White Leagues, 74, 75, 76, 129–130
white supremacists, 5, 145–146

Why the Solid South? (Barksdale),
    100–101
Williamson, Hugh, 9
Wilson, Edmund, 53–54, 56, 58, 59,
    159
Wilson, Woodrow, 26–27
Wiltse, Charles M., 139–141
Winsor, Justin, 20
Wisconsin, 167–172
With Malice Toward None (Oates),
    61–63, 148
Wofford, J. L., 108
Wolf, George, 87–88

Woodburn, J. A., 83
Woodward, C. Vann, 157
Woody, Robert H., 86
Works (Jefferson), 11
World War I, 162
World War II, 162
Wright, Donald R., 155, 156

Yazoo (Morgan), 102
Young Man Luther (Erikson), 4

Zangwill, Israel, 172

About the Author

Richard Nelson Current is one of the most distinguished American historians. He has won a number of awards, including the Bancroft Prize. He is a graduate of Oberlin (B.A., 1934), the Fletcher School of Law and Diplomacy (M.A., 1935), and the University of Wisconsin (Ph.D., 1940). He is now University Distinguished Professor Emeritus of the Univesity of North Carolina at Greensboro, where he taught for twenty-three years. He has taught also at Mills College, the University of Illinois, and the University of Wisconsin in Madison, and, as lecturer, at universities in England, Germany, Chile, Australia, India, and Japan, and, for the U.S. Navy, in Antarctica. Current has written thirteen other books. He lives in South Natick, Massachusetts.

About the Book

Arguing With Historians was composed in Trump Mediaeval by G&S Typesetters of Austin, Texas. It was printed on 60-pound Glatfelter paper and bound by Braun-Brumfield of Ann Arbor, Michigan. Design by Joyce Kachergis Book Design and Production of Bynum, North Carolina.

Wesleyan University Press, 1987